FOUR CORNERS

Second Edition

Student's Book
with Digital Pack

JACK C. RICHARDS & DAVID BOHLKE

CAMBRIDGE

i

Shaftesbury Road, Cambridge CB2 8EA, United Kingdom

One Liberty Plaza, 20th Floor, New York, NY 10006, USA

477 Williamstown Road, Port Melbourne, VIC 3207, Australia

314–321, 3rd Floor, Plot 3, Splendor Forum, Jasola District Centre, New Delhi – 110025, India

103 Penang Road, #05–06/07, Visioncrest Commercial, Singapore 238467

Cambridge University Press & Assessment is a department of the University of Cambridge.

We share the University's mission to contribute to society through the pursuit of education, learning and research at the highest international levels of excellence.

www.cambridge.org
Information on this title: www.cambridge.org/9781009286473

© Cambridge University Press & Assessment 2012, 2019, 2023

First published 2012
Second edition 2019

20 19 18 17 16 15 14 13 12 11 10 9 8 7 6 5 4 3 2 1

Printed in Mexico by Litográfica Ingramex, S.A. de C.V.

A catalogue record for this publication is available from the British Library

ISBN 978-1-009-28633-6   Student's Book with Digital Pack 2
ISBN 978-1-009-28645-9   Student's Book with Digital Pack 2A
ISBN 978-1-009-28645-9   Student's Book with Digital Pack 2B
ISBN 978-1-108-65228-5   Teacher's Edition with Complete Assessment Program 2
ISBN 978-1-009-28647-3   Full Contact with Digital Pack 2
ISBN 978-1-009-28648-0   Full Contact with Digital Pack 2A
ISBN 978-1-009-28649-7   Full Contact with Digital Pack 2B
ISBN 978-1-009-28594-0   Presentation Plus Level 2

Additional resources for this publication at www.cambridge.org/fourcorners

Authors' acknowledgments

Many people contributed to the development of *Four Corners*. The authors and publisher would like to particularly thank the following **reviewers**:

Nele Noe, **Academy for Educational Development, Qatar Independent Secondary School for Girls**, Doha, Qatar; Pablo Stucchi, **Antonio Raimondi School** and **Instituto San Ignacio de Loyola**, Lima, Peru; **Nadeen Katz, Asia University, Tokyo, Japan;** Tim Vandenhoek, **Asia University**, Tokyo, Japan; Celso Frade and Sonia Maria Baccari de Godoy, **Associação Alumni**, São Paulo, Brazil; Rosane Bandeira, **Atlanta Idiomas**, Manaus, Brazil; Cacilda Reis da Silva, **Atlanta Idiomas**, Manaus, Brazil; Gretta Sicsu, **Atlanta Idiomas**, Manaus, Brazil; Naila Maria Cañiso Ferreira, **Atlanta Idiomas**, Manaus, Brazil; Hothnã Moraes de Souza Neto, **Atlanta Idiomas**, Manaus, Brazil; Jacqueline Kurtzious, **Atlanta Idiomas**, Manaus, Brazil; José Menezes Ribeiro Neto, **Atlanta Idiomas**, Manaus, Brazil; Sheila Ribeiro Cordeiro, **Atlanta Idiomas**, Manaus, Brazil; Juliana Fernandes, **Atlanta Idiomas**, Manaus, Brazil; Aline Alexandrina da Silva, **Atlanta Idiomas**, Manaus, Brazil; Kari Miller, **Binational Center**, Quito, Ecuador; Alex K. Oliveira, **Boston University**, Boston, MA, USA; Noriko Furuya, **Bunka Gakuen University**, Tokyo, Japan; Robert Hickling, **Bunka Gakuen University**, Tokyo, Japan; John D. Owen, **Bunka Gakuen University**, Tokyo, Japan; Elisabeth Blom, **Casa Thomas Jefferson**, Brasília, Brazil; Lucilena Oliveira Andrade, **Centro Cultural Brasil Estados Unidos (CCBEU Belém)**, Belém, Brazil; Marcelo Franco Borges, **Centro Cultural Brasil Estados Unidos (CCBEU Belém)**, Belém, Brazil; Geysa de Azevedo Moreira, **Centro Cultural Brasil Estados Unidos (CCBEU Belém)**, Belém, Brazil; Anderson Felipe Barbosa Negrão, **Centro Cultural Brasil Estados Unidos (CCBEU Belém)**, Belém, Brazil; Henry Grant, **CCBEU – Campinas**, Campinas, Brazil; Maria do Rosário, **CCBEU – Franca**, Franca, Brazil; Ane Cibele Palma, **CCBEU Inter Americano**, Curitiba, Brazil; Elen Flavia Penques da Costa, **Centro de Cultura Idiomas – Taubaté**, Taubaté, Brazil; Inara Lúcia Castillo Couto, **CEL LEP – São Paulo**, São Paulo, Brazil; Sonia Patricia Cardoso, **Centro de Idiomas Universidad Manuela Beltrán**, Barrio Cedritos, Colombia; Geraldine Itiago Losada, **Centro Universitario Grupo Sol (Musali)**, Mexico City, Mexico; Nick Hilmers, **DePaul University**, Chicago, IL, USA; Monica L. Montemayor Menchaca, **EDIMSA**, Metepec, Mexico; Angela Whitby, **Edu-Idiomas Language School**, Cholula, Puebla, Mexico; Mary Segovia, **El Monte Rosemead Adult School**, Rosemead, CA, USA; Dr. Deborah Aldred, **ELS Language Centers, Middle East Region**, Abu Dhabi, United Arab Emirates; Leslie Lott, **Embassy CES**, Ft. Lauderdale, FL, USA; M. Martha Lengeling, **Escuela de Idiomas**, Guanajuato, Mexico; Pablo Frias, **Escuela de Idiomas UNAPEC**, Santo Domingo, Dominican Republic; Tracy Vanderhoek, **ESL Language Center**, Toronto, Canada; Kris Vicca and Michael McCollister, **Feng Chia University**, Taichung, Taiwan; Flávia Patricia do Nascimento Martins, **First Idiomas**, Sorocaba, Brazil; Andrea Taylor, **Florida State University in Panama**, Panamá, Panama; Carlos Lizárraga González, **Groupo Educativo Angloamericano**, Mexico City, Mexico; Bo-Kyung Lee, **Hankuk University of Foreign Studies**, Seoul, South Korea; Dr. Martin Endley, **Hanyang University**, Seoul, South Korea; Mauro Luiz Pinheiro, **IBEU Ceará**, Ceará, Brazil; Ana Lúcia da Costa Maia de Almeida, **IBEU Copacabana**, Copacabana, Brazil; Maristela Silva, **ICBEU Manaus**, Manaus, Brazil; Magaly Mendes Lemos, **ICBEU São José dos Campos**, São José dos Campos, Brazil; Augusto Pelligrini Filho, **ICBEU São Luis**, São Luis, Brazil; Leonardo Mercado, **ICPNA**, Lima, Peru; Lucia Rangel Lugo, **Instituto Tecnológico de San Luis Potosí**, San Luis Potosí, Mexico; Maria Guadalupe Hernández Lozada, **Instituto Tecnológico de Tlalnepantla**, Tlalnepantla de Baz, Mexico; Karen Stewart, **International House Veracruz**, Veracruz, Mexico; Tom David, **Japan College of Foreign Languages**, Tokyo, Japan; Andy Burki, **Korea University, International Foreign Language School**, Seoul, South Korea; Jinseo Noh, **Kwangwoon University**, Seoul, South Korea; Neil Donachey, **La Salle Junior and Senior High School**, Kagoshima, Japan; Rich Hollingworth, **La Salle Junior and Senior High School**, Kagoshima, Japan; Quentin Kum, **La Salle Junior and Senior High School**, Kagoshima, Japan; Geoff Oliver, **La Salle Junior and Senior High School**, Kagoshima, Japan; Martin Williams, **La Salle Junior and Senior High School**, Kagoshima, Japan; Nadezhda Nazarenko, **Lone Star College**, Houston, TX, USA; Carolyn Ho, **Lone Star College-Cy-Fair**, Cypress, TX, USA; Kaoru Kuwajima, **Meijo University**, Nagoya, Japan; Alice Ya-fen Chou, **National Taiwan University of Science and Technology**, Taipei, Taiwan; Raymond Dreyer, **Northern Essex Community College**, Lawrence, MA, USA; Mary Keter Terzian Megale, **One Way Línguas-Suzano**, São Paulo, Brazil; B. Greg Dunne, **Osaka Shoin Women's University**, Higashi-Osaka, Japan; Robert Maran, **Osaka Shoin Women's University**, Higashi-Osaka, Japan; Bonnie Cheeseman, **Pasadena Community College** and **UCLA American Language Center**, Los Angeles, CA, USA; Simon Banha, **Phil Young's English School**, Curitiba, Brazil; Oh Jun Il, **Pukyong National University**, Busan, South Korea; Carmen Gehrke, **Quatrum English Schools**, Porto Alegre, Brazil; John Duplice, **Rikkyo University**, Tokyo, Japan; Wilzania da Silva Nascimento, **Senac**, Manaus, Brazil; Miva Silva Kingston, **Senac**, Manaus, Brazil; Lais Lima, **Senac**, Manaus, Brazil; Yuan-hsun Chuang, **Soo Chow University**, Taipei, Taiwan; Mengjiao Wu, Shanghai Maritime University, Shanghai, China; Wen hsiang Su, **Shih Chien University Kaohsiung Campus**, Kaohsiung, Taiwan; Lynne Kim, **Sun Moon University (Institute for Language Education)**, Cheon An City, Chung Nam, South Korea; Regina Ramalho, **Talken English School**, Curitiba, Brazil; Tatiana Mendonça, **Talken English School**, Curitiba, Brazil; Ricardo Todeschini, **Talken English School**, Curitiba, Brazil; Monica Carvalho da Rocha, **Talken English School**, Joinville, Brazil; Karina Schoene, **Talken English School**, Joinville, Brazil; Diaña Peña Munoz and Zira Kuri, **The Anglo**, Mexico City, Mexico; Christopher Modell, **Tokai University**, Tokyo, Japan; Song won Kim, **TTI (Teacher's Training Institute)**, Seoul, South Korea; Nancy Alarcón, **UNAM FES Zaragoza Language Center**, Mexico City, Mexico; Laura Emilia Fierro López, **Universidad Autónoma de Baja California**, Mexicali, Mexico; María del Rocío Domínguez Gaona, **Universidad Autónoma de Baja California**, Tijuana, Mexico; Saul Santos Garcia, **Universidad Autónoma de Nayarit**, Nayarit, Mexico; Christian Meléndez, **Universidad Católica de El Salvador**, San Salvador, El Salvador; Irasema Mora Pablo, **Universidad de Guanajuato**, Guanajuato, Mexico; Alberto Peto, **Universidad de Oaxaca**, Tehuantepec, Mexico; Carolina Rodriguez Beltan, **Universidad Manuela Beltrán, Centro Colombo Americano**, and **Universidad Jorge Tadeo Lozano**, Bogotá, Colombia; Nidia Milena Molina Rodriguez, **Universidad Manuela Beltrán** and **Universidad Militar Nueva Granada**, Bogotá, Colombia; Yolima Perez Arias, **Universidad Nacional de Colombia**, Bogotá, Colombia; Héctor Vázquez García, **Universidad Nacional Autónoma de Mexico**, Mexico City, Mexico; Pilar Barrera, **Universidad Técnica de Ambato**, Ambato, Ecuador; Doborah Hulston, **University of Regina**, Regina, Canada; Rebecca J. Shelton, **Valparaiso University, Interlink Language Center**, Valparaiso, IN, USA; Tae Lee, **Yonsei University**, Seodaemun-gu, Seoul, South Korea; Claudia Thereza Nascimento Mendes, **York Language Institute**, Rio de Janeiro, Brazil; Jamila Jenny Hakam, **ELT Consultant**, Muscat, Oman; Stephanie Smith, **ELT Consultant**, Austin, TX, USA.

Scope and sequence

Functional language	Listening and Pronunciation	Reading and Writing	Speaking
			• Discussion about English words
Interactions: Asking for repetition Asking someone to speak more slowly	**Listening:** About a party An unusual interest **Pronunciation:** Intonation in *yes / no* and *Wh-* questions	**Reading:** "What's your hobby?" Social media posts **Writing:** An interest	• Interview about interests • *Keep talking:* Board game about favorites • Class contact list • Interview about sports and exercise • *Keep talking:* "Find someone who" activity about free-time activities • Discussion about other people's interests
Interactions: Saying you think something is true Saying you think something isn't true	**Listening:** People's personalities An online profile **Pronunciation:** *Is he* or *Is she*	**Reading:** "Online Profiles" A webpage **Writing:** Guess who!	• Descriptions of family member personalities • *Keep talking:* Quiz about confidence • Discussion about people at a party • Guessing game about physical appearances • *Keep talking:* Different physical appearances • Personal descriptions
Interactions: Asking for an opinion Giving an opinion	**Listening:** Weather in different cities A good time to visit places **Pronunciation:** Reduction of *would you*	**Reading:** "Canada Through the Seasons" A brochure **Writing:** An email to a friend	• True or false information about the weather • *Keep talking:* Information gap activity about the weather • Opinions about the weather • Decisions about things to do • *Keep talking:* Things to do someday • Discussion about places to visit
Interactions: Making a request Agreeing to a request	**Listening:** Friendly requests A tour of Graceland **Pronunciation:** Intonation in requests	**Reading:** "Unusual Homes from Around the World" An online article **Writing:** Dream home	• Discussion about homes • *Keep talking:* Memory game about a home • Problems and requests • Interview about chores • *Keep talking:* Decisions about chores • Discussion of a dream home
Interactions: Saying how you feel Wishing someone well	**Listening:** What's wrong? Creative ways to manage stress **Pronunciation:** Reduction of *and*	**Reading:** "Feeling Stressed?" An online article **Writing:** Managing stress	• Instructions • *Keep talking:* Exercises at your desk • Role play about health problems and not feeling well • Questions about healthy habits • *Keep talking:* Quiz about health • Tips for living with stress
Interactions: Agreeing with an opinion Disagreeing with an opinion	**Listening:** What to watch on TV Favorite TV shows **Pronunciation:** Sentence stress	**Reading:** "Reality Shows" An online article **Writing:** My favorite TV show	• "Find someone who" activity about TV preferences • *Keep talking:* Debate about things to watch • Opinions about television • List of shows to record • *Keep talking:* Plans for tomorrow • Discussion about reality TV shows

Scope and sequence

Functional language	Listening and Pronunciation	Reading and Writing	Speaking
Interactions: Bargaining for a lower price Suggesting a different price	**Listening:** Bargaining at a yard sale A weekend market in London **Pronunciation:** Linked sounds	**Reading:** "Chatucak Weekend Market" A webpage **Writing:** An interesting market	• Comparison of two products • *Keep talking:* Comparing several products • Role play of a bargaining situation • Discussion about clothes • *Keep talking:* Different clothing items • Discussion about good places to shop
Interactions: Asking for a recommendation Giving a recommendation	**Listening:** Cities At a tourist information desk **Pronunciation:** Word stress	**Reading:** "Austin or San Antonio?" A message board **Writing:** A message board	• Discussion about things to do in one day • *Keep talking:* Discussion of possible things to do • Role play at a tourist information desk • Comparison of places in a town or a city • *Keep talking:* City quiz • Discussion about aspects of a city
Interactions: Expressing certainty Expressing uncertainty	**Listening:** Friends playing a board game People who made a difference **Pronunciation:** Simple past -*ed* endings	**Reading:** "A Different Kind of Banker" A biography **Writing:** A biography	• Guessing game about famous people • *Keep talking:* Information gap activity about people from the past • Group quiz about famous people • Descriptions of admirable people • *Keep talking:* Discussion about inspiring people • Description of a person who made a difference
Interactions: Ordering food Checking information	**Listening:** Customers ordering food Restaurant impressions **Pronunciation:** *The* before vowel and consonant sounds	**Reading:** "Restaurants with a Difference" A webpage **Writing:** A review	• Discussion about eating out • *Keep talking:* A menu • Role play of a restaurant situation • Discussion about food experiences • *Keep talking:* Board game about food experiences • Restaurant recommendations
Interactions: Asking for suggestions Giving a suggestion	**Listening:** Fun things to do An influential world musician **Pronunciation:** Reduction of *of*	**Reading:** "Everybody Loves a Sing-Off" An online article **Writing:** A popular musician	• Movie talk • *Keep talking:* Movie favorites • Suggestions about the weekend • Class musical preferences • *Keep talking:* Class survey about music • A playlist
Interactions: Reacting to bad news Reacting to good news	**Listening:** Sharing news An interview with an athlete **Pronunciation:** Contraction of *will*	**Reading:** "An Olympic Dream Flies High" An online article **Writing:** A dream come true	• Discussion about changes • *Keep talking:* Reasons for doing things • Good news and bad news • Predictions about the future • *Keep talking:* Predictions about next year • Dream planner

Welcome

▮1 Working with a partner

A 🎧 Complete the conversations with the correct sentences. Then listen and check your answers.

- Can I borrow your pen?
- Let's compare our answers!
- Whose turn is it?
- Are you ready?

B PAIR WORK Practice the conversations.

2

2 Asking for help

A Match the questions and answers. Then practice with a partner.

1 How do you spell this word? ___d___
2 How do you pronounce this word? ___c___
3 What does this word mean? ___b___
4 How do you say *bienvenidos* in English? ___a___

a You say "welcome." ✓
b It means "not common." ✓
c /ˈhɑbi/ (hobby). ✓
d I-N-T-E-R-A-C-T-I-O-N-S. ✓

B Write these four questions in the conversations. Then compare with a partner.

> What does this word mean? ✓
> How do you pronounce this word? ✓
> How do you say *Boa sorte* in English?
> How do you spell your first name? ✓

1 A How do you pronounce this word?
  B /ˈkɑntɛkst/ (context).
  A Oh, that's easy!

2 A what does this word mean?
  B I think it means "working together."
  A Just like us!

3 A How do you spell your first name?
  B E-M-I-K-O.
  A That's a nice name.

4 A How do you say Boa Sorte in English?
  B You say "Good luck."
  A I see. Well, good luck!

C 🎧 Listen and check your answers. Then practice the conversations with a partner.

3 Speaking Do you know? *sabes*

A **PAIR WORK** Think of two English words you know. Ask your partner about them.

A: What *does* the word *kitten* mean? *(kiten) Que significa la palabra gatito*
B: It means "baby cat." *significa*

B **PAIR WORK** Look at a page in the book and find two words. Write one word in each *(cada)* blank. Ask about the words. *pregunta sobre las palabras*

How do you spell this word? _____   How do you pronounce this word? _____

C **GROUP WORK** Think of words or expressions that you want to know in English. Ask your group how to say them. Can they answer?
como se dice
A: How *do* you say _____ in English?
B: You say "_____."

Classroom language

A Write these actions below the correct picture. Then compare with a partner.

> Close your books.   Look at the picture.   Turn to page ...
> Listen.   ✓ Open your books.   Work in groups.
> Look at the board.   Raise your hand.   Work in pairs.

1   Open your books.

2   Look at the board

3   listen

4   Work in groups

5   Raise your hand

6   work in pairs

7   Look at the picture

8   close your books

9   Turn to page

A: What's number one?

B: It's ...

B 🎧 Listen and check your answers.

C 🎧 Listen to seven of the actions. Do each one.

1 My interests

Lesson A
- Interests
- Present of *be*

Lesson B
- Asking for repetition
- Asking someone to speak more slowly

Lesson C
- Sports and exercise
- Simple present

Lesson D
- Reading: "What's your hobby?"
- Writing: An interest

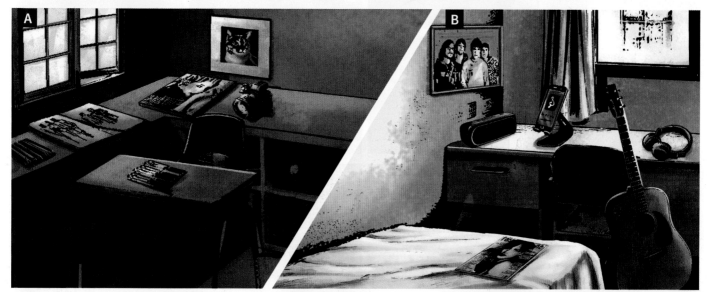

Warm Up

A Name the things in the pictures. What do you think each person likes? Why?

B Do you like similar things?

A I'm interested in fashion.

1 Vocabulary Interests

A 🎧 Match the words and the pictures. Then listen and check your answers.

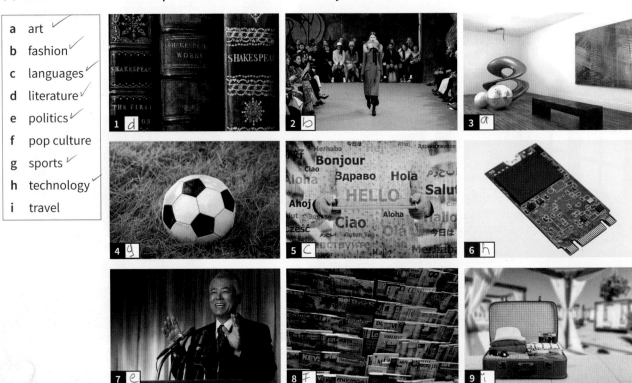

a art ✓	
b fashion ✓	
c languages ✓	
d literature ✓	
e politics ✓	
f pop culture	
g sports ✓	
h technology ✓	
i travel	

1 d
2 b
3 a
4 g
5 c
6 h
7 e
8 f
9 i

2 Language in context Find new friends!

A Read the survey. Then complete the survey with your own information.

LOOKING FOR NEW FRIENDS?
FIND SOMEONE WITH SIMILAR INTERESTS!

What's your name?_____

Where are you from? _____

How old are you? _____

Are you single or married? _____

Are you interested in . . . ?

travel	☐yes	☐no
sports	☐yes	☐no
fashion	☐yes	☐no

Who's your favorite . . . ?

actor_____

actress_____

singer_____

What's your favorite . . .?

TV show_____

movie_____

video game_____

B **GROUP WORK** Compare your information. Who are you similar to? How?

"Ming and I are similar. Our favorite movie is . . ."

3 Grammar 🎧 Present of *be*

Where **are** you from? *de dónde eres*	**Are** you interested in travel?
I'**m** from South Korea.	Yes, I **am**. No, I'**m not**.
How old **is** he? *cuantos años trienel*	**Is** he single?
He'**s** 22 years old.	Yes, he **is**. No, he'**s not**. / No, he **isn't**.
What **are** your friends' names?	**Are** they married?
Their names **are** Ming and Kathy.	Yes, they **are**. No, they'**re not**. / No, they **aren't**.

A Complete the conversations with the correct form of *be*. Then practice with a partner.

1   A What '*s* _____ your name?
    B Diego.
    A Where __*are*__ you from?
    B Mexico City.
    A __*are*__ you single?
    B No, I *am* ____ not. I _____ married.
    A __*are*__ you interested in fashion?
    B Not really. I _____ interested in sports.

2   A Where _____ your parents from?
    B My mother _____ from Osaka.
    A _____ your father from Osaka, too?
    B No, he _____. He _____ from Nagoya.
    A What _____ they interested in?
    B Art, languages, and literature.
    A _____ they interested in travel?
    B No, they _____.

B Read the answers. Write the possible questions. Then compare with a partner.

1   _What are you interested in?_   Technology.
2   _How old are you?_   I'm 20 years old.
3   _who is your favorite Singer?_   Taylor Swift.
4   _Are you Hong Kong?_   No, I'm from Seoul.
5   _Are you an English teacher?_   Yes, I am.
    Eres profesora de Inglés.

C **PAIR WORK** Ask and answer the questions in Part B.
Answer with your own information.

4 Speaking What are you interested in?

A **PAIR WORK** Interview your partner. Take notes.

1 Are you interested in literature? **YES** → *Who's your favorite writer?* **NO** → *What books are in your house?*
2 Are you interested in technology? **YES** → *What's a good cell phone?* **NO** → *How old is your cell phone?*
3 Are you and your friends interested in similar things? **YES** → *What are you and your friends interested in?* **NO** → *What are your friends interested in?*

B **PAIR WORK** Tell another classmate about your partner's answers.

"Elena is interested in literature. Her favorite author is Jane Austen."

5 Keep talking!

Go to page 125 for more practice.

I can ask and talk about interests. ☑

B Can you repeat that, please?

1 Interactions Asking for repetition

A Look at the pictures. Where are the people? What do you think they're talking about?

B 🎧 Listen to the conversations. Were your guesses from Part A correct? Then practice the conversations.

Fred	Fun party.
Carlos	Yeah, it is. Um, do you have the time?
Fred	It's . . . 9:50.
Carlos	I'm sorry. Can you repeat that, please?
Fred	Sure. It's 9:50.
Carlos	Wow! It's late.

Meg	So call me. OK?
Melissa	Sure. What's your number?
Meg	It's 629-555-0193.
Melissa	Can you say that more slowly, please?
Meg	Oh, sure. It's 629-555-0193.
Melissa	Got it. Thanks.

C 🎧 Listen to the expressions. Then practice the conversations again with the new expressions.

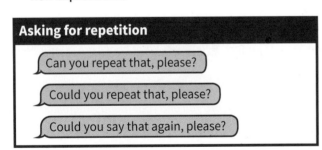

Asking for repetition	**Asking for someone to speak more slowly**
Can you repeat that, please?	Can you say that more slowly, please?
Could you repeat that, please?	Could you say that more slowly, please?
Could you say that again, please?	Could you speak more slowly, please?

D Put the words in order. Then practice the questions with a partner.

1 you / can / that / please / repeat   _Can you repeat that, please?_

2 slowly / please / say / you / can / more / that   _____

3 again / could / say / you / that / please   _____

4 slowly / please / more / you / speak / could   _____

8

2 Pronunciation Intonation in *yes / no* and *Wh-* questions

A 🎧 Listen and repeat. Notice the intonation in *yes / no* and *Wh-* questions.

Do you have the time? ↗   Are you interested in fashion? ↗

Where are you from? ↘   What's your number? ↘

B 🎧 Listen and mark the intonation in the questions. Then practice with a partner.

1   Who's your favorite actress?   3   Are you from here?

2   Do you like parties?   4   What's your email address?

3 Listening Could you . . .?

A 🎧 Listen to Clara's phone calls. Who does she talk to? Number the pictures from 1 to 3.

B 🎧 Listen again. Check (✓) the question that Clara is going to ask at the end of each conversation.

1   ☐ Can you repeat that, please?   ☐ Can you say that more slowly, please?

2   ☐ Could you repeat that, please?   ☐ Could you say that more slowly, please?

3   ☐ Could you say that again, please?   ☐ Could you speak more slowly, please?

4 Speaking Class contact list

A **GROUP WORK** Ask four classmates their name, email address, and birthday.
Make a list. Ask them to repeat or speak more slowly if necessary.

	Full name	Email address	Birthday
1			
2			
3			
4			

A: What's your full name?

B: It's Maria Sanchez.

A: I'm sorry. Could you . . .?

B Share your information and create a class contact list.

I can ask someone to speak more slowly. ✓

9

C Do you play sports?

1 Vocabulary Sports and exercise

A 🎧 These people are very active. Match the sentences and the pictures. Then listen and check your answers.

They . . .
bowl. _____
ski. _____
swim. _____

They play . . .
baseball. _____
golf. _____
table tennis. _____

They do . . .
gymnastics. _____
karate. _____
yoga. _____

B **PAIR WORK** Which sports and exercises in Part A do you do? Tell your partner.

"I swim and play baseball."

2 Conversation A ski sale

A 🎧 Listen and practice.

Clerk Can I help you?

Gina Yes, thank you. I want something for my boyfriend. It's his birthday tomorrow.

Clerk OK. What sports does he like? Does he play baseball?

Gina No, he doesn't.

Clerk How about table tennis? You can play together.

Gina No, we don't really like table tennis.

Clerk Well, does he ski?

Gina Yes! He skis all the time. Do you sell skis?

Clerk Yes, we do. And there's a ski sale right now.

Gina Great!

B Listen to the conversation between Gina and her boyfriend. Where are they?

3 Grammar 🎧 *Simple present*

What sports **do** you **like**?	**Do** you **sell** skis?
I **like** golf and karate.	Yes, I **do.** No, I **don't.**
I **don't like** basketball.	**Does** he **play** baseball?
What sports **does** he **play**?	Yes, he **does.** No, he **doesn't.**
He **plays** soccer.	**Do** they **like** table tennis?
He **doesn't play** baseball.	Yes, they **do.** No, they **don't.**
Where **do** they **do** yoga?	
They **do** yoga at home.	
They **don't do** yoga in the park.	

A Complete the paragraph with the simple present forms of the verbs. Then compare with a partner.

Every year, over a thousand men and women _____
(compete) in the Hawaii Ironman Triathlon. A triathlon _____
(have) three parts, but it _____ (not / have) three winners.
The person with the best time for the three races _____ (win).
They _____ (swim) for 3.86 km, _____ (bike)
for 180 km, and then _____ (run) for 42.2 km. The winner
_____ (get) $100,000.

B Put the words in order. Then ask and answer the questions. Answer with your own information.

1 soccer / do / play / on the weekend / you   _____

2 family / like / does / what sports / your   _____

3 best friend / your / where / does / exercise   _____

4 bowl / friends / do / your / on the weekend   _____

4 Speaking Do you . . . ?

A **PAIR WORK** Complete the questions in the chart. Then interview your partner. Take notes.

1 Do you play sports on the weekend? **YES** ➡ *What sports do you play?*
    NO ➡ *What do you do on the weekend?*   I walking every day

2 Do you watch sports on TV? **YES** ➡ What sports _do you watch on t.v_ ?
    NO ➡ What _do yo watch sport_ on TV?

3 Do you exercise in the morning? **YES** ➡ What _do you exercise in the morning_ ?
    you   **NO** ➡ When _do you exercise._ ?

B **PAIR WORK** Tell another classmate about your partner's answers.

"Ricardo plays basketball and does karate on the weekend."

5 Keep talking!

Go to page 126 for more practice.

I can ask and talk about sports and exercise habits. ✓

D Free time

1 Reading 🎧

A Look at the pictures. What is each person's hobby? Guess.

B Read the social media posts and check your guesses.

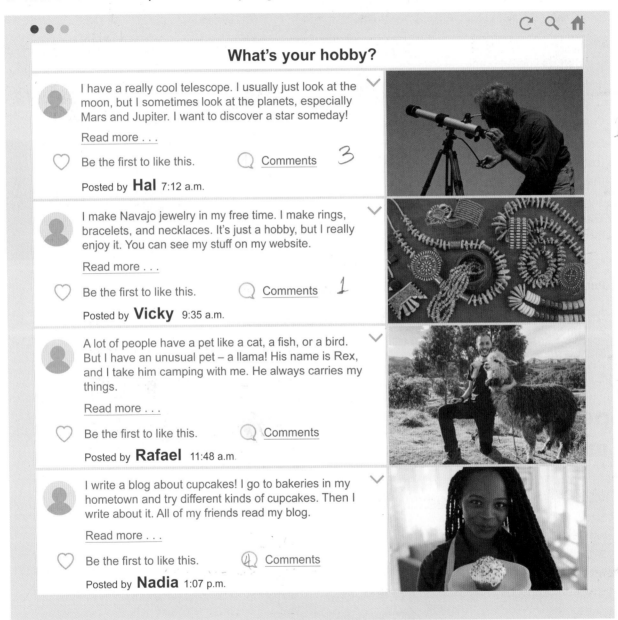

What's your hobby?

I have a really cool telescope. I usually just look at the moon, but I sometimes look at the planets, especially Mars and Jupiter. I want to discover a star someday!

Read more . . .

♡ Be the first to like this.   ◯ Comments *3*

Posted by **Hal** 7:12 a.m.

I make Navajo jewelry in my free time. I make rings, bracelets, and necklaces. It's just a hobby, but I really enjoy it. You can see my stuff on my website.

Read more . . .

♡ Be the first to like this.   ◯ Comments *1*

Posted by **Vicky** 9:35 a.m.

A lot of people have a pet like a cat, a fish, or a bird. But I have an unusual pet – a llama! His name is Rex, and I take him camping with me. He always carries my things.

Read more . . .

♡ Be the first to like this.   ◯ Comments

Posted by **Rafael** 11:48 a.m.

I write a blog about cupcakes! I go to bakeries in my hometown and try different kinds of cupcakes. Then I write about it. All of my friends read my blog.

Read more . . .

♡ Be the first to like this.   ◯ Comments

Posted by **Nadia** 1:07 p.m.

C Read the social media posts again. Which comment follows each post? Number the comments from 1 to 4.

1 Your stuff is great! Do you sell it?

2 So where's a good place to get one?

3 Good luck! Oh, what would you name it?

4 I love the picture. What does he eat?

D **PAIR WORK** Which social media post do you like best? Write a comment for one of the people. Discuss your ideas.

washing the fish

2 Listening Is that a fish?

A 🎧 Listen to John tell his friend about *gyotaku*. Number the pictures from 1 to 4.

B 🎧 Listen again. Answer the questions.

1 Where is *gyotaku* from? ___Japan___

2 Who does John work with? ___her sister___

3 Is it fun? _____

4 What does John sell? ___pictures.___

3 Writing An interest

A Think of an interest you have. Answer the questions.

- What are you interested in?
- What do you do?
- What do you like about it?

B Write a blog post about an interest you have. Use the model and your answers in Part A to help you.

Collecting Autographs

I'm interested in autographs. I collect them from baseball players. Sometimes players write their names on pieces of paper. Sometimes they write on their photos. My favorite is an autographed baseball. It's just a hobby, but I really enjoy it.

C **PAIR WORK** Share your writing. Ask and answer questions for more information.

4 Speaking Other people's interests

GROUP WORK Think about people you know. Which of the things below do they do? Ask and answer questions for more information.

writes a blog	wears cool clothes	has a favorite sports team
collects something	cooks a lot	makes something
travels a lot	has an unusual pet	reads a lot

A: My friend Masao writes a blog.

B: What does he write about?

A: He usually writes about sports.

C: How often do you read it?

I can *talk about people's free-time activities.* ✓

Wrap-up

1 Quick pair review

Lesson A Brainstorm!
Make a list of interests. How many do you know? You have one minute.

> fashion
>
> politics

Lesson B Do you remember?
Check (✓) the questions you can ask when someone is speaking too fast or
you want someone to repeat something. You have one minute.

____✓____ Could you repeat that, please?

_____ Can you say that more slowly, please?

_____ What does this mean?

_____ Could you say that again, please?

_____ Can I speak to Rita, please?

_____ Can you repeat that, please?

_____ Could you speak more slowly, please?

_____ How do you spell that?

Lesson C Test your partner!
Say the names of sports and exercises. Can your partner say the correct verb?
You have one minute.

Student A:    **Student B:**   yoga

A: Baseball

B: Play baseball.

Lesson D Guess!
Describe or act out an interest or a sport, but don't say its name. Can your partner
guess what it is? Take turns. You and your partner have two minutes.

A: I write online every day. Other people read my writing.

B: Do you write a blog?

A: Yes, I do.

2 In the real world

Who has unusual interests? Go online and find someone
with one of these interests. Then write about it.

has an unusual pet	collects something
makes something	plays an unusual sport

Unusual pets

A woman in the U.S. has ducks
as pets . . . .

2 Descriptions

LESSON A
- Personality adjectives
- *What . . . like?*; *be* + adjective (+ noun)

LESSON B
- Saying you think something is true
- Saying you think something isn't true

LESSON C
- Appearance
- *What . . . look like?*; order of adjectives

LESSON D
- Reading: "Online Profiles"
- Writing: Guess who!

Warm Up

A Match the comments and the people in the pictures.

    4   "We love your new car!"   3   "That's very good. Good job!"

    2   "What a great place!"   1   "I wonder what's going to happen next."

B What else can you say about the people in the pictures?

A He's talkative and friendly.

1 Vocabulary Personality adjectives

A 🎧 Match the words and pictures. Then listen and check your answers.

a confident
b creative *crieitl*
c friendly
d funny
e generous
f hardworking
g serious
h shy *(shai)*
i talkative

timido
totati
hablador

I em

 1 g

 2 d

 3 h

 4 a

 5 f

 6 b

 7 e

 8 c

 9 f

B PAIR WORK Which words describe you? Tell your partner.

"I'm hardworking and creative. Sometimes I'm shy."

2 Language in context Find an e-pal!

A 🎧 Read Nick's answers to an online form. Then complete the form with your own information.

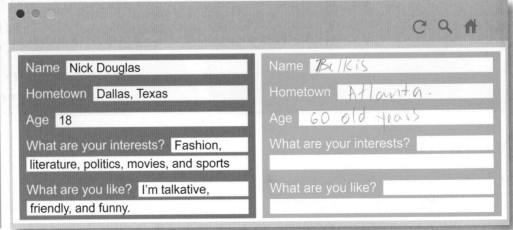

Name Nick Douglas

Hometown Dallas, Texas

Age 18

What are your interests? Fashion, literature, politics, movies, and sports

What are you like? I'm talkative, friendly, and funny.

Name Belkis

Hometown Atlanta.

Age 60 old years

What are your interests?

What are you like?

B Is Nick a good e-pal for you? Why or why not?

3 Grammar 🎧 *What . . . like?; be* + adjective (+ noun)

What are you like?	**What's she like?**	**What are they like?**
I'm talkative and friendly.	She's shy but friendly.	They're hardworking.
I'm **a** friendly and talkative **person**.	She's **a** shy but friendly **girl**.	They're hardworking **students**.

A Put the words in order. Then compare sentences with a partner.

1 teacher / a / Mrs. Jenkins / creative / is
2 Melissa / student / serious / a / is
3 funny / Bruno / is / talkative / and
4 are / Rodrigo and Miguel / confident / men
5 women / Marina and Elisa / are / hardworking
6 is / and / generous / Carrie / friendly

[handwritten:]
Mrs Jenkins
Melissa serious student
Bruno is talkative and Funny
Rodrigo and Miguel are con/
Marina and Elisa are hardworking women

B Read the answers. Write the *What . . . like?* questions. Then practice with a partner.

1 What are you like? — I'm serious but friendly.
2 *[handwritten:]* what is she like — Eva is a very funny girl.
3 *[handwritten:]* what are you like? — Matt and I are talkative people.
4 *[handwritten:]* what are they like? — Mr. and Mrs. Park are generous.
5 *[handwritten:]* what are you like? — I'm very serious and hardworking.
6 *[handwritten:]* what is he like? — His brother Sam is a creative guy.

4 Speaking He's hardworking.

A **PAIR WORK** Choose three people from your family. Describe them to your partner.

brother	father	grandfather	husband
sister	mother	grandmother	wife

A: My brother's name is Gi-woo.

B: What's he like?

C: Well, he's very hardworking. He's 26 and he's an accountant. He works late every day.

B **GROUP WORK** Are the people you know similar or different?

A: My brother is really hardworking.

B: Really? My mother is hardworking, too. She's a . . .

5 Keep talking!

Go to page 127 for more practice.

I can ask and talk about people's personalities. ✓

B I don't think so.

1 Interactions When you're not sure

A Look at the picture. Where are the people?

B 🎧 Listen to the conversation. Do Will and Joe know Mike well? Then practice the conversation.

Will What's your new roommate like?	**Will** Does he know many people here?
Joe Mike? Oh, he's nice, but he's not very talkative.	**Joe** I don't think so.
Will Really? Is he shy?	**Will** Well, maybe we can all go out together sometime.
Joe I think so.	**Joe** That's a great idea.

C 🎧 Listen to the expressions. Then practice the conversation again with the new expressions.

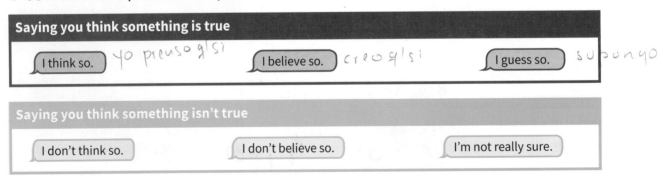

Saying you think something is true

I think so.   *yo pieuso g/si*   I believe so.   *creo g/si*   I guess so.   *supongo*

Saying you think something isn't true

I don't think so.   I don't believe so.   I'm not really sure.

D Complete each response with one of the expressions from Part C. Then practice with a partner.

1 A Is Rafael hardworking?   B *I guess so* _____ He studies a lot.

2 A Is Marilyn married?   B _____ She doesn't have a ring.

3 A Is David creative?   B _____ He paints a lot.

4 A Is Maria interested in travel?   B _____ She doesn't have a passport.

5 A Is Sun-hee friendly?   B *I think so* _____ People like her.

2 Pronunciation *Is he* or *Is she*

A 🎧 Listen and repeat. Notice the pronunciation of *Is he* and *Is she*.

/IZi/   /IʃI/

Is he hardworking?   **Is she** a good student?

B 🎧 Listen and write *he* or *she*. Then practice with a partner.

1 Is _____She_____ a creative person?   3 Is _____He_____ a serious student?

2 Is _____He_____ your new roommate?   4 Is _____she_____ generous?

3 Listening People we know

A 🎧 Listen to two friends talk about different people. Who are they talking about? Check (✓) the correct answers.

1 ☑ a teacher   2 ☑ a classmate   3 ☐ best friends
   ☐ a student   ☐ a father   ☑ classmates *clasmeit*
   ☐ a friend   ☑ a neighbor   ☐ teachers

B 🎧 Listen again. Circle the words you hear.

1 generous   2 (talkative)   3 (serious)
  (great)   hardworking   confident
  (funny)   (shy) *shai*   (nice)
   creative   (friendly) *Friendly*   (talkative) *tokedef*

4 Speaking Is he friendly?

A **PAIR WORK** Talk about the people at the party. Use the words in the box and your own ideas.

| friendly |
| talkative |
| shy |
| creative |
| serious |
| funny |
| single |
| married |
| a student |
| a teenager |
| a parent |

A: Is Jun friendly?

B: I believe so.

A: Is he married?

B: I don't think so.

B **PAIR WORK** You want to meet one person at the party. Who do you talk to? Why?

I can say I think something is true and not true. ✓   19

C What do they look like?

1 Vocabulary Appearance

A 🎧 Complete the descriptions with the correct words. Then listen and check your answers.

bald	middle-aged	mustache	red	short	tall

1 They're **young**. Rob is **short** and **overweight**, and May is ___tall___ and **thin**. Rob has **straight brown hair**. May has **blond** hair. It's ___short___ and **wavy**.

2 They're _____. Lou and Jill have **curly** ___short___ hair. Jill has **shoulder-length hair**. Lou has **little round glasses**.

3 They're **elderly**. They're **medium height**. Tony is ___bald___ and has **a short white beard** and a ___mustache___. Angela has **long gray** hair.

B PAIR WORK Describe people in your family using the words in Part A.

"My brother is young. He's ten. My father has a mustache. And my . . ."

2 Conversation That's not my husband!

A 🎧 Listen and practice.

Waiter Good evening. Can I help you?

Mrs. Gray Yes, thank you. Is Ken Gray here? He's my husband.

Waiter Mr. Gray? I don't know. What does he look like?

Mrs. Gray He's tall, thin, and has black hair. And he has glasses.

Waiter Does he have a mustache?

Mrs. Gray Yes, he does.

Waiter I think he's over there.

Mrs. Gray No, that's not my husband! My husband has short hair.

B 🎧 Listen to the rest of the conversation. Who is Mr. Gray with?

3 Grammar 🎧 *What . . . look like?;* order of adjectives

What do you look like?

I'm short and overweight.

I have glasses.

What does he look like?

He's tall and thin.

He has a mustache.

What do they look like?

They're middle-aged.

They have curly red hair.

The order of adjectives is usually size, age, shape, and color.

She has **long gray** hair. (size + color)

She has **new green** glasses. (age + color)

He has **little round** glasses. (size + shape)

They have **curly red** hair. (shape + color)

A Look at the picture. Complete the sentences with two adjectives. Then compare with a partner.

grande ~ | big | brown | long | (round) ~round | short | thin | (wewi) ~ wavy | young (yan) |
largo ~ redonda ~ corta ~ dolgada ~ ongola ~ joven

1 He is a __young__ and __thin__ man.

2 He has __long wavy__ hair.

3 He has a __short brown__ beard.

4 He has __big round__ glasses.

B Put the words in order. Then ask and answer the questions. Answer with your own information.

1 like / what / do / look / you __what do you like.__

2 best friend / look / what / does / your / like __what does your best friend look like__

3 what / like / look / does / favorite singer / your __what does your look favorite singer look like__

4 Speaking Who is it?

PAIR WORK Describe a person in one of the pictures below, but don't say his or her name! Your partner guesses the person. Take turns.

Cara   Adam

Maggie   Lucy   Beth

Bo   Hai
Mei
Yi-Yin
Shen   Jiang

"This person is tall and has short black hair."

5 Keep talking!

Student A go to page 128 and Student B go to page 130 for more practice.

I can ask and talk about people's appearances. ✓

D People's profiles

1 Reading 🎧

A Read the webpage profiles. What is each person like?

Online profiles

Name: Adriano   **Home:** Belo Horizonte, Brazil *(wer)*
(hom)
Appearance: I'm tall and have long brown hair. I wear only black.
Personality: I'm a very creative person. I like to make different things from paper. I do it just for fun. I can make airplanes, birds, boats, and flowers.

Name: Bea   **Home:** London, U.K.
Appearance: I'm 60, with red hair. I always wear green glasses.
Personality: I think I'm a very generous person. I have a lot of free time, so I do a lot of volunteer work at local schools. To me, it's very important to give back to my community.

Name: Suchin   **Home:** Bangkok, Thailand
Appearance: I'm 30. I'm medium height and I have short hair.
Personality: I'm friendly and hardworking. I work as a salesclerk in a clothing store. We sell clothing from northern Thailand there. In my free time, I play the *seung*, a traditional musical instrument.

Name: Marco   **Home:** Iquitos, Peru
Appearance: I'm tall and handsome, with long black hair.
Personality: I'm talkative and friendly. I have a part-time job. Iquitos is in the Amazon, so piranha fishing is very popular. I take tourists fishing, but we never keep the fish.

B Read the webpage again. Adriano, Bea, Suchin, and Marco later uploaded these photos to their profiles. Write the name of the person under the correct photo.

Marco

Bea

Suchin

Adiano

C Who wrote each sentence? Write the names.

1 ___Marco___ But there's one problem – I can't swim!

2 ___Suchin___ My neighbors complain about the noise.

3 ___Bea___ I especially like to work with children.

4 ___Adriano___ I spend a lot of money on paper!

D **PAIR WORK** Which person do you think is interesting? Why? Tell you partner.

2 Listening Starting a profile

A 🎧 Listen to Brian help his mother join a social networking site. Check (✓) the picture that Linda posts on the site.

B 🎧 Listen again. Check (✓) the information Brian's mother includes in her profile.

☐ Age ☑ Appearance ☑ Favorite actress ☑ Favorite singer ☐ Personality

3 Writing and speaking Guess who!

A Think about your appearance and personality. Answer the questions.

- How old are you?
- What do you look like?
- What are you like?

B Write a description of yourself, but don't write your name! Use the model and your answers in Part A to help you.

Guess who

I'm 18 years old. I'm thin and medium height. I have short black hair and glasses. I'm a friendly and talkative person, but sometimes I'm shy. I'm creative and very interested in art and fashion.

C GROUP WORK Put your papers face down on the table. Take one paper and read the description. Your group guesses who it is. Take turns.

A: This person is interested in art and fashion.

B: I think I know. Is it Marta?

A: No, Marta has long hair.
This person has short hair.

B: Oh, OK.

C: Is it . . . ?

I can describe my personality and appearance. ✓

23

Wrap-up

1 Quick pair review

Lesson A Brainstorm!

Make a list of personality adjectives. How many do you know? You have two minutes.

Lesson B Test your partner!

Ask your partner the questions. Can your partner give the correct answers? You have one minute.

Student A: What are three ways to say you think something is true?

Student B: What are three ways to say you think something isn't true?

Lesson C Do you remember?

Look at the picture. Circle the correct word for each sentence. You have one minute.

1   This is Eduardo. He's **young** / **elderly**.

2   He has **short** / **long** gray hair.

3   His hair is **straight** / **curly**.

4   He has **little** / **big** glasses.

5   He has a **mustache** / **beard**.

Lesson D Find out!

Are any of your and your partner's friends similar? Take turns. You and your partner have two minutes.

A: My friend is tall and has long black hair. She's very funny.

B: My friend is tall and has long black hair. She's funny, too.

2 In the real world

Who are you like? Go online and find a musician, an actor, or an actress who is similar to you. Then write a description of him or her.

- What does he or she look like?
- What is he or she like?

Scarlett Johansson

Scarlett Johansson is similar to me. She's medium height. She has blond hair . . .

3 Rain or shine

(Rein) *(or)* *(Shain)*
lluvia *o* *sol*

Lesson A
- Weather
- Adverbs of intensity; quantifiers with verbs

Lesson B
- Asking for an opinion
- Giving an opinion

Lesson C
- Indoor activities
- *Would like* + infinitive

Lesson D
- Reading: "Canada Through the Seasons"
- Writing: An e-mail to a friend

Warm-up

A Describe the pictures. Where are the people? What are they doing?

B Do you ever do these activities? When do you do them?

A It's extremely cold.

(ires) (estrim) (lou)
hace mucho frio
(wether)

1 Vocabulary Weather *clima*

A 🎧 Label the pictures with the correct words. Then listen and check your answers.

Weather				
(claury)	*(reini)*	*(snoowii)*	*(sani)*	*(windi)*
cloudy	rainy	snowy	sunny	windy
nublado	*lluvioso*	*nevado*	*soleado*	*vientos*

Temperature *(tempecher)*			
(kold)	*(ku)*	*(jat)*	*(worm)*
cold	cool	hot	warm
fria	*frio*	*caliente*	*calida*

6 ___Hot___
7 ___Wear___
8 ___cold___
9 ___cool___

1 __Sunny__   2 __cloudy__   3 __windy__   4 __rainy__   5 __snowy__

B **PAIR WORK** What's the weather like in your country in each season? Complete the chart with the words from Part A. Then compare answers.

Primavera

spring	summer *(samer)*	fall *(fol)*	winter		rainy season *(drai) (sisen)*	dry season
	verano	*otoño* autumm *(aron)*	*invierno*		*Temporada de lluvias*	*estacion seca*

2 Language in context Favorite seasons

A 🎧 Listen to people talk about their favorite season. Which places are cool?

My favorite season is spring. It's fairly cool, and rains quite a bit, but it's a good time to see the flowers.

–Jan, Lisse, Holland

I like summer a lot. It's very windy – great for windsurfing! And it doesn't rain at all.

– Fouad, Essaouira, Morocco

Fall is my favorite. It's sunny and cool, and in late October, 150 million butterflies arrive!

– Juan, Morelia, Mexico

I love winter. It's extremely cold, and it snows a lot, but that's when the Sapporo Snow Festival is.

– Rie, Sapporo, Japan

B What about you? What's your favorite season? What's the weather like then?

3 Grammar 🎧 Adverbs of intensity; quantifiers with verbs

Adverbs of intensity	Quantifiers with verbs
It's **extremely** cold.	It snows **a lot**.
It's **very** windy.	It rains **quite a bit**. *llueve bastante*
It's **really** hot.	It snows **a little**.
It's **pretty** sunny. *soleado*	It doesn't rain **very much**. *no esta lloviendo mucho*
It's **fairly** cool. *esta fresco*	It doesn't rain **at all**. *no esta lloviendo*
It's **somewhat** cloudy. *mas o menos*	

Add the adverbs and quantifiers to the sentences. Then compare with a partner.

1   It snows in Moscow in the winter. (a lot)

2   It rains in Seattle in the winter. (quite a bit)

3   It's cold in Busan in January. (extremely)

4   It's cool in Rabat in the rainy season. (fairly)

5   It snows in Lima in July. (not . . . at all)

6   It's windy in Wellington all year. (pretty)

It snows a lot in Moscow in the winter.

It rains quite a bit in Seattle in the winter too.

it's extremely cold in Busan in January

it's fairly cool in Rabat in the rainy season

_____

it's _____

4 Listening Think about the weather!

A 🎧 **Listen to people talk about the weather in three cities. Which city is one of the people planning to visit? Circle the city.**

1   Istanbul, Turkey   It's _____ cold in the winter.

2   Antigua, Guatemala   The _____ season is from November to April.

3   Beijing, China   It's _____ and _____ in the spring.

B 🎧 **Listen again. Complete the sentences with the correct words.**

5 Speaking True or false?

A   Write two true sentences and two false sentences about the weather where you live. Use these words and expressions.

pretty sunny	rain a lot	somewhat cloudy
extremely hot	very windy	fairly cool
really cold	snow	

B   **PAIR WORK** Read your sentences. Your partner corrects the false sentences. Take turns.

A: It's pretty sunny in the winter.

B: I think that's false. It's somewhat cloudy in the winter.

6 Keep talking!

Student A go to page 129 and Student B go to page 131 for more practice.

I can talk about the weather and seasons. ✓

B In my opinion, . . .

1 Interactions Opinions

A Do you ever videochat? What do you like about it? What don't you like?

B 🎧 Listen to the conversation. Where are the three people? Then practice the conversation.

Cindy   So, Luk, how are things in Bangkok?

Luk   Great. It's warm and sunny today.

Brian   It's really cold here in Chicago. So when are you coming to see us?

Luk   Well, when is a good time to visit?

Cindy   Hmm . . . I'm not sure.

Luk   Brian? What do you think?

Brian   I think fall is a good time. The weather is great, and there's a lot to do.

Cindy   Yeah, we can all go to a baseball game then.

Luk   That would be great!

C 🎧 Listen to the expressions. Then practice the conversation with the new expressions.

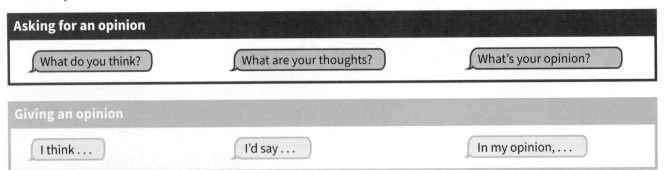

Asking for an opinion		
What do you think?	What are your thoughts?	What's your opinion?

Giving an opinion		
I think . . .	I'd say . . .	In my opinion, . . .

D Number the sentences from 1 to 6. Then compare with a partner.

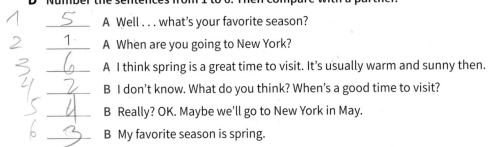

1   __5__   **A** Well . . . what's your favorite season?

2   __1__   **A** When are you going to New York?

3   __6__   **A** I think spring is a great time to visit. It's usually warm and sunny then.

4   __2__   **B** I don't know. What do you think? When's a good time to visit?

5   __4__   **B** Really? OK. Maybe we'll go to New York in May.

6   __3__   **B** My favorite season is spring.

2 Listening When's a good time to visit?

A 🎧 Listen to three people talk to friends about the best time to visit these cities. Are their friends' opinions the same or different? Circle your answers.

Rio de Janeiro, Brazil

Queenstown, New Zealand

Marseille, France

1   the same / different

2   the same / different

3   the same / different

B 🎧 Listen again. Write T (true) or F (false) next to the sentences.

1   Gabriel is from Rio de Janeiro, but Bianca isn't. ___F___

2   It's very hot in Rio de Janeiro in February. _____

3   Patricia thinks it's fine to visit New Zealand anytime. _____

4   It's extremely cold in New Zealand in July and August. _____

5   Sophie is from Marseille. _____

6   A lot of stores and restaurants in France close in August. _____

[handwritten: chilly = cold]

3 Speaking Good time, bad time

A **PAIR WORK** Discuss the weather and seasons where you live. Give your opinions.

● When's a good season to visit?

● What months are especially good?

● What's the weather like then?

● What kinds of things do people do then?

● When's not a good time to visit? Why not?

A: I think spring is a good time to visit Mexico. What do you think?

B: Yes, I'd say May is good.

A: The weather is warm then.

B: And there are some great festivals.

B **GROUP WORK** Share your opinions with another pair. Do you have the same opinions?

I can ask for and give an opinion. ✓

C I'd like to play chess.

1 Vocabulary Indoor activities

A 🎧 Complete the phrases with the correct words. Then listen and check your answers.

a board game	cookies	a jigsaw puzzle	popcorn
chess	a crossword	a nap	a video

a bake _cookies_   b do _a crossword_   c do _jigsaw puzzle_   d make _a video_

e make _popcorn_   f play _a board game_   g play _chess_   h take _a nap_

B **PAIR WORK** Rank these activities from 1 (fun) to 8 (not fun at all). Then compare answers.

A: I do a crossword every day, so I think that's really fun. How about you?

B: I never take a nap. I don't think that's fun at all. It's my number eight.

2 Conversation It's raining!

A 🎧 Listen and practice.

Joanie Oh, no! It's raining!

Evan We can't go on our picnic.

Joanie No. So, what would you like to do?
Would you like to do a jigsaw puzzle?

Evan Not really. Would you like to play chess?

Joanie Um, yeah, I would.

Evan We can make some popcorn, too.

Joanie Great idea. But let's play a little later.

Evan OK. Why?

Joanie I'd like to take a short nap.

B 🎧 Listen to their conversation later in the day.
What does Evan want to do?

3 Grammar 🎧 *Would like* + infinitive

What **would** you **like to do**?	**Would** you **like to do** a jigsaw puzzle?
I**'d like to play** chess.	Yes, I **would.** No, I **wouldn't.**
Where **would** he **like to play** chess?	Would they **like to take** a nap?
He**'d like to play** right here.	Yes, they **would.** No, they **wouldn't.**

A Circle the correct words. Then practice with a partner.

1 A Which game would you like **play** / **to play**?

   B **I'd like to** / **I would to** play chess.

2 A Would you like **do** / **to do** a crossword now?

   B No, **I'd not** / **I wouldn't.** I don't like crosswords.

3 A What **do** / **would** you like to do tonight?

   B **I'd like** / **I would** to watch TV with my friends.

B PAIR WORK Make true sentences with *I'd like to* or *I wouldn't like to*. Tell your partner.

have class outside	play chess after class	stay in this weekend	take a nap right now

4 Pronunciation Reduction of *would you*

A 🎧 Listen and repeat. Notice how *would you* is pronounced /wʊdʒə/.

Would you like to play a board game?   Which game **would you** like to play?

B PAIR WORK Practice the questions in Exercise 3A again. Reduce *would you* to /wʊdʒə/.

5 Speaking I'd like to . . .

A PAIR WORK Look out these windows and describe the weather. Then decide what you'd like to do together on each day. Take notes.

1   2   3

A: It's cool and rainy today. What would you like to do?

B: I'd like to do a jigsaw puzzle. How about you?

B GROUP WORK Share your ideas with another pair. Ask and answer questions for more information.

6 Keep talking!

Go to page 132 for more practice. ▶

I can talk about what I would like to do. ✓   31

D Where would you like to go?

1 Reading 🎧

A Read the article. Where do you think it is from? Check (✓) the correct answer.

☐ a vacation blog ☐ a tourist brochure ☐ a textbook ☐ a weather report

Canada Through the Seasons

The weather is very different in this large country, so there's something to do for everyone in every season.

Pacific Ocean · **British Columbia** · Churchill · *Hudson Bay* · **CANADA** · Calgary · **Alberta** · **Manitoba** · Victoria · **Saskatchewan** · **Ontario** · **Quebec** · **UNITED STATES** · Toronto · *Atlantic Ocean*

SPRING can arrive in February in Victoria on the west coast. In other parts of Canada, it gets warm in early April, and spring weather continues until June. In British Columbia, you can kayak, camp, or take a train trip through the Rocky Mountains.

SUMMER brings warm to hot weather from May to September. This is a great time to fish in one of Canada's many lakes; kayak among the whales in Churchill, Manitoba; or have some Wild West fun at the Calgary Stampede.

FALL brings cool temperatures in September and October. It's a good time of year to see the fall leaves in eastern Canada, enjoy hiking, visit museums, or go to the Toronto International Film Festival.

Snow begins to fall in November, and temperatures drop. Days are short in **WINTER**, but you can ski, go to an ice festival, or see the northern lights. In parts of British Columbia, the snow doesn't stay long and you can golf all year!

B Read the article again. When can you use these things? Write the season.

_____ _____ _____ _____

C GROUP WORK Imagine you can visit Canada. When and where would you go? Why? Discuss your ideas.

2 **Writing** An email to a friend

A Think of a place and a friend you would like to visit. Answer the questions.

- What is your friend's name?
- Where does your friend live?
- When do you plan to visit?
- What would you like to do there?

B Write an email to a friend about your travel plans. Use the model and your answers in Part A to help you.

Reply   Forward

From: Kate Spencer
  To: Hee-jin Choi

Hi, Hee-jin,

I have good news. I can visit you in Seoul this summer! Tell me about Seoul. What's the weather like in the summer? Is it really hot?

As you know, I'm very interested in art and food. So I'd like to visit the National Museum and go to some really good restaurants. What about you? What would you like to do?

This is so exciting! See you soon.

Kate

C **PAIR WORK** Share your writing. Ask and answer questions for more information.

3 **Speaking** A place I'd like to visit

A Think about a place you'd like to visit in your own country or a different country. Take notes.

Place: _____ When would you like to go?	Why would you like to go then?	What would you like to do there?

B **GROUP WORK** Share your ideas. Ask and answer questions for more information.

A: I'd really like to go to Kyoto in the spring.

B: Why would you like to go then?

A: Because I'd like to see the cherry blossoms.

C: What else would you like to do there?

I can talk about a place I'd like to visit. ✓

Wrap-up

1 Quick pair review

Lesson A Brainstorm!

Make a list of words for weather and words for temperature. How many do you know?
You have two minutes.

Lesson B Do you remember?

Check (✓) the questions you can ask when you want someone's opinion. You have one minute.

- ☐ What's your opinion?
- ☐ What's your teacher's name?
- ☐ What's the weather like today?
- ☐ What are your thoughts?
- ☐ What are you like?
- ☐ What do you think?

Lesson C Find out!

What is one thing both you and your partner would like to do outside this weekend? What is one thing you both would like to do inside? Take turns. You and your partner have two minutes.

A: I'd like to play chess inside. Would you?

B: No. I'd like to bake cookies. Would you?

A: Yes, I would.

Lesson D Guess!

Describe a famous place in your country, but don't say its name. Can your partner guess where it is? Take turns. You and your partner have two minutes.

A: It's hot, and it's a big city. People have parties on the beach.

B: Is it Rio de Janeiro?

A: Yes, it is.

2 In the real world

Where would you like to go? Go online and find the typical weather for that place in every season. Then write about it.

Chicago

I'd like to go to Chicago. There are four seasons. It's extremely cold in the winter. It's very windy in the spring . . .

4 Life at home

Warm Up

A These are the homes of world leaders. Match the countries and the pictures. Check your answers on page 44.

_____ Brazil   _____ France   _____ Iceland   _____ Japan

B Rank the homes you would like to visit from 1 (really want to visit) to 4 (don't want to visit).

A There's a lot of light.

1 Vocabulary Things in a home

A 🎧 Label the pictures with the correct words. Then listen and check your answers.

bathtub   bed   coffee table   refrigerator

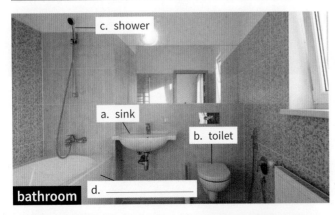

c. shower
a. sink
b. toilet
d. _____
bathroom

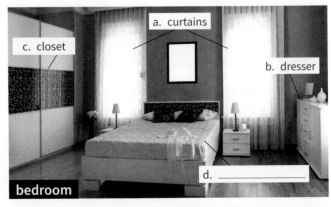

a. curtains
c. closet
b. dresser
d. _____
bedroom

a. _____
b. cupboards
c. stove
d. dishwasher
kitchen

b. shelves
c. armchairs
a. sofa
d. _____
living room

B PAIR WORK Which of the things in Part A do you have in your home? Tell your partner.

2 Language in context A new apartment

A 🎧 Listen to the conversation. Beth has a new apartment. Which room does Lori like?

Lori Your new place is nice. How many rooms are there?

Beth There are four – a kitchen, a living room, a bathroom, and a bedroom.

Lori I really like your kitchen.

Beth Thanks. There aren't many cupboards, and there isn't much space, but that's OK. I hardly ever cook.

Lori Look at all the windows in your living room!

Beth Yeah, there's a lot of light in here. But . . . there's also a lot of noise!

B What about you? What is important to you when you move into a new house or apartment?

3 Grammar 🎧 *How many/much;* quantifiers before nouns

How many cupboards are there?		
	a lot of	
There are	**some**	cupboards.
	a few	
There are**n't**	**many**	cupboards.
	any	

How much light is there?		
	a lot of	
There's	**some**	light.
	a little	
There is**n't**	**much**	light.
	any	

A Complete the questions with *many* or *much*. Answer the questions about the home in Exercise 1. Then practice with a partner.

1 How _____ space is there in the kitchen? _____

2 Are there _____ cupboards in the kitchen? _____

3 How _____ chairs are there in the living room? _____

4 Are there _____ shelves in the bathroom? _____

5 How _____ light is there in the bedroom? _____

B **PAIR WORK** Ask and answer questions about the apartment in Exercise 2.

rooms / apartment   cupboards / kitchen   space / kitchen

light / living room   windows / living room   noise / apartment

A: *How many rooms are there in the apartment?*

B: *There are four rooms. Are there many cupboards in the kitchen?*

4 Speaking My home

PAIR WORK Add three questions below. Then interview your partner. **Find out three things that are similar about your homes.**

● Do you live in a house or apartment?

● How many rooms are there?

● Are there many closets in the bedroom?

● Is there much space in the bathroom?

_____

_____

_____

A: *Do you live in a house or apartment?*

B: *I live in a small apartment.*

A: *Me, too.*

house

apartment

5 Keep talking!

Go to page 133 for more practice. ▶

I can ask and answer questions about my home. ✅   37

B Can you turn down the music?

1 Interactions Requests

A What are your neighbors like? Do you like them?

B 🎧 Listen to the conversation. Why does Keisha call her neighbor? Then practice the conversation.

Carlos Hello?

Keisha Hi. It's Keisha from downstairs. Are you having a party?

Carlos Uh-huh. Are we being noisy?

Keisha I'm afraid so. Can you turn down the music, please?

Carlos Sure. I can do it now.

Keisha Thank you. I have an exam tomorrow, and I'm trying to study.

Carlos I understand.

Keisha Thanks again.

C 🎧 Listen to the expressions. Then practice the conversation again with the new expressions.

Making a request
Can you turn down the music, please?
Could you turn down the music, please?
Would you turn down the music, please?

Agreeing to a request
Sure.
No problem.
I'd be happy to.

D Match the requests and the responses. Then practice with a partner.

1 Can you turn down your TV, please?
2 Can you move your car, please?
3 Could you answer the phone, please?
4 Would you open the curtains, please?

a I'd be happy to. I'm going to work now, anyway.
b Sure. I think it's for me.
c No problem. Sorry about the noise.
d Sure. There isn't much light in here.

2 **Pronunciation** Intonation in requests

A 🎧 **Listen and repeat. Notice the falling intonation in these requests.**

Can you turn down the music, please?   Can you move your car, please?

B PAIR WORK **Practice the questions in Exercise 1D again. Pay attention to your intonation.**

3 **Listening** Friendly requests

A 🎧 **Listen to three people call their neighbors. Where does each caller live? Circle the correct answers.**

1   apartment / house   2   apartment / house   3   apartment / house

B 🎧 **Listen again. What does each caller want the neighbor to do? Check (✓) the correct answers.**

1   ☐ stop the party   2   ☐ get the cat   3   ☐ stop exercising
    ☐ turn down the TV   ☐ move the car   ☐ exercise earlier
    ☐ turn down the music   ☐ buy some milk   ☐ stop the party

4 **Speaking** Neighbor to neighbor

A **Match the requests and the problems.**

1   Can you move it, please?   3   Could you come and get it, please?

2   Could you put it in the garbage can, please?   4   Would you keep it down, please?

Your neighbor's cat is at your door.

Your neighbor's guests are very noisy.

Your neighbor's car is in your parking space.

Your neighbor's garbage isn't in the garbage can.

B PAIR WORK **Call your neighbor. Identify yourself and explain the situation. Make a request. Take turns.**

A: Hello.

B: Hi. It's Mike from downstairs. Your cat is at my door. Could you come and get it, please?

A: Sure. I'd be happy to.

C PAIR WORK **Think of two more requests. Then call your partner to make the requests. Take turns.**

I can make and agree to requests. ☑   39

C I always hang up my clothes!

1 Vocabulary Household chores

A 🎧 **Label the pictures with the correct words. Then listen and check your answers.**

clean out the closet	drop off the dry cleaning	pick up the magazines	take out the garbage
clean up the yard	hang up the clothes	put away the dishes	wipe off the counter

1 _____

2 _____

3 _____

4 _____

5 _____

6 _____

7 _____

8 _____

B **PAIR WORK** **Which chores in Part A do you do? Tell your partner.**

"I always clean up the yard on the weekend. I also drop off the dry cleaning."

2 Conversation Let's clean it up!

A 🎧 **Listen and practice.**

Ken This place is a mess. Let's clean it up before Mom and Dad get home.

Paul Good idea. Well, I can put the dishes away and wipe off the counter.

Ken And, the garbage is full. Could you take it out?

Paul Sure. No problem.

Ken And you know, your bedroom is a mess, too. Your clothes are all over the floor. Would you pick them up, please?

Paul Yeah, I guess.

Ken And then hang them up in the closet?

Paul OK, but what are *you* going to do?

B 🎧 **Listen to the rest of the conversation. What chore is Ken going to do?**

3 Grammar 🎧 Separable two-word phrasal verbs

I **take out** the garbage.	Could you **hang up** your clothes, please?
I **take** the garbage **out**.	Could you **hang** your clothes **up**, please?
I **take** it **out**.	Could you **hang** them **up**, please?
Not: ~~I take out it.~~	*Not:* ~~Could you hang up them, please?~~

A Rewrite the sentences. Then compare with a partner.

1 Let's hang up the dry cleaning.   _Let's hang the dry cleaning up._

2 Could you put away your clothes, please?   _____

3 How often do you take out the garbage?   _____

4 I clean out my closets once a year.   _____

B Complete the sentences with the correct verbs. Use either *it* or *them*. Then compare with a partner.

clean out	drop off	pick up	take out
✓ clean up	hang up	put away	wipe off

1 The living room is a mess. Let's _____ _clean it up_ _____ before the party.

2 Why is your coat on the chair? Can you _____ in the closet?

3 The garbage is full. Could you _____ right away, please?

4 This closet is full of old clothes and books. Let's _____.

5 The dishes are in the dishwasher. Would you _____ for me?

6 This table isn't clean. Can you _____ before dinner, please?

7 These books belong to the library. Could you _____ for me?

8 Your magazines are all over the floor. Would you _____, please?

4 Speaking What a chore!

A **PAIR WORK** Interview your partner. Check (✓) his or her answers.

How often do you . . .?	My partner	How often do you . . .?	My partner
1 put away the dishes		4 clean out your closet	
2 clean up your bedroom		5 hang up your clothes	
3 take out the garbage			

B **GROUP WORK** Tell your group about your partner's answers. Who does a lot of chores? Who doesn't?

"Daniel does a lot of chores. He puts away the dishes and takes out the garbage every day."

5 Keep talking!

Go to page 134 for more practice.

I can talk about household chores. ✓

41

D What a home!

1 Reading 🎧

A Look at the pictures. Describe each home.

B Read the article. Check (✓) the best title for the article.

☐ Crazy Houses in the United States   ☐ Daily Life in a Strange House

☐ Unusual Homes from Around the World   ☐ How to Build Your Dream Home

The Storybook House

The classic children's story "Hansel and Gretel" inspired this unusual home in the U.S. The owners built the house by hand and included five fireplaces inside.

The Shoe House

This house in the U.S. has a living room, two bathrooms, a kitchen, and three bedrooms. There's even a shoe mailbox. The owner had a few shoe stores. No one lives there now, but there are tours of the house.

The Crazy House

People in Vietnam call this house the Crazy House because it looks strange. Part of the house is a tree, and it has unusual twists and turns. You can also see big animals on the outside. The house is a hotel and a tourist attraction.

The Upside-down House

In this house in Poland, the furniture hangs from the ceiling! No one lives there, but it's a popular tourist attraction. It took the workers a long time to build the house. They often felt sick inside.

C Read the article again. Answer the questions.

1 How did the owners build the Storybook House? _____

2 How many rooms are there in the Shoe House? _____

3 What can you see on the outside of the Crazy House? _____

4 What is unusual about the inside of the Upside-down House? _____

D PAIR WORK Which house would you like to stay in? Why? Tell your partner.

2 Listening A tour of Graceland

A Graceland was Elvis Presley's home in Memphis, Tennessee. Look at the pictures in Part B of four rooms in the home. What do you see? What do you think the house is like?

B 🎧 Listen to Sam and Haley take a tour of Graceland. Number the rooms from 1 to 4.

TV room

kitchen

dining room

living room

C 🎧 Listen again. What is each person's favorite room? Complete the sentences.

1 Sam's favorite room is the _____.

2 Haley's favorite room is the _____.

3 Writing and speaking Dream Home

A Imagine your dream home. Answer the questions.

- Where is your dream home?
- How many rooms does it have?
- What does it look like?
- Is there anything unusual about your home?

B Write a description of your dream home. Use the model and your answers from Part A to help you.

C PAIR WORK Share your writing. Ask and answer questions for more information.

> My Dream Home
> My dream home is on the beach in Hawaii. It's a very big house. It has five bedrooms, five bathrooms, and a lot of light and space. There are two kitchens. One kitchen is inside the house. The other kitchen is outside because we have a lot of barbecues on the beach!

A: What color is the house?

B: It's white.

A: What is your favorite part of the house?

B: The swimming pool.

I can describe a home. ✓

43

Wrap-up

1 Quick pair review

Lesson A `Brainstorm!`

Make a list of the rooms in a house and the things that go in each room. How many do you know?
You have two minutes.

Lesson B `Do you remember?`

Complete the conversations with the correct words. You have two minutes.

1 A <u>Could</u>_____ you turn down the music, please?

   B No p_____.

2 A W_____ you answer the phone, please?

   B I'd be h_____ to.

3 A Could you buy some milk, p_____?

   B S_____.

Lesson C `Test your partner!`

Act out a chore. Can your partner guess what it is? Take turns. You and your partner
have two minutes.

Lesson D `Guess!`

Describe a room in your house, but don't say its name. Can your partner guess what
room it is? Take turns.
You and your partner have two minutes.

A: This is my favorite room. There are three posters on the wall.

B: Is it your bedroom?

A: Yes, it is.

2 In the real world

Go online and find information in English about an unusual house.
Then write about it.

- Why is it unusual?
- What are the rooms like?
- Find a picture of the home, if possible.

An Unusual Home

Fallingwater is a famous house at
the top of a waterfall. It has rooms
that look like ...

Answers to Warm-up Part A (page 35)
a. Japan   b. Iceland   c. Brazil   d. France

5 Health

Warm Up

A Describe the pictures. Which activities are good for you? Which ones aren't?

B Do you ever do any of the things in the pictures? Which ones?

A Breathe deeply.

1 Vocabulary Parts of the body

A 🎧 Label the pictures with the correct words. Then listen and check your answers.

a	arm	d	finger	g	head	j	mouth	m	shoulder
b	ear	e	foot (feet)	h	knee	k	neck	n	stomach
c	eye	f	hand	i	leg	l	nose	o	wrist

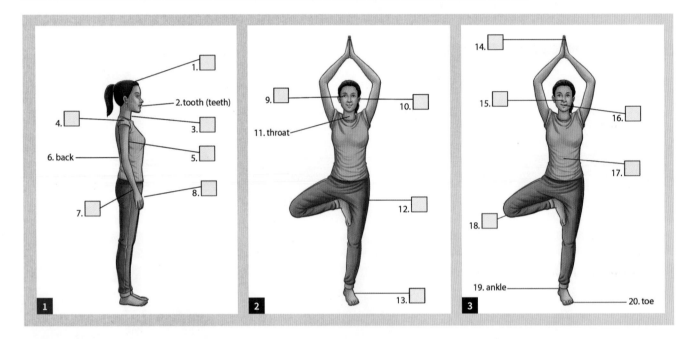

B **PAIR WORK** Point to a part of your body. Your partner names it. Take turns.

"That's your arm. And those are your ears."

2 Language in context Yoga for beginners

A 🎧 Match the exercises with the yoga pictures in Exercise 1. Listen and check your answers.

A. _____ Place your right foot carefully on your left leg. Stretch your arms over your head. Hold for 30 seconds. Lower your arms and foot slowly.

B. _____ Repeat on the other side. Place your left foot carefully on your right leg. Stretch your arms over your head. Hold for 30 seconds.

C. _____ Stand up. Hold your stomach in. Keep your back and neck straight. Relax your arms. Don't hold your breath. Breathe slowly and deeply.

B What about you? Do you do yoga? If not, would you like to try it? Why or why not?

3 Gram... of manner

Adjective	Adverb
slow	slowly
careful	carefully
deep	deeply
noisy	noisily

Breathe
deeply.
Stretch
Hold fo
Repea

A Comp... m. Then compare with a partner.

✓ d

1
2
3

4 _____ some water.
5 _____ a big meal before you exercise.
6 _____ twice a week.

B Circ
1
2
3
4
5

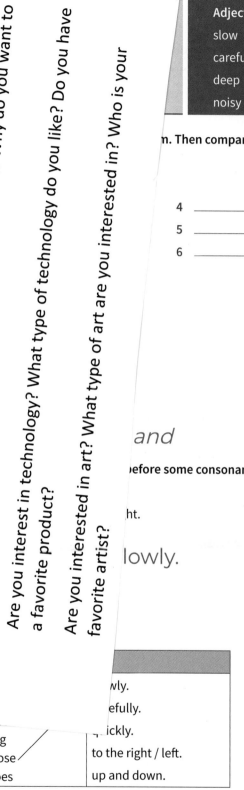

Are you interested in literature? Who is your favorite author? Do you have a favorite book?

Are you interested in sports? Which sport are you interested in? Which is your favorite team? Do you have a favorite player?

Are you interested in travel? Where would you like to travel? Why do you want to travel there?

Are you interest in technology? What type of technology do you like? Do you have a favorite product?

Are you interested in art? What type of art are you interested in? Who is your favorite artist?

4 Pr... *and*

🎧 L... before some consonant sounds.

Brea... ...ht.

5 S...

PA
You
"P...

A			
S			...wly.
I			...efully.
Point to	your		...ickly.
Move		leg	
Raise		nose	to the right / left.
Touch		toes	up and down.

6 Keep talking!

Go to page 135 for more practice.

B I'm not feeling well.

1 Health problems

🎧 Listen. Then act out a health problem. Your partner guesses it.

a backache   a cold   a cough   an earache   a fever

the flu   a headache   a sore throat   a stomachache   a toothache

"Do you have a cold?"

2 Interactions   When you're not feeling well

A 🎧 Listen to the conversation. What's wrong with Margaret? Then practice the conversation.

Debbie   Hey, Margaret. How are you?

Margaret   I'm not feeling well.

Debbie   Oh? What's wrong?

Margaret   I have a headache. I think I'd like to go home and rest.

Debbie   That's fine. Take it easy.

B 🎧 Listen to the expressions. Then practice the conversation again with the new expressions.

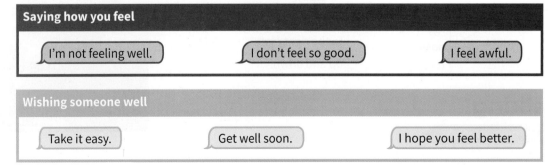

Saying how you feel

I'm not feeling well.   I don't feel so good.   I feel awful.

Wishing someone well

Take it easy.   Get well soon.   I hope you feel better.

3 **Listening** What's wrong?

A 🎧 Listen to four phone conversations. Number the pictures from 1 to 4.

B 🎧 Listen again. How does each caller wish the person well? Write the expression.

1 _____   3 _____

2 _____   4 _____

4 **Speaking** We're not feeling well.

CLASS ACTIVITY Role-play these situations. Then change roles.

Group A: Walk around the class and ask people in Group B how they feel. Use expressions from Exercise 2.

Group B: Imagine you have a health problem. Tell the people in Group A about it. Use expressions from Exercise 2.

A: How are you?

B: I don't feel so good.

A: Oh? What's wrong?

B: I have a stomachache.

A: I'm sorry to hear that. I hope you feel better.

I **can** wish someone well. ✓

C How healthy are you?

1 Vocabulary Healthy habits

A 🎧 Complete the phrases with the correct verbs. Then listen and check your answers.

| eat | eat | exercise | get | go | lift | protect | wash |

1 _____
a balanced diet

2 _____
your hands

3 _____
your skin

4 _____
weights

5 _____
for a walk

6 _____
daily

7 _____
enough sleep

8 _____
a good breakfast

B **PAIR WORK** Which of the healthy habits in Part A do you have? Tell your partner.

2 Conversation I don't have much energy.

A 🎧 Listen and practice.

Laura What's wrong, Hal? Are you OK?

Hal Oh, hi, Laura. I don't know. I just don't have much energy.

Laura Hmm. Do you eat breakfast every day?

Hal Sure. And I exercise. I lift weights at my gym.

Laura And how often do you go there?

Hal Three or four days a week.

Laura That's not bad. How long do you spend there?

Hal Oh, about an hour a day.

Laura That's good. And how much sleep do you get?

Hal Quite a bit, about ten hours a night.

Laura Ten hours? That's why you don't have any energy. I think that's too much sleep!

B 🎧 Listen to the rest of the conversation. What else does Laura ask about?

3 Grammar 🎧 *How* questions

How often do you go to the gym?	**How healthy** are your eating habits?
Three or four days a week.	Somewhat healthy.
How long do you spend at the gym?	**How many** meals do you eat a day?
About an hour.	Five small meals.
How well do you follow your diet?	**How much** sleep do you get?
Not very well.	Quite a bit.

A Complete the questions with a *How* question. Then compare with a partner.

1 _____ do you protect your skin from the sun?

   a Extremely well.   **b** Pretty well.   **c** Not very well.

2 _____ are your eating habits?

   a Very healthy.   **b** Quite healthy.   **c** Not healthy at all.

3 _____ coffee do you drink in a week?

   a A lot.   **b** Quite a bit.   **c** Not much.

4 _____ do you eat red meat?

   a Every day.   **b** Several times a week.   **c** Never.

5 _____ do you spend on the computer every week?

   a 40 hours.   **b** 20 hours.   **c** Five hours.

6 _____ times a day do you wash your hands?

   a About six times.   **b** About three times.   **c** Once.

B **PAIR WORK** Ask and answer the questions in Part A. Circle your partner's answers.

A: How well do you protect your skin from the sun?

B: Not very well. I sometimes wear a hat, but I rarely use sunscreen.

4 Speaking Good question!

A **GROUP WORK** Look at the pictures. How many different *How* questions can you make for each picture? Ask the questions.

  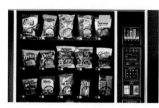 

A: How many times a week do you lift weights?

B: Never. I go to the gym once a week, but I don't lift weights.

C: How long do you spend at the gym?

B How healthy do you think you are?

5 Keep talking!

Go to page 136 for more practice. ▶

I can ask and talk about healthy habits. ✓

D Don't stress out!

1 Reading 🎧

A 🎧 Read the article. Write the correct headings above the paragraphs.

| Communicate | Breathe | Do Nothing | Move! | Laugh | Get Organized |

FEELING STRESSED?

Everyone feels stress, and a little stress is OK. It's what gives you energy and pushes you to do well at school or work. But too much stress is not good. There are ways to manage stress. Try one or more of these tips the next time you feel stressed out.

1. _____

Take a deep breath. Breathe slowly and deeply every time you begin to feel stress. Make this a habit, and you can often stop a little stress from becoming a lot of stress.

2. _____

Make a "to do" list, and decide what you need to do right away and what can easily wait. Clean up your study or work space. Do the same with your computer desktop.

3. _____

Go for a swim. Run. Ride your bicycle. Do aerobics. Hike up a mountain. It doesn't really matter what you do. Just do something that you enjoy.

4. _____

Have a problem? Don't keep it inside. Talk to a friend, a family member, or even your cat. Don't want to talk? Write it down in a stress journal.

5. _____

See a funny movie. Tell some jokes. Watch some silly pet videos on the Internet. Laughter – yours or someone else's – is often the best medicine.

6. _____

That's right . . . nothing. Close the door. No TV, computer, or phone. Sit down and take a break from life. Close your eyes, and feel the stress . . . disappear.

B Read the article again. Write the tip next to what each person does to manage stress.

_____	Jill	I watch my favorite TV show, and I laugh and laugh.
_____	Rachid	I go jogging. It makes me feel better.
_____	Paul	I just sit quietly. That's all I do!
_____	Valerie	I clean my house and put everything away.
_____	Ming	I stop and breathe deeply.
_____	Eduardo	I call a good friend and talk for a while.

C **PAIR WORK** Which tips in Part A do you think work? Tell your partner.

2 Listening It works for me!

A 🎧 Listen to four people talk about how they manage stress. What do they do? Number the pictures from 1 to 4. There are two extra items.

 ☐

 ☐

 ☐

 ☐

 ☐

 ☐

B 🎧 Listen again. What else do the people do to manage stress? Write the activities.

1 _____   3 _____

2 _____   4 _____

3 Writing Managing stress

A Think about how you manage stress. Answer the questions.

- How much stress do you feel?
- What makes you stressed?
- How well do you manage stress?
- What do you do?

B Write a paragraph about how you manage stress. Use the model and your answers in Part A to help you.

C **PAIR WORK** Share your writing. Do the same things stress you out?

How I Manage Stress

I don't often feel stressed, but Mondays are sometimes difficult. I'm a full-time student, but I have a part-time job on Mondays. Here are a few ways I manage stress on Mondays. I eat a good breakfast and lift weights. Then I go to school early and talk with friends. It really helps.

4 Speaking Living with stress

PAIR WORK Imagine you are one of these people. Ask your partner for tips to help you manage your stress.

- A mother with two young children and no time
- A young man before his wedding
- A soccer player before a big game
- A student before a big test

A: I'm very tired and my children never stop. What can I do?

B: Talk to your friends and find out what they do.

I can discuss ways to manage stress. ✓   53

Wrap-up

1 Quick pair review

Lesson A `Test your partner!`

Say the name of a sport. Can your partner say what parts of the body you use for the sport?
Take turns. You have one minute.

A: *Soccer.*

B: *Legs, feet, head, . . .*

Lesson B `Brainstorm!`

Make a list of ways to say how you feel and ways to wish someone well. You have two minutes.

Lesson C `Do you remember?`

Complete the questions with *much*, *well*, *healthy*, *many*, and *long*. You have one minute.

1 How _____ apples do you eat a week?

2 How _____ stress do you have at work?

3 How _____ do you work on Saturdays?

4 How _____ is your lifestyle?

5 How _____ do you manage stress?

Lesson D `Guess!`

Act out a way to manage stress. Can your partner guess what it is? Take turns.
You have one minute.

A: *Are you exercising?*

B: *Yes, I am.*

2 In the real world

What other ways can you manage stress? Go online and find three ideas in English.
Then write about them.

Three Ways to Manage Stress

Turn off your computer and your phone
for an hour. Then turn on some relaxing
music. Open a good book . . .

6 What's on TV?

LESSON A	LESSON B	LESSON C	LESSON D
● Types of TV shows ● Verb + infinitive or gerund	● Agreeing with an opinion ● Disagreeing with an opinion	● Television ● Present continuous for future plans	● Reading: "Reality Shows" ● Writing: My favorite TV show

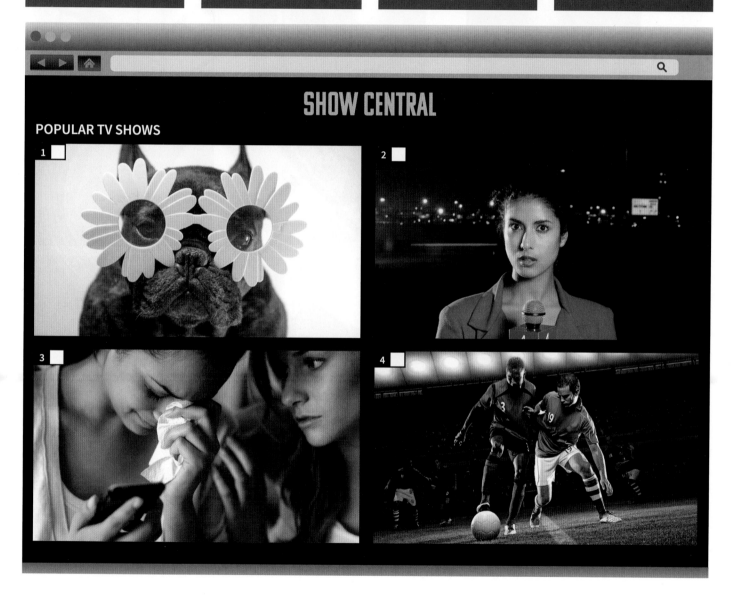

SHOW CENTRAL

POPULAR TV SHOWS

1
2
3
4

Warm Up

A Match the words with TV shows in the online menu.

a exciting   b funny   c serious   d sad

B Can you name some TV shows from your country? What kinds of TV shows do you like to watch?

A I love watching game shows.

1 Vocabulary Types of TV shows

A 🎧 Match the TV shows and the pictures. Then listen and check your answers.

a   a cartoon   d   a game show   g   a sitcom
b   a documentary   e   the news   h   a soap opera
c   a drama   f   a reality show   i   a talk show

1 [c]   2 [g]   3 [ ]
4 [ ]   5 [ ]   6 [ ]
7 [ ]   8 [ ]   9 [ ]

B **PAIR WORK** What was the last show you watched on TV? What type of show was it? Tell your partner.

"I watched a sitcom with my parents. It was . . ."

2 Language in context TV preferences

A 🎧 Listen to four people talk about their TV preferences. Who doesn't watch TV very much?

I watch a lot of TV. I really enjoy baseball.
And I hope to get a big new TV soon.

– Jessica

I love soap operas. My favorite is *Our Life*.
I like seeing my favorite actors.

– Lucas

I don't like reality shows at all. I love to watch
documentaries and game shows.

– Gustavo

I hardly ever watch TV. I prefer to listen to the
radio. I hate to miss the news.

– Min-hwa

B Which person in Part A are you similar to?

3 Grammar ⌕ Verb + infinitive or gerund

Verb + infinitive
I **hope to get** a big TV.
I **want to see** every baseball game.

Verb + gerund
I **enjoy watching** football games.
I **dislike watching** TV.

Verb + infinitive or gerund
I **like to see** / **seeing** my favorite actors.
I **love to watch** / **watching** game shows.
I **prefer to listen** / **listening** to the radio.
I **hate to miss** / **missing** the news.

A **Circle the correct verb forms. If both forms are correct, circle both.**
Then practice with a partner.

1 A What types of TV shows do you like **to watch** / **watching** late at night?

B Actually, I dislike **to watch** / **watching** TV at night. I prefer **to be** / **being** online.

2 A What do you want **to watch** / **watching** on TV tonight? A reality show?

B I hate **to watch** / **watching** those shows. I enjoy **to watch** / **watching** dramas.

3 A Do you want **to see** / **seeing** a movie tonight?

B No, not tonight. My favorite TV show is on, and I hate **to miss** / **missing** it.

B **Complete the questions with a correct form of the verb. Then compare**
with a partner.

1 Do you enjoy _____ (watch) cartoons on TV?

2 What do you want _____ (watch) on TV this weekend?

3 Do you like _____ (guess) the answers on game shows?

4 What types of TV shows do you dislike _____ (watch)?

C PAIR WORK **Ask and answer the questions in Part B. Answer with your own information.**

4 Speaking TV Talk

A **Add one more thing to the chart.**

Find someone who . . .	Name
1 enjoys watching documentaries	
2 wants to buy a new TV	
3 hopes to meet a famous actress or actor	
4 hates missing soap operas	
5	

B CLASS ACTIVITY **Find a classmate for each sentence. Write their names.**

A: *Do you enjoy watching documentaries?*

B: *Yes, I do.*

5 Keep talking!

Go to page 137 for more practice.

I can talk about types of TV shows I like. ✓

B I don't really agree.

1 Interactions Agreeing and disagreeing

A Look at the picture. What are the people doing? Do you think they like the TV show?

B 🎧 Listen to the conversation. Why doesn't Vasco like talk shows?
Then practice the conversation.

Fred	Let's see what's on TV. . . .Oh, no! I don't like this talk show at all. I think it's terrible.	**Fred**	Really? I disagree. I think some of them are pretty interesting.
Vasco	I agree. Actually, I hate all talk shows. I think they're really boring.	**Vasco**	I don't think any talk shows are interesting.
		Fred	Well, would you like to watch something else?

C 🎧 Listen to the expressions. Then practice the conversation again with the new expressions.

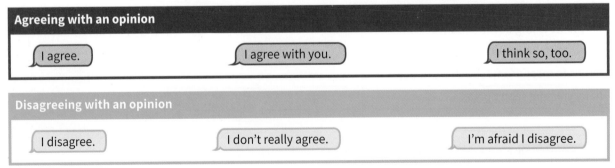

Agreeing with an opinion

I agree.   I agree with you.   I think so, too.

Disagreeing with an opinion

I disagree.   I don't really agree.   I'm afraid I disagree.

D Complete each response with one of the expressions from Part C. Then practice with a partner.

1 **A** Most TV sitcoms are funny.   **B** _____ I never laugh at them.

2 **A** Reality shows are great.   **B** _____ I watch them all the time.

3 **A** Game shows are exciting.   **B** _____ I think they're boring.

4 **A** It's good to watch the news.   **B** _____ I watch it every night.

5 **A** Cartoons are just for children.   **B** _____ They're for adults, too.

2 Listening What else is on?

A 🎧 Listen to Dan and Amy discuss what is on TV. Number the TV shows from 1 to 5. (There is one extra picture.)

The Forbidden City

Santa Monica

Big City Lights

On Your Own

The Maxine Weber Show

Just My Luck
ROUND 1

B 🎧 Listen again. Look at Amy's opinion of each show. Write Dan's opinion.

Amy's opinions: Dan's opinions:

1 boring   1 _____

2 great   2 _____

3 interesting   3 _____

4 exciting   4 _____

5 fantastic   5 _____

3 Speaking My opinion

A Check (✓) the statements you agree with. Then make the statements you disagree with true for you.

☐ Documentaries are ~~boring~~. *exciting*

☐ Talk shows are very interesting.

☐ All sports programs are exciting.

☐ Most sitcoms are very funny.

☐ It's important to watch the TV news.

☐ Reality shows are boring.

B GROUP WORK Share your ideas.

A: In my opinion, documentaries are exciting.

B: I don't really agree. I think they're pretty boring.

C: What about talk shows? I think they're very interesting.

A: I agree with you.

I can agree and disagree with an opinion. ✓

59

C I'm recording a documentary.

1 Vocabulary Television

A 🎧 Match the words and the definitions. Then listen and check your answers.

1 I often **record** my favorite show. ___C___
2 I often **fast-forward** through the boring parts of shows. _____
3 I always **skip** the sad parts of movies. _____
4 I watch **reruns** of old sitcoms. _____
5 I never lose the **remote control**. _____
6 Most **commercials** are funny. _____
7 You can learn a lot from **public TV**. _____
8 I think **satellite TV** is great. _____

a to play a show at high speed
b to not watch something
c to store a show to watch it later
d advertisements for products
e a nonprofit TV network
f a service that sends TV shows to homes through a dish
g repeat showings of a TV show
h a device used to control a TV from a distance

B **PAIR WORK** Which sentences in Part A describe your opinions or habits? Tell your partner.

A: I often record my favorite show.

B: Really? I never record my favorite show.

2 Conversation I'm going away this weekend.

A 🎧 Listen and practice.

Nora Hi, Zack. How are you?

Zack Oh, hi, Nora. I'm fine. Actually, I'm going away this weekend, so I want to record some TV shows.

Nora Really? Which shows?

Zack On Friday night, I'm recording the soccer game. The Hawks are playing the Lions.

Nora Oh, I'm watching that at Lisa's. She's having a soccer party. She has satellite TV now.

Zack Well, I'm watching it on Sunday night. That way I can fast-forward and skip the commercials.

Nora Good idea. I hate watching commercials. So what else are you recording?

Zack On Saturday, I'm recording a documentary on Channel 11 called *TV Is Dead*.

B 🎧 Listen to the rest of the conversation. What is Nora watching on TV this weekend?

3 **Grammar** 🎧 Present continuous for future plans

I'm **recording** the soccer game. I'm **not recording** the sitcom. She's **having** a soccer party this week. She's **not visiting** her family. They're **playing** the Lions this weekend. They're **not playing** the Sharks.

Is Zack **watching** the game on Sunday?
   Yes, he **is**.   No, he's **not**. / No, he **isn't**.
Are they **watching** the game on Sunday?
   Yes, they **are**.   No, they're **not**. / No, they **aren't**.
What else **are** you **recording** on Friday?
   I'm also **recording** a movie.

A Complete these conversations with the present continuous form of the verbs. Then practice with a partner.

1 A What _____ you _____ (do) this weekend? _____
      you _____ (go) anywhere?

   B No, I _____ (stay) home all weekend. Some friends _____ (come)
      over to watch a basketball game. The Tigers _____ (play).

2 A I _____ (get) satellite TV on Wednesday – finally! What _____
      you _____ (do) on Friday? Do you want to come over?

   B I'd love to, but I can't. Joe and I _____ (visit) his parents this weekend.
      We _____ (leave) on Friday after work.

B What are you doing this weekend? Use these verbs to write about your weekend plans. Then tell your partner.

1 (meet) _____   3 (play) _____

2 (watch) _____   4 (go out) _____

4 **Pronunciation** Sentence stress

🎧 Listen and repeat. Notice how the important words in a sentence are stressed.

I'm **going** to **Colombia** on **Monday**.   She's **staying home** this **weekend**.

5 **Speaking** What are you recording?

A Imagine you are going away next week, and you can't watch TV. Decide where you're going and make a list of five shows you are recording.

B **CLASS ACTIVITY** Compare lists. Is anyone recording the same shows? Find classmates with a similar list.

A: I'm visiting my mother next Tuesday, so I'm recording . . .

B: Me, too. I love . . ., and I'm recording . . .

6 **Keep talking!**

Go to page 138 for more practice.

I can describe future plans. ✓

D Popular TV

1 Reading 🎧

A 🎧 Read the article. Match the headings to the descriptions of the reality shows.

a Improvement shows   b Game-style shows   c Documentary-style shows

REALITY SHOWS

You either love them or you hate them! But did you realize there are different types of reality shows? Read on and find out more. . .

In this type of reality show, **contestants** try to win a prize. The prize is often money or, in some cases, a job. Each week, one person leaves the show until there is only one – the winner. Sometimes the contestants vote on who stays or goes, sometimes the TV **viewers** at home vote, and other times the show's **judges** choose. One example is *Master Chef*. In this show, contestants cook dishes for the **host** and the three judges. The winner usually receives money, a course, and a trophy.

This type of reality show looks like a soap opera, but it is about one or more real people and their daily lives. Some of the shows are about people on the job, such as police officers, firefighters, or hospital workers. Others are about regular people in unusual situations, and some even follow famous people. One example of this type is *Keeping Up with the Kardashians*. This show is about the daily life of the Kardashian family in Los Angeles, CA. In these types of shows, there is no prize money and no winner.

These shows are about a person or people who need a change. Other people help this person in one area, such as home, style, health, or relationships. An example of this is *The Property Brothers*. On each show, identical twin brothers help a couple buy and transform an inexpensive house into their dream home. The couple needs to help with the transformation and stay on budget.

B Read the article again. Look at the questions. Check (✓) the correct answer.

Which show . . .?	Master Chef	Keeping Up with the Kardashians	The Property Brothers
has a host	☐	☐	☐
gives a trophy	☐	☐	☐
shows people's daily lives	☐	☐	☐
is about home improvement	☐	☐	☐
is like a soap opera	☐	☐	☐

C Find the words in bold in the article. What do they mean? Match the definitions and the correct word.

A person / People who . . .

a presents a TV show _____

b participate in a competition _____

c watch a television program _____

d decide who wins or loses _____

D **PAIR WORK** Imagine you can be on one type of reality show. Which would you choose? Why? Tell your partner.

2 Listening Favorite shows back home

A 🎧 Listen to three students talk about their favorite TV shows in their countries. What type of show does each like? Write it in the chart.

	Type of show	Favorite thing about the show	
Valerie		the models	the end of each show
Young-ho		the costumes	the actors
Claudia		the teenagers	the stories

B 🎧 Listen again. What is their favorite thing about the show? Circle the correct answers.

3 Writing My favorite TV show

A Think of your favorite TV show. Answer the questions.

- What type of show is it?
- What happens on the show?
- Why do you enjoy watching it?
- Is there anything you don't like about it?

> My Favorite TV Show
> I like to watch the reality show "Project Runway." The contestants are fashion students. The winner receives money and an article in a fashion magazine. I enjoy watching the show because the clothes are fantastic, but sometimes I disagree with the judges.

B Write a paragraph about your favorite TV show. Use the model and your answers in Part A to help you.

C GROUP WORK Share your writing. Do you agree with each other's opinions?

4 Speaking Reality shows

A GROUP WORK Read about these reality shows. Which ones sound interesting? Why?

The Amazing Race
the U.S.
Pairs race one another around the world. The winners receive a million dollars.

The Genius Game
South Korea
Reality-style game show where contestants compete to solve logic puzzles and games.

The Grand Tour
the U.K.
Three British men drive a variety of motor vehicles on adventures around the world.

B Do you ever watch similar shows in your country? Why or why not?

"I watch a show similar to *The Amazing Race*. I don't really like it, but I always watch it!"

I can give my opinions about popular TV shows. ✓

Wrap-up

1 Quick pair review

Lesson A `Brainstorm!`

Make a list of types of TV shows. How many do you remember? You have one minute.

Lesson B `Do you remember?`

Write *A* for expressions that show you agree with an opinion. Write *D* for expressions that show you disagree. You have one minute.

1 I disagree. _____
2 I think so, too. _____
3 I agree. _____
4 I don't really agree. _____
5 I'm afraid I disagree. _____
6 I agree with you. _____

Lesson C `Find out!`

What are three things both you and your partner are doing next week? Take turns. You and your partner have two minutes.

A: I'm watching a baseball game next week. Are you?

B: Yes, I am.

Lesson D `Guess!`

Describe your favorite TV show, but don't say its name. Can your partner guess the name and type of show it is? Take turns. You and your partner have two minutes.

A: In this TV show, celebrities dance with professional dancers.

B: Is it a reality show?

A: Yes, it is.

B: Is it *Dancing with the Stars*?

A: Yes, it is.

2 In the real world

What new shows are on TV this year? Look at a TV schedule or go online and find information about a new TV show in English. Then write about it.

- What's the name of the TV show?
- What type of TV show is it?
- What's it about?
- When is it on?

A New TV Show

"The Crown" is a drama. It's about the life of Queen Elizabeth II of the U.K.

Answers to Warm-up, Part A:
1. e 2007   2. b 1994   3. c 1999   4. f 2009   5. d 2002   6. a 1989

7 Shopping

Warm up

A Describe the pictures. How many things can you name?

B Where do you usually shop? What do you like to buy?

A It's lighter and thinner.

1 Vocabulary Opposites

A 🎧 Label the pictures with the correct words. Then listen and check your answers.

| big | expensive | heavy | loud | slow | thick |

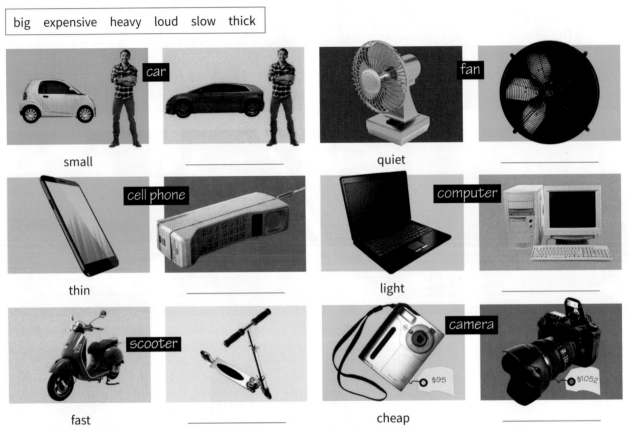

small   _____

quiet   _____

thin   _____

light   _____

fast   _____

cheap   _____

B **PAIR WORK** Use the words in Part A to describe things you own. Tell your partner.

"My cell phone is thin and light."

2 Language in context Which is better?

A 🎧 Read the message board. Then label the pictures.

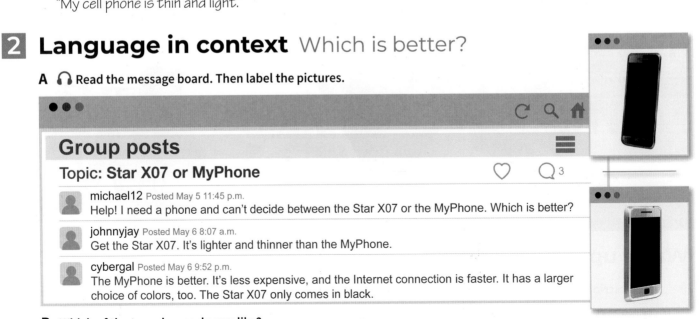

Group posts

Topic: **Star X07 or MyPhone** ♡ ◯ 3

michael12 Posted May 5 11:45 p.m.
Help! I need a phone and can't decide between the Star X07 or the MyPhone. Which is better?

johnnyjay Posted May 6 8:07 a.m.
Get the Star X07. It's lighter and thinner than the MyPhone.

cybergal Posted May 6 9:52 p.m.
The MyPhone is better. It's less expensive, and the Internet connection is faster. It has a larger choice of colors, too. The Star X07 only comes in black.

B Which of the two phones do you like?

3 **Grammar** 🎧 Comparative adjectives

The Star X07 is **lighter than** the MyPhone.

The MyPhone is **heavier than** the Star X07.

Which cell phone is **more expensive**?

The Star X07 is **more expensive than** the MyPhone.

The MyPhone is **less expensive than** the Star X07.

Is the MyPhone **better than** the Star X07?

No, I don't think it's **better**. It's **worse**.

Adjective	Comparative
light	light**er**
nice	nic**er**
thin	thin**ner**
heavy	heav**ier**
difficult	**more / less** difficult
good	**better**
bad	**worse**

Complete the sentences with the correct comparative form. Add *than* **if necessary. Then compare with a partner.**

1 Is your new printer _____ (fast) your old one?

2 Are desktop computers always _____ (heavy) laptops?

3 This new camera is really cheap! It's _____ (expensive) than my old one.

4 I like this TV, but I think I want a _____ (big) one.

5 This phone has a big screen, so it's _____ (expensive) than other phones.

6 My new camera isn't _____ (good) my old one. In fact,
it's _____ (bad)!

4 **Speaking** Let's compare

A **PAIR WORK** **Compare these products. How many sentences can you make?**

Car A

Watch A

Camera A

Car B

Watch B

Camera B

A: Car A is older than Car B.

B: And it's slower. Do you think Car A is quieter?

B **PAIR WORK** **Which product in each pair do you prefer? Why?**

5 **Keep talking!**

Go to page 139 for more practice.

I can describe and compare products. ✓

B Would you take $10?

1 Interactions Bargaining

A Do you ever bargain for lower prices? Where? For what? Do you enjoy bargaining?

B 🎧 Listen to the conversation. Does Eve buy the lamp? Then practice the conversation.

Eve	Excuse me. How much is this lamp?	**Rob**	No, I'm sorry. $20 is a good price.
Rob	Oh, it's only $20.	**Eve**	Well, thanks anyway.
Eve	Wow, that's expensive! How about $10?	**Rob**	Wait! You can have it for $15.
		Eve	$15? OK. I'll take it.

C 🎧 Listen to the expressions. Then practice the conversation again with the new expressions.

Bargaining for a lower price

How about . . . ?　　　Will you take . . . ?　　　Would you take . . . ?

Suggesting a different price

You can have it / them for . . .　　　I'll let you have it / them for . . .　　　I'll give it / them to you for . . .

D Number the sentences from 1 to 7. Then practice with a partner.

_____ **A** I'll take them. Thank you very much.

_____ **A** $30? That's pretty expensive. Would you take $20?

_____ **A** OK. Well, thank you anyway.

_____ **A** Excuse me. How much are these earrings?

_____ **B** Just a moment. I'll give them to you for $25.

_____ **B** No, I'm sorry. $30 is the price.

_____ **B** They're only $30.

2 Pronunciation Linked sounds

A 🎧 Listen and repeat. Notice how final consonant sounds are often linked to the vowel sounds that follow them.

How much is this lamp?   It's only $20.

B 🎧 Listen and mark the linked sounds. Then practice with a partner.

1   How much are the earrings?   2   Just a moment.   3   Thanks anyway.

3 Listening How much is it?

A 🎧 Listen to four people shopping at a yard sale. Number the pictures from 1 to 4. (There is one extra picture.)

$ _____ $ _____ $ _____ $ _____ $ _____

B 🎧 Listen again. Write the price the buyer and seller agree on.

4 Speaking What a bargain!

A Write the prices on the tags.

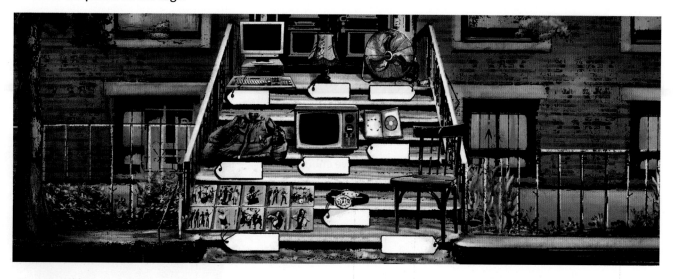

B **PAIR WORK** Role-play the situations. Then change roles.

Student A: Sell the things. You want to sell them for a good price.

Student B: Buy the things. Bargain for lower prices.

A: Excuse me. How much is the computer?

B: It's only $250.

A: That's very expensive. Would you take . . .?

I can bargain. ✓

C This hat is too small.

1 Vocabulary Adjectives to describe clothing

A 🎧 Complete the phrases with the correct words. Then listen and check your answers.

baggy	comfortable	pretty	ugly
bright	plain	tight	uncomfortable

1 a _____
shirt

2 _____
jeans

3 _____
shoes

4 a _____
blouse

5 a _____
tie

6 a _____
dress

7 _____
pants

8 an _____
hat

B **PAIR WORK** Describe your clothing today. Tell your partner.

"I think my shirt is plain, but comfortable. My jeans are a little baggy."

2 Conversation Try it on!

A 🎧 Listen and practice.

Allie Let's look at the jackets.

Paul OK, but I have a class at 3:00. Do we have enough time?

Allie Sure. It's only 1:30. Hey! Look at this black one.

Paul It's cool. Try it on.

Allie OK. What do you think? Does it fit?

Paul No, it's too small. Try this red one.

Allie OK. How does it look? Is it big enough?

Paul I think so. Yeah, it looks good on you.

Allie How much is it? Can you see the tag?

Paul Let's see . . . it's $120.

Allie Oh, no! I only have $60. I don't have enough money. I can't afford it.

B 🎧 Listen to the rest of the conversation. What else does Allie try on?

3 **Grammar** 🎧 *Enough* and *too*

Enough *means the right amount.* Too *means more than enough.*

Enough *before nouns*

I have **enough** time.

I don't have **enough** money.

Enough *after adjectives*

The jacket is big **enough**.

The pants aren't long **enough**.

Too *before adjectives*

The jacket is **too** small.

The pants aren't **too** long.

A Complete the sentences with the correct words. Use *too* and *enough*. Then compare with a partner.

| big ✓ long money uncomfortable |

1 How do these pants look? Do you think they're _____long enough_____ ?

2 These shoes look nice, but they're _____. I can't walk at all.

3 Oh, no! I don't have _____. This belt is $30, and I only have $20.

4 The shirt I ordered online is _____. It fits very well.

B Rewrite the sentences. Use *enough* and *too*. Then compare with a partner.

1 Those boots are too small. (enough)   *These boots aren't big enough.*

2 That belt is $10. I have $10. (enough) _____

3 The jacket is expensive. I can't afford it. (too) _____

4 That belt is $12. I have $10. (enough) _____

5 I wear a large size. This T-shirt isn't big enough. (too) _____

6 These pants aren't long enough. (too) _____

4 **Speaking** Things I never wear

A Think of your closet at home. Complete the chart with pieces of clothing. Write reasons why you don't wear them.

Things I don't like wearing	Things I never wear
Ties – too ugly	

B GROUP WORK Share your ideas. What do you have in common?

5 **Keep talking!**

Student A go to page 140 and Student B go to page 144 for more practice.

I can describe how clothing looks and fits. ✓

D A shopper's paradise

1 Reading 🎧

A Read the webpage. Which paragraph includes information about these topics? Number the topics from 1 to 4.

☐ transportation ☐ number of visitors ☐ prices and money ☐ hours

CHATUCHAK WEEKEND MARKET

1 With more than 15,000 shops and 200,000 visitors every Saturday and Sunday, Bangkok's Chatuchak Weekend Market is a popular place with visitors to Thailand. You can find plants, flowers, music, jewelry, clothes, food, and even animals!

2 The market is a great place to find bargains, and prices are **generally** low. Most people bargain, but some don't, so don't worry if you don't want to bargain. Just go with a friendly smile and have enough cash in your pocket. There are ATMs for cash, but they are difficult to find, and many **vendors** don't take credit cards. The market is **huge**, and many people walk in circles, even with a map. Don't try to see it all in one day!

3 The market is open from 8:00 to 6:00 Saturday and Sunday. It's good to get there early, before it gets too busy. Wear light, comfortable clothing and bring a bottle of water. And for lunch, try some of Thailand's famous snacks, such as fried scorpions!

4 The market is very easy to get to. It's only a five-minute walk from Mo Chit station on Bangkok's Skytrain. Many people come by train but leave by taxi. It's easier to get your **purchases** back to your hotel that way!

B Read the webpage again. Find the words in **bold**, and check (✓) the correct meaning.

1 **generally** ☐ usually   3 **huge**   ☐ easy to find
              ☐ rarely   ☐ very large

2 **vendors**   ☐ buyers   4 **purchases** ☐ things you buy
              ☐ sellers   ☐ things you sell

C Check (✓) the tips you think the writer would agree with.

☐ Pay the first price the vendor offers.   ☐ Bring a credit card, not cash.
☐ Arrive in the morning.   ☐ Take the bus home after shopping.

D **PAIR WORK** What would you like about Bangkok's Weekend Market? What wouldn't you like? Tell your partner.

2 Listening Portobello Road Market

A 🎧 **Listen to two friends talk about Portobello Road Market. Answer the questions.**

1 What city is the market in? _____

2 How many days is the outdoor market open? _____

3 When's a good time to visit? _____

4 What's a good way to get there? _____

B 🎧 **Listen again. What can you buy at the market on Saturday? Circle the words you hear.**

animals   cell phones   clothes   fruit   jewelry   meat   vegetables

3 Writing An interesting market

A Think about a market you know. Answer the questions.

- What is the name of the market?
- Where is it?
- When is it open?
- When's a good time to visit?
- What can you buy there?

B Write a description of an interesting market. Use the model and your answers in Part A to help you.

The Farmers' Market is near my home. It's open every Saturday from 9:00 to 4:00. You can buy the best fruits and vegetables there. A good time to visit is late in the afternoon. It's not too busy then. You don't bargain at this market, but some vendors lower their prices at the end of the day.

C PAIR WORK **Share your writing. How are the markets similar? How are they different?**

4 Speaking A good place to shop

A Think about things you buy. Add two more things to the list. Then complete the rest of the chart.

Things I buy	Place	Reason
fruits and vegetables		
shoes		
old furniture		
computers and cell phones		

B GROUP WORK **Share your ideas. Ask and answer questions for more information.**

"I always go to the market to buy fruits and vegetables. They are always fresh, and the people are friendly."

I can discuss good places to shop. ✓

Wrap-up

1 Quick pair review

Lesson A Test your partner!

Say an adjective. Can your partner say its opposite? Take turns. You have one minute.

A: Small.

B: Big.

Lesson B Do you remember?

Complete the conversation with the correct word. You have two minutes.

A How much is this TV?

B $50

A Will you _____ $30?
             1

B You can _____ it for $45.
             2

A How _____ $35?
         3

B I'll _____ it to you for $40.
       4

A OK.

Lesson C Brainstorm!

Make a list of adjectives to describe clothing. Take turns. You and your partner have two minutes.

Lesson D Find out!

What are two things both you and your partner buy at a market? Take turns. You and your partner have two minutes.

A: I buy music at a market. Do you?

B: No, I don't. I buy music online.

2 In the real world

What outdoor markets are famous? Go online and find information in English about an outdoor market. Then write about it.

- What's the name of the market?
- When is it open?
- Where is it?
- What do they sell at the market?

The Otavalo Market
The Otavalo Market is in Ecuador. It's open every day, but Saturdays are very busy . . . .

8 Fun in the city

<table>
<tr>
<td>

LESSON A

- Places to see
- *Should; can*

</td>
<td>

LESSON B

- Asking for a recommendation
- Giving a recommendation

</td>
<td>

LESSON C

- Adjectives to describe cities
- Superlative adjectives

</td>
<td>

LESSON D

- Reading: "Austin or San Antonio?"
- Writing: A message board

</td>
</tr>
</table>

Warm Up

A Describe the pictures. What is happening in each picture?

B Which of these things do you like about city life? Which don't you like?

A You shouldn't miss it!

1 Vocabulary Places to see

A 🎧 Match the words and the pictures. Then listen and check your answers.

a	botanical garden	c	fountain	e	palace	g	square
b	castle	d	monument	f	pyramid	h	statue

 1
 2
 3
 4

 5
 6
 7
 8

B **PAIR WORK** Which of the places in Part A do you have where you live? Discuss the places.

"There's a nice statue in the center of the square."

2 Language in context Attractions in the city

A 🎧 Read about what to do in these three cities. Which cities are good for shopping?

Guayaquil, Ecuador
Enjoy shopping, cafés, fountains, and statues on El Malecón, a popular walking area. It's a fantastic place to take a long, slow walk or ride on a tour boat.

Seoul, South Korea
You shouldn't miss the small neighborhood of Insadong. It's a great place to shop for books, pottery, and paintings. Later, you can walk to a nearby palace or relax at an old teahouse.

Cairo, Egypt
Love history? Then you should visit the Egyptian Museum. You can't see it all in one day, so be sure to see King Tut's treasure and the famous "mummy room."

B What about you? Which city in Part A would you like to visit? Why?

3 **Grammar** 🎧 *Should; can*

Should for recommendations	*Can* for possibility
Where **should** I go?	What **can** I do there?
You **should** visit the Egyptian Museum.	You **can** enjoy cafés, shops, and fountains.
They **shouldn't** miss Insadong.	You **can't** see all of the museum in one day.
(= They should see Insadong.)	**Can** they take a taxi?
Should she go to Cairo?	Yes, they **can**. No, they **can't**.
Yes, she **should**. No, she **shouldn't**.	

Complete the conversation with *should*, *shouldn't*, *can*, or *can't*. Then practice with a partner.

A   ___Should___ I rent a car in Seoul?

B   No, I think you _____ take the subway. You _____ get around
quickly and easily.

A   Oh, good. And what places _____ I visit?

B   Well, you _____ miss the palace, and you _____ also go to the
art museum. You _____ see it all in one day because it's very big, but
you _____ buy really nice art books and postcards there.

A   OK. Thanks a lot!

4 **Listening** My city

A   **Listen to three people describe their cities. Number the pictures from 1 to 3.**

☐   Istanbul

☐   Mexico City

☐   Florence

1 _____   1 _____   1 _____

2 _____   2 _____   2 _____

B   🎧 **Listen again. Write two things the people say visitors should do in their cities.**

5 **Speaking** Only one day

A   **PAIR WORK**   **Imagine these people are planning to visit your town or city for only one day.
What places should they visit?**

- a family with teenage children
- two college students
- a businessperson from overseas
- young children on a school trip

"I think the family should visit the town square. They can eat and shop there."

B   **GROUP WORK**   **Compare your answers from Part A. Do you agree?**

6 **Keep talking!**

Go to page 142 for more practice.

I can say what people should do in a city. ☑

B I'd recommend going . . .

1 Interactions Recommendations

A Look at the pictures. What do you think the woman is going to do soon?

B 🎧 Listen to the conversation. Was your guess from Part A correct? Then practice the conversation.

Lucy	Hi, Alex.		Alex	I'd recommend going to a samba club.
Alex	Oh, hi, Lucy. Are you ready for your trip to Brazil?		Lucy	A samba club? Really?
Lucy	Almost, but I don't really know much about Rio. What would you recommend doing there?		Alex	Yeah. You can dance or just listen to the music. Everyone has a good time.
			Lucy	Great. That sounds fun!

C 🎧 Listen to the expressions. Then practice the conversation again with the new expressions.

Asking for a recommendation

What would you recommend doing there?	What would you suggest doing there?
What do you think I should do there?	

Giving a recommendation

I'd recommend going . . .	I'd suggest going . . .	I think you should go . . .

D Put the words in order. Then compare with a partner.

1 you / there / recommend / what / seeing / would _____?

2 I'd / the castle / visiting / suggest _____.

3 the square / I / should / think / you / go to _____.

4 suggest / would / doing / what / you / in Tokyo _____?

5 bus / recommend / I'd / the / taking _____.

78

2 Listening One day in Taipei

🎧 **Listen to Carrie and David get information from the tourist information desk in Taipei. Check (✓) the recommendations you hear.**

1 ☐ I'd suggest visiting Taipei 101.
   ☐ You should visit Taipei 101.

2 ☐ I'd recommend going to the night market.
   ☐ You shouldn't miss the night market.

3 ☐ I'd suggest going to the Fine Arts Museum.
   ☐ I'd recommend going to the Fine Arts Museum.

4 ☐ I think you should take the subway.
   ☐ I'd recommend taking the subway.

3 Speaking Role play

PAIR WORK **Role—play the situation. Then change roles.**

Student A: You are a tourist in London. Ask for recommendations for three things to do.

Student B: You work at a tourist information desk. Give recommendations for three things to do.

TOP LONDON ATTRACTIONS

The British Museum
See the famous Rosetta Stone.

The Tate Modern
See great art for free.

The London Eye
Enjoy views of 55 famous places.

Trafalgar Square
Take your picture by the lion statues.

Tower Bridge
Walk across the bridge. Fantastic city views!

Buckingham Palace
See one of the Royal Family's many homes.

A: Hello. Can I help you?

B: Yes. This is my first time in London. What would you suggest doing here?

A: Well, there are a lot of things to do, but I think you should definitely visit the British Museum. You can see . . .

I can ask for and give a recommendation. ✓

C The best and the worst

1 Vocabulary Adjectives to describe cities

A 🎧 Match the words and pictures. Then listen and check your answers.

a beautiful	b dangerous	c dirty	d modern	e stressful

1

2

3

4

5

B 🎧 Write the opposites. Use the words in Part A. Then listen and check your answers.

clean	relaxing	safe	traditional	ugly
dirty	_____	_____	_____	_____

C **PAIR WORK** Describe where you live using the words in Parts A and B.

"Our city is beautiful and clean, but life here can be stressful."

2 Conversation Life in Sydney

A 🎧 Listen and practice.

Peter So, Akemi, how do you like living in Sydney?

Akemi I miss Japan sometimes, but I love it here. I think it's the most beautiful and one of the most exciting cities in the world.

Peter But do you find it stressful?

Akemi Not at all. I know Sydney is the biggest city in Australia, but remember, I'm from Tokyo.

Peter Oh, yeah. What else do you like about living here?

Akemi A lot of things. It's very clean and safe. The people are friendly. Oh, and the food here is fantastic.

Peter I agree. I think Sydney has the best restaurants in the country.

Akemi Hey, do you want to get something to eat?

Peter Sure. I know a nice café. It's cheap but good.

B 🎧 Listen to their conversation in the café. How does Akemi describe the café? How does Peter describe the food?

3 **Grammar** 🎧 Superlative adjectives

Sydney is **the biggest** city in Australia.

Sydney is one of **the most exciting** cities in the world.

Sydney has **the best** restaurants in the country.

What is **the cleanest** city in your country?

What city has **the most traditional** restaurants?

Is it the **worst** restaurant?

    Yes, it is.   No, it isn't.

Adjective	Superlative
clean	**the** cleanest
safe	**the** safest
big	**the biggest**
ugly	**the** ugliest
stressful	**the most** stressful
good	**the best**
bad	**the worst**

A Complete the questions with the superlative form of the adjectives. Then compare with a partner.

1 What's one of _____ (old) universities in your country?

2 What's _____ (big) city in your country?

3 What's _____ (modern) city in your country?

4 What's _____ (beautiful) national park?

5 What city has _____ (good) restaurants?

6 What city has _____ (bad) weather?

B Ask and answer the questions in Part A. Discuss your ideas.

University of Cambridge

4 **Pronunciation** Word stress

A 🎧 Listen and repeat. Notice the stress in the names of these cities.

● •	• ●	● • •	• ● •
Sydney	Ma**drid**	**Can**berra	New **Del**hi

B 🎧 Listen and write the cities in the correct columns in Part A. Then practice with a partner.

Amsterdam   Berlin   Caracas   Lima

5 **Speaking** What's the . . .?

PAIR WORK Ask and answer questions about your town or city.

expensive / hotel	exciting / neighborhood	modern / building
beautiful / park	big / department store	relaxing / place

A: What's the most expensive hotel?

B: I'm not sure it's the most expensive, but the Grand Hotel is very expensive.

6 **Keep talking!**

Go to page 143 for more practice.

I can make comparisons about my city. ✓

D The best place to go

1 Reading 🎧

A Read the message board. Who answers Miguel's question about safety?

Group posts

Topic: Austin or San Antonio?

♡   ◯ 7

> **miguel** Posted May 17 7:06 p.m.
> Hi! I live in Mexico and am planning to visit my uncle in Dallas, Texas, next year. I'd also like to visit Austin or San Antonio for a few days. I like the outdoors, local music, good food, friendly people, etc. Are both cities safe? Any other tips appreciated. Thanks! Miguel

> **rocker** Posted May 17 7:23 p.m.
> I'm a musician and I live in Austin. I think the music here is the best in Texas. In fact, Austin's nickname is "the Live Music Capital of the World." I can send you the names of some cool music clubs. We have fantastic restaurants here, too.

> **biker68** Posted May 17 8:54 p.m.
> Definitely visit San Antonio. The River Walk is one of the most popular things for visitors to do. There's a lot to do outdoors here, too. And everyone in Texas is friendly. Check out my pics: **myphotos**

> **susanp** Posted May 17 11:09 p.m.
> I disagree with rocker. I think the music is better in San Antonio. I've lived in both cities. There is a lot to do outdoors in San Antonio, but there's just more to do in Austin.

> **richard** Posted May 18 6:45 a.m.
> Both cities are safe, by the way, so don't worry. I live in Houston. It's the largest city in Texas. You should visit here, too.☺ Read my travel blog at richard23.cup.org.

> **traveler** Posted May 10 10:31 a.m
> San Antonio has the best food in Texas. Do you like Tex-Mex food? You should go in spring or fall (summer is hot!). I suggest traveling by bus. It's not expensive. Email me with any questions.

> **miguel** Posted May 18 3:22 p.m.
> Miguel here again. Thanks, everyone!

B Read the message board again. Answer the questions. Check (✓) your answers.

Who . . .?	rocker	biker68	susanp	richard	traveler
lives in Houston	☐	☐	☐	☐	☐
gives a link to see pictures	☐	☐	☐	☐	☐
writes about the weather	☐	☐	☐	☐	☐
prefers the music in San Antonio	☐	☐	☐	☐	☐
has a travel blog	☐	☐	☐	☐	☐
is a musician	☐	☐	☐	☐	☐

C **PAIR WORK** What do you do when you need advice or a recommendation? Who do you talk to? Tell your partner.

82

2 **Writing** A message board

A Choose a topic for a message board. Then write a question asking for a recommendation about your topic. Use the model to help you.

- food
- music
- outdoor activities
- transportation

B GROUP WORK Pass your question to the classmate on your right. Read and answer your classmate's question. Continue to pass, read, and answer all the questions in your group.

C Read the answers to your question. Which recommendation is the best?

> Can you suggest a good restaurant near our school?
>
> **1.** You should go to Mickey's. It's fantastic, but it's expensive.
> **2.** I think Thai Palace has the best food.
> **3.** I agree. It's the most popular restaurant near here.

3 **Speaking** The best of the city

A PAIR WORK Complete the chart with information about the best things in your city or town. Give reasons.

The best things about _____	Reasons

A: I think the best thing about our city is the people. They are very friendly and helpful.

B: I agree.

B GROUP WORK Compare your ideas with another pair. Do you agree?

C CLASS ACTIVITY Make a list of all things from Parts A and B. Which is the most popular?

Wrap-up

1 Quick pair review

Lesson A Brainstorm!
Make a list of fun places to see in a city. How many do you know? You have one minute.

Lesson B Do you remember?
Check (✓) the questions you can ask when you want a recommendation. You have one minute.

☐ What would you recommend doing there?

☐ Which place is more expensive?

☐ When are you going to China?

☐ What would you suggest doing there?

☐ What are you going to do in Brazil?

☐ What do you think I should do there?

Lesson C Test your partner!
Say an adjective to describe a city. Can your partner say the superlative? Take turns. You have one minute.

A: Modern.

B. The most modern.

Lesson D Guess!
Describe a city, but don't say its name. Can your partner guess what it is? Take turns. You and your partner have two minutes.

A: It's an old city in Europe. It's beautiful. It has a lot of squares and fountains.

B: Is it Florence?

A: Yes, it is.

2 In the real world

What city would you like to visit? Go to a travel website and find information about the city in English. Then write about it.

- What country is it in?
- What's it like?
- What is there to do in the city?
- What's it famous for?

Montreal
I would like to go to Montreal. It's in Canada.
It's modern and safe . . .

84

9 People

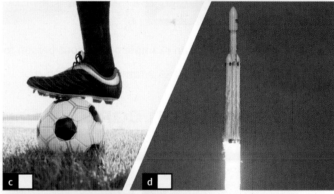

Warm-up

A Match the people and the things they are famous for. Check your answers on page 94.

B Which of the people in Part A would you like to meet? Why?

A Where was he born?

1 Vocabulary Careers

A 🎧 Match the words and the pictures. Then listen and check your answers.

a	astronaut	c	composer	e	director	g	politician
b	athlete	d	designer	f	explorer	h	scientist

 1 ☐

 2 ☐

 3 ☐

 4 ☐

 5 ☐

 6 ☐

 7 ☐

 8 ☐

B PAIR WORK Give an example of a famous person for each category.

"Guillermo del Toro is a famous director."

2 Language in context Famous firsts

A 🎧 Read about these famous firsts. Which famous first happened first?

Emilio Palma was born at Argentina's Esperanza Base in Antarctica in 1978. He was the first person born on the continent.

The first person on the moon in 1969 was American astronaut Neil Armstrong. He was on the moon for only two and a half hours.

Junko Tabei was the first woman to climb Mt. Everest in 1975. She was also the first woman to climb the highest mountains on all seven continents.

Venus and Serena Williams are great athletes. They were the first sisters to win Wimbledon in 2000.

B Which people from Part A would you like to meet? What question would you ask them?

3 Grammar 🎧 *Was / were born; past of be*

Where **was** Emilio Palma **born**? 　He **was born** in Antarctica. 　He **wasn't born** in Argentina. Where **were** Venus and Serena **born**? 　They **were born** in the U.S. 　They **weren't born** in Canada. **Was** he **born** in Antarctica? 　Yes, he **was**.　　No, he **wasn't**.	How long **was** Neil Armstrong on the moon? 　He **was** there for two and a half hours. 　He **wasn't** there for very long. Where **were** his parents from? 　They **were** from Argentina. 　They **weren't** from Antarctica. **Were** they Wimbledon champions in 2000? 　Yes, they **were**.　　No, they **weren't**.

A Complete the sentences with the correct past form of *be*. Then compare with a partner.

1　Coco Chanel _____ an amazing French designer.

2　Albert Einstein _____ born in Germany.

3　Alfred Hitchcock _____ a great director.

4　Diego Rivera and Frida Kahlo _____ born in Mexico.

5　Mozart and Beethoven _____ famous composers.

B Correct the false sentences. Then compare with a partner.

1　Ronald Reagan was a British politician. (American)

　　He wasn't a British politician. He was an American politician.

2　Zheng He was an early Chinese scientist. (explorer)

　　_____

3　Artist Vincent van Gogh was born in the 20th century. (19th century)

　　_____

4　Gianni Versace and Yves Saint Laurent were explorers. (designers)

　　_____

5　Venus and Serena Williams were born in the late 1970s. (early 1980s)

　　_____

4 Speaking Famous people

GROUP WORK Choose a person from the past. Your group asks questions and guesses the person's name. Take turns.

A: He was from Mexico. He was a politician.

B: Is it . . . ?

A: No, sorry. He was born in the 19th century.

C: I think I know. Is it Benito Juárez?

5 Keep talking!

Student A go to page 141 and Student B go to page 145 for more practice.

I can ask and talk about people from the past. ✓

B I'm not sure, but I think . . .

1 Interactions Certainty and uncertainty

A Look at the pictures. Where are the people? What are they doing?

B 🎧 Listen to the conversation. Does Mike know the answer to both questions? Then practice the conversation.

Mike	Let's go over more questions before our test tomorrow.	**Jenny**	Correct! This one's more difficult. Who was Plato's teacher?
Jenny	OK. What was the original name of New York City?	**Mike**	I'm not sure, but I think it was Aristotle.
Mike	It was New Amsterdam.	**Jenny**	Actually, Aristotle was Plato's student. Socrates was his teacher.
Jenny	Are you sure?	**Mike**	Oh, right.
Mike	I'm positive.		

C 🎧 Listen to the expressions. Then practice the conversation again with the new expressions.

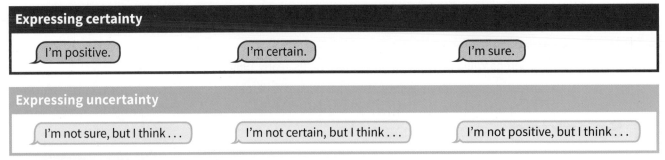

Expressing certainty

> I'm positive.   I'm certain.   I'm sure.

Expressing uncertainty

> I'm not sure, but I think . . .   I'm not certain, but I think . . .   I'm not positive, but I think . . .

D Circle the answer you think is correct. Practice with a partner and use expressions from Part C. Then check your answers on page 94.

1 Barack Obama was president of the **U.S.** / **U.K.**

2 Mozart was born in the **16ᵗʰ** / **17ᵗʰ** / **18ᵗʰ** century.

3 Neymar da Silva Santos, Jr's first soccer team was **Barcelona** / **Paris Saint-Germain** / **Santos**.

4 Che Guevara was born in **Bolivia** / **Argentina** / **Cuba**.

5 The 2016 Olympics were in **Sochi** / **Rio** / **Sydney**.

A: Barack Obama was the president of the U.S.

B: Are you sure?

A: I'm positive.

2 **Listening** Sorry, that's not right.

A Do you know the answers to these questions? Write your guesses in the first column.

		Your guess	Player's guess	
1	Where were the 2016 Olympics?			☐
2	Who was the winner of the 2014 World Cup?			☐
3	In what century was Pablo Picasso born?			☐
4	Who was the author of the play *Hamlet*?			☐
5	How long was Barack Obama president of the U.S.?			☐

B 🎧 Listen to four friends play a board game. Write the players' guesses in the second column.

C 🎧 Listen again. Check (✓) the players' guesses that are correct.

3 **Speaking** Do you know?

A **PAIR WORK** Look at the pictures and the categories. Add another category. Then write two questions for each category. Be sure you know the answers!

Actors and actresses

Athletes

Singers and musicians

B **GROUP WORK** Ask your questions. Use expressions of certainty or uncertainty in the answers.

A: Where was Brad Pitt born?

B: I'm not sure, but I think he was born in . . .

A: How old is he?

I can express certainty and uncertainty. ✓

C People I admire

1 Vocabulary Personality adjectives

A 🎧 **Match the words in the paragraphs and the definitions. Then listen and check your answers.**

I admire U.S. President Abraham Lincoln. He was **honest**[1] as a lawyer and often worked for free. He was **brave**[2] and kept the country together during war. He was a very **inspiring**[3] person.

–Jin Ju

Nobel Prize in Literature winner Kazuo Ishiguro is very **passionate**[4] about his writing. He's very **intelligent**[5], and I really admire his novels.

–Celia

Bono is a **talented**[6] musician, but he's also a **caring**[7] person. I admire him for his fight against world poverty. He's very **determined**[8], and he's helping a lot of poor people.

–Mark

_____ very good at something	_____ making other people want to do something
__1__ open, telling the truth	_____ able to understand things quickly and easily
_____ not afraid of anything	_____ trying everything possible to do something
_____ nice to other people	_____ showing a strong feeling about something

B **PAIR WORK** **What other personality adjectives can you think of? Discuss your ideas.**

2 Conversation I really admire him.

A 🎧 **Listen and practice.**

Paul Did you finish your report, Emma?

Emma Yeah, I did. I finished it two days ago.

Paul Good for you! So who did you write about?

Emma Jacques Cousteau. I really admire him.

Paul I don't think I know him. What did he do?

Emma A lot! He was a French scientist and explorer. He loved nature and studied the sea. He made documentaries and wrote books about the world's oceans. He won a lot of prizes for his work.

Paul Wow! He sounds like an inspiring guy.

Emma He was. He was really passionate about his work.

B 🎧 **Listen to the rest of the conversation. When did Jacques Cousteau die?**

3 Grammar ∩ Simple past; *ago*

Who **did** you **write** about? I **wrote** about Jacques Cousteau. I **didn't write** about his son. What **did** he **do**? He **made** documentaries. **Did** you **finish** your report? Yes, I **did**. No, I **didn't**.	**Period of time +** *ago* I finished the report **two days ago**. I researched it **a week ago**. I saw a documentary **four years ago**. He died **a long time ago**.

A Complete the conversation with the simple past form of the verbs. Then practice with a partner.

A Why _____ you _____ (decide) to write about Serena Williams for your report?

B Well, I _____ (want) to write about an athlete. And I think she's very inspiring. In 2008, she _____ (start) the Serena Williams Foundation. It builds schools. Then in 2010, she _____ (write) the book *My Life: Queen of the Court*.

A What else did she do?

B Well, in 2016, she _____ (dance) in her friend Beyoncé's video. In September 2017, she _____ (have) a baby girl!

B PAIR WORK Ask and answer questions about when Serena Williams did these things. Use *ago* in the answers.

have a baby	dance in a video	start a foundation	write a book

4 Pronunciation Simple past *-ed* endings

∩ Listen and repeat. Notice the different ways the past simple endings are pronounced.

/t/		/d/		/id/	
finished	asked	played	admired	wanted	created

5 Speaking What did they do?

GROUP WORK Use the adjectives to describe people you know. What did the people do?

brave	caring	honest	intelligent	talented

"My sister Megumi is very brave. She traveled alone in Canada and . . ."

6 Keep Talking

Go to page 146 for more practice.

I can describe people I admire. ☑

D Making a difference

1 Reading 🎧

A Read the biography. How did Dr. Muhammad Yunus make a difference?

   a He won the Nobel Peace Prize.   **b** He helped the poor.   **c** He studied economics.

A DIFFERENT KIND OF BANKER

Dr. Muhammad Yunus, a banker and economist, was born in Bangladesh in 1940. He studied economics at Dhaka University in Bangladesh. He taught for a few years and then went to the United States to continue his studies. He returned home to Bangladesh in 1972 and started teaching again.

One day in 1976, Yunus visited a poor **village** in his home country. There he met some women who wanted to make furniture, but they didn't have enough money. He decided to help them and gave them $27 of his own money.

They made and sold the furniture, **made a profit**, and then returned the money to Dr. Yunus. At that point, he saw how very little money could help a lot. He decided to help poor people. A bank **loaned** him the money. In 1983, Yunus started Grameen Bank. This bank loans money to poor people. Dr. Yunus and Grameen Bank received the 2006 Nobel Peace Prize for their work with the poor.

In 2009, the bank had 7.95 million customers, and 97% of these customers were women. The success of the bank inspired other people in many different countries to start similar banks. Yunus once said, "**Conventional** banks look for the rich; we look for the absolutely poor."

B Number these events from Dr. Yunus's life from 1 to 8.

_____ He returned to Bangladesh.	_____ He studied at Dhaka University.
_____ He was born in 1940.	_____ He gave money to some women in 1976.
_____ He started the Grameen Bank.	_____ He won the Nobel Peace Prize.
_____ He studied in the United States.	_____ He inspired other people.

C Read the biography again. Find the words in **bold**, and check (✓) the correct meaning.

  1 A **village** is:

     ☐ a very small town   ☐ a big place where a lot of people live

  2 If you **made a profit**, you:

     ☐ lost money   ☐ made money

  3 If someone **loaned** you money, you:

     ☐ gave back the money   ☐ kept the money

  4 A **conventional** bank is:

     ☐ usual   ☐ unusual

D **PAIR WORK** How would you describe Dr. Yunus? Tell your partner.

2 **Writing** A biography

A PAIR WORK Discuss famous people who made a big difference in people's lives. Answer the questions.

- What are their names?
- What do you know about their lives?
- What did they do?
- How did they make a difference?

B Write a short biography about a famous person who made a difference. Use the model and the answers in Part A to help you.

José Antonio Abreu
José Antonio Abreu is a Venezuelan economist. He is also a talented musician. In 1975, he started a music school for poor children. He wanted to help these children and was determined to change their lives with music. Today, children all over Venezuela are playing in orchestras.

C GROUP WORK Share your writing. Who do you think made the biggest difference?

3 **Listening** Life lessons

A 🎧 Listen to three people describe the people who made a difference in their lives. Check (✓) the qualities they use to describe those people.

	Qualities		What did the people teach them?
1	☐ caring ☐ talented	☐ intelligent ☐ creative	a. how to sing b. to be a musician
2	☐ brave ☐ honest	☐ generous ☐ determined	a. never to quit b. how to play soccer
3	☐ determined ☐ caring	☐ honest ☐ inspiring	a. how to teach English b. the qualities of a good teacher

B 🎧 Listen again. What did the people teach them? Circle the correct answers.

4 **Speaking** In my life

GROUP WORK Tell your group about a person who made a difference in your life. Use the questions below and your own ideas.

- How do you know this person?
- What did he or she teach you?
- What did he or she do?
- How would you describe him or her?

A: *My aunt made a difference in my life.*

B: *Oh, yeah? Why?*

A: *She taught me to think of other people.*

Wrap-up

1 Quick pair review

Lesson A Brainstorm!

Make a list of careers. How many do you know? You have two minutes.

Lesson B Guess!

Say the name of a famous person. Does your partner know where he or she was born?
Take turns. You have two minutes.

A: Albert Einstein.

B: He was born in Germany.

A: Are you sure?

B: I'm positive.

B: Oprah Winfrey.

A: I'm not sure, but I think she was born
in Mississippi.

Lesson C Test your partner!

Say six verbs. Can your partner write the simple past form of the verbs correctly?
Check his or her answers. Take turns. You and your partner have two minutes.

1 _____ 3 _____ 5 _____
2 _____ 4 _____ 6 _____

Lesson D Find out!

Who are two people both you and your partner think made a difference in the world?
What qualities do they have? Take turns. You and your partner have two minutes.

A: I think Nelson Mandela made a difference.

B: Me, too. He was determined and inspiring.

A: Yes, he was.

2 In the real world

Who do you admire? Go online and find five things that he or she did
that you think are interesting. Then write about this person.

Sheryl Sandberg
I admire Sheryl Sandberg. She is the Chief
Operating Officer of Facebook. She's a great
businessperson. She also helps a lot of women
and children . . .

10 In a restaurant

LESSON A
- Menu items
- Articles

LESSON B
- Ordering food
- Checking information

LESSON C
- Interesting food
- Present perfect for experience

LESSON D
- Reading: "Restaurants with a Difference"
- Writing: A review

Warm Up

A What kinds of food do you think each place serves?

B Check (✓) the top three places you would like to try. Why?

A The ice cream is fantastic!

1 Vocabulary Menu items

A 🎧 Label the menu with the correct words. Then listen and check your answers.

Appetizers   Desserts   Main dishes   Side dishes

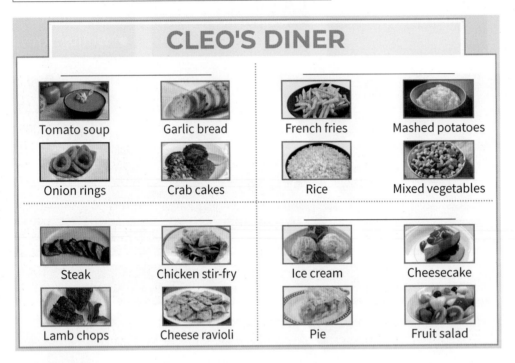

CLEO'S DINER

Tomato soup   Garlic bread   French fries   Mashed potatoes

Onion rings   Crab cakes   Rice   Mixed vegetables

Steak   Chicken stir-fry   Ice cream   Cheesecake

Lamb chops   Cheese ravioli   Pie   Fruit salad

B **PAIR WORK** Give an example of another menu item for each category.

"Another example of a main dish is spaghetti with meatballs. Another side dish . . ."

2 Language in context Any recommendations?

A 🎧 Listen to Jeff chat with his friends online. Who recommends the ice cream?

Jeff I'm thinking of eating out tonight. Any recommendations?

Junko I'd recommend going to Cleo's Diner. They have great food and good service.

Tony12 Yeah, Cleo's is amazing. Get an appetizer there. They're excellent.

Jeff GR8! How are the main dishes?

Tony12 I had steak with some French fries. The steak was great, but the fries weren't.

Junko You should try a dessert there, too. The ice cream is fantastic!

Jeff I love ice cream! THX. 😊 Does anyone want to join me?

B What about you? What do you do when you need a recommendation for a restaurant?

3 **Grammar** 🎧 Articles

Use a / an *to talk about nonspecific singular count nouns*	*Use* the *to talk about specific count and noncount nouns.*
Try **a** dessert.	I had **the** crab cakes.
Get **an** appetizer.	**The** ice cream is fantastic.
Use some *before plural count and noncount nouns.*	*Use* the *to name count and noncount nouns a second time.*
Let's order **some** French fries.	I had a steak and some French fries.
Let's order **some** garlic bread.	**The** steak was great, but **the** fries weren't.

Circle the words. Then compare with a partner.

A   I'm glad we came here. It's a great place.

B   So, do you want to share **an** / **some** appetizer?

A   Sure. How about **an** / **the** onion rings?

B   Perfect!

A   And do you want to get **a** / **some** crab cakes?

B   I don't think so. I'm not *that* hungry.

A   I'm going to get **a** / **the** lamb chops with **a** / **some** rice.

B   I think I want **a** / **the** steak. I heard it's delicious.

A   **A** / **The** desserts are good. I love **an** / **the** ice cream.

B   Yeah, we should order **a** / **an** dessert later.

A   Let's find **the** / **some** waiter. Where is he?

4 **Pronunciation** *The* before vowel and consonant sounds

A 🎧 **Listen and repeat. Notice how *the* is pronounced before vowel and consonant sounds.**

/i/		
the **a**ppetizer	the **i**ce cream	the **o**range

/ə/		
the lamb	the fruit	the pie

B PAIR WORK **Practice the conversation in Exercise 3.**

5 **Speaking** What to order?

A PAIR WORK **Do you usually order an appetizer, a main dish, a side dish, and a dessert in restaurants? Discuss your ideas.**

A: *I usually order a main dish and a side dish. I don't really like desserts.*

B: *I sometimes order an appetizer, but I always order a dessert.*

B PAIR WORK **Look at the menu in Exercise 1. What would you order?**

"The chicken stir-fry and the rice look good. I'd order that."

6 **Keep talking!**

Go to page 147 for more practice.

I can talk about menus and eating out. ✓

B I'll have the fish, please.

1 Interactions At a restaurant

A When was the last time you went to a restaurant? Who did you go with? What did you order?

B 🎧 Listen to the conversation. What does Maria order? Then practice the conversation.

Waiter	Are you ready to order?
Maria	Yes, I think so.
Waiter	What would you like?
Maria	I'll have the fish with some rice, and a small salad, please.
Waiter	Anything else?

Maria	No, I don't think so.
Waiter	All right. Let me check that. You'd like the fish, with rice, and a small salad.
Maria	Yes, that's right.
Waiter	Would you like some water?
Maria	Sure, that would be great. Thank you.

C 🎧 Listen to the expressions. Then practice the conversation again with the new expressions.

Ordering food

I'll have . . ., please.   I'd like . . ., please.   Can I have . . .,please?

Checking information

Let me check that.   Let me read that back.   Let me repeat that.

D PAIR WORK Have conversations like the one in Part B. Use the food below.

2 Listening Food orders

A 🎧 Listen to people order food. How many people order dessert? Circle the correct answer.

one   two   three

B 🎧 Listen again. Correct any wrong information on these orders.

1

Mickey's 🌶

chicken

rice

mixed vegetables

apple pie

2

Mickey's 🌶

crab cakes

lamb chops

French fries

small salad

water

chocolate cake

medium mushroom pizza

iced tea

3 Speaking Role play

PAIR WORK Role-play the situation. Then change roles.

Student A: You are waiter or waitress at Puck's Place. Greet the customer, take his or her order, and then check the information.

Student B: You are a customer at Puck's Place. Order from the menu.

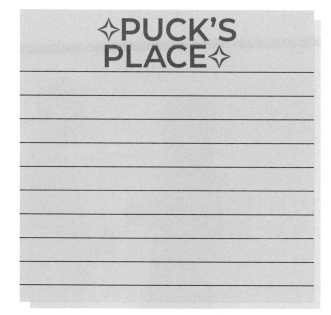

✧PUCK'S PLACE✧

Appetizers
Chicken salad • Pasta salad • Onion soup
Chicken soup • Crab cakes • Garlic bread

Main dishes
Lamb chops • Steak
Chicken stir-fry • Fish • Cheese ravioli

Sides
French fries • Rice
Mixed vegetables • Mashed potatoes

Desserts
Apple pie • Chocolate ice cream • Fruit salad

Drinks
Tea • Coffee • Lemonade • Soda

A: Hello. Are you ready to order?

B: Yes. I'll have the onion soup. And can I have the fish and some white rice, please? Also, . . .

I can order food in a restaurant. ✓

C Have you ever . . .?

1 Vocabulary Interesting food

A 🎧 Complete the chart with the correct words. Then listen and check your answers.

avocados   blue cheese   carrot juice   dates   frozen yogurt

oysters   plantains   seaweed   soy milk   squid

Dairy	Seafood	Fruits / Vegetables	Drinks

B **PAIR WORK** Which food in Part A do you like? do you dislike? would you like to try? Tell your partner.

"I like oysters. I don't like carrot juice. I'd like to try squid."

2 Conversation Dinner plans

A 🎧 Listen and practice.

Ellen   What are you doing tonight?

Peter   I'm going to World Café with my brother. Have you ever been there?

Ellen   No, I haven't. But I heard it's good.

Peter   I looked at their menu online this morning. They serve some really interesting food.

Ellen   Oh, yeah? Like what?

Peter   Fresh oysters. I've never had oysters, so I want to try them. Have you ever eaten them?

Ellen   Yeah, I have. I think they're delicious.

Peter   I've had squid. Are they similar?

Ellen   Um, not really. Do they only serve seafood?

Peter   No, they serve a little of everything.

B 🎧 Listen to Peter's message to Ellen the next day. What food did he like?

3 Grammar ♫ Present perfect for experience

I've **been** to World Café.	I **haven't tried** the desserts.
I've **had** squid.	I've never **eaten** oysters.

Have you **ever been** to World Café?

Yes, I **have.**   No, I **haven't.**

Contractions   I've = I have   I haven't = I have not.

Past participles	
be	**been**
drink	**drunk**
eat	**eaten**
have	**had**
try	**tried**

A Complete the conversations with the present perfect form of the verbs. Then practice with a partner.

1 A This place looks fun. I _____ (never / be) here.

   B I love it here. I _____ (be) here many times.

   A Everything looks delicious.

   B _____ you _____ (ever / eat) Mexican food before?

   A I _____ (have) tacos, but I'd like to try some-
     thing new.

2 A I _____ (never / try) frozen yogurt. Can you
     recommend a flavor?

   B I _____ (have) most flavors, and they're
     all good.

   A _____ you _____ (ever / try) the green tea flavor?

   B No, I _____ (have / not), but you should try it!

B Make sentences about your food experiences.

1 be / to a Turkish restaurant _____

2 eat / oysters _____

3 drink / soy milk _____

4 have / plantains _____

5 try / blue cheese _____

C **PAIR WORK** Ask *Have you ever . . .?* questions about the experiences in Part B.

4 Speaking Food experiences

A Add two more food experiences to the list.

eat / dates	have / seaweed	_____ / _____
try / Vietnamese food	drink / carrot juice	_____ / _____

B **PAIR WORK** Discuss your experiences. What food would you like to try?

A: Have you ever tried Vietnamese food?

B: Yes, I have. It's delicious.

5 Keep talking!

Go to page 148 for more practice. ▶

| I can ask about and describe food experiences. ✓ | 101 |

D Restaurant experiences

1 Reading 🎧

A 🎧 Read the web page. Which sentence describes all three restaurants? Check (✓) the correct answer.

☐ They don't have a lot of light.   ☐ They are in good locations.

☐ They're not very expensive.   ☐ They are very unusual.

RESTAURANTS WITH A DIFFERENCE

Ninja Akasaka is a popular restaurant in Tokyo. A ninja in dark clothes greets guests at the door and takes them through the dark hallways of the ninja house to their tables. The waiters also dress as ninjas. Ninja Akasaka has over a hundred delicious dishes to choose from. There's also a branch of the restaurant in Manhattan – Ninja New York.

♡ ◯ 95 likes   Follow

Annalakshmi is a vegetarian restaurant in Chennai, India, with additional restaurants in three other countries. There are no prices on the menu, so guests pay what they can! The people who work there are volunteers and take turns serving customers, cleaning tables, and washing dishes. Indian art covers the walls, and there are even live music and dance performances.

♡ ◯ 78 likes   Follow

At *Dans Le Noir* (In the Dark) in Paris, guests order their food in a place with a lot of light, but then they eat in darkness. They focus on the touch, smell, and taste of the food. The waiters there are blind, so when guests are ready to leave, they call the waiter's name. Their waiter then takes them back to the place where they ordered the food. There are additional restaurants in London and Moscow.

♡ ◯ 64 likes   Follow

B Read the web page again. Write T (true), F (false), or NI (no information) next to the sentences.

1 Guests dress as ninjas at Ninja Akasaka. _____

2 Ninja New York is more popular than Ninja Akasaka. _____

3 Annalakshmi has restaurants in four countries. _____

4 Every guest at Annalakshmi pays the same price. _____

5 Guests never see their food at Dans Le Noir. _____

6 The cooks at Dans Le Noir are blind. _____

C **PAIR WORK** Which restaurants in Part A do you think you'd enjoy? Why? Have you ever been to an unusual restaurant? Tell your partner.

2 Listening So, what did you think?

A 🎧 Listen to three couples talk about the restaurants in Exercise 1. Where did each couple eat? Number the restaurants from 1 to 3.

☐ Ninja Akasaka   ☐ Annalakshmi   ☐ Dans Le Noir

B 🎧 Listen again. Check (✓) the things each couple liked about the experience.

	the service	the prices	the location	the food
1	☐	☐	☐	☐
2	☐	☐	☐	☐
3	☐	☐	☐	☐

3 Writing A review

A Think of a restaurant you like. Answer the questions.

- What is the name of the restaurant?
- What type of food does it serve?
- When were you there last?
- What would you recommend ordering?
- What do you like about the restaurant?

B Write a short review of your favorite restaurant. Use the model and your answers from Part A to help you.

My Favorite Restaurant
Seoul Barbecue is my favorite restaurant. It serves delicious, healthy Korean food. I went there last week and loved it. I ordered beef, and I had some small side dishes. I would recommend doing that. It's fun because you cook your own meat at the table. It's a little expensive, but I really liked the service. I'd recommend this restaurant.

C **CLASS ACTIVITY** Post your reviews around the room. Read your classmates' reviews. Then get more information about the restaurant that interests you the most.

4 Speaking Restaurant recommendations

PAIR WORK Recommend a good place to go for each situation. Discuss your ideas.

- take an overseas visitor
- meet a big group of friends
- have a child's birthday party
- have a quiet dinner for two
- get a quick, cheap lunch
- enjoy live music

A: What's a good place to meet a big group of friends?
B: How about . . .? There's a private room for big groups.

I can describe restaurant experiences. ✓   103

Wrap-up

1 Quick pair review

Lesson A Brainstorm!

Make a list of menu items. How many do you know? You have two minutes.

Lesson B Do you remember?

Check (✓) the things you can say to order food. You have one minute.

- [ ] I'll have some French fries, please.
- [ ] Try the cheesecake, please.
- [ ] What would you like?
- [ ] Can I have the steak, please?
- [ ] Let me check that.
- [ ] I'd like some pie, please.

Lesson C Find out!

What interesting food have you and your partner both tried? Take turns.
You and your partner have two minutes.

A: I've eaten squid.

B: I haven't. I've eaten . . .

Lesson D Guess!

Describe a restaurant in your city, but don't say its name. Can your partner
guess which one it is? Take turns. You and your partner have two minutes.

A: This restaurant is on Main Street. It has good seafood, and the food is cheap. The service
is fantastic.

B: Is it Big Fish?

A: Yes, it is.

2 In the real world

What would you like to order? Go online and find a menu for a restaurant
in English. Then write about it.

- What is the name of the restaurant?
- What appetizers, main dish, and side dishes would you like to order?
- What drink would you like to try?
- What dessert would you like to eat?

Alphabet Café
I'd like to eat at Alphabet Café. I'd like
some garlic bread and the spaghetti . . .

11 Entertainment

LESSON A
- Types of movies
- *So, too, either,* and *neither*

LESSON B
- Asking for suggestions
- Giving a suggestion

LESSON C
- Types of music
- Determiners

LESSON D
- Reading: "Everybody Loves a Sing-Off"
- Writing: A popular musician

Warm Up

A Match the words and the pictures.

_____ an amusement park   _____ a dance performance   _____ a play

_____ a concert   _____ a movie   _____ a soccer game

B Which of these types of entertainment do you want to go to? Rank them from 1 (really want to go) to 6 (don't really want to go).

A I'm not a fan of dramas.

1 Vocabulary Types of movies

A 🎧 Match the types of movies and the pictures. Then listen and check your answers.

a	an action movie	**c**	a comedy	**e**	a horror movie	**g**	a science fiction movie
b	an animated movie	**d**	a drama	**f**	a musical	**h**	a western

1 `g`

2 `d`

3 ☐

4 ☐

5 ☐

6 ☐

7 ☐

8 ☐

B **PAIR WORK** What are your favorite types of movies? Give an example of the types you like. Tell your partner.

"I love action movies and dramas. My favorite movies are . . ."

2 Language in context At the movies

A 🎧 Listen to two friends at the movies. What type of movie are they watching?

I'm not usually late for movies.
Neither am I.

I like to sit in the front row.
So do I.

I love musicals!
I don't. I prefer horror movies.

B What about you? Are you ever late for movies? Do you like to sit in the front, middle, or back?

3 Grammar 🎧 *So, too, either,* and *neither*

I'm a fan of science fiction movies. 　　**So** am I / I am, **too**. 　　Oh, I'm not. I like comedies. I like to sit in the front row. 　　**So** do I. / I do, **too**. 　　Really? I don't. I prefer the back row.	I'm not usually late for movies. 　　**Neither** am I. / I'm not, **either**. 　　Oh, I am. I'm always late. I don't buy popcorn. 　　**Neither** do I. / I don't, **either**. 　　Oh, I do. And I always get a soda.

A Respond to the sentences in two different ways. Use *so, too, either,* or *neither*. Compare with a partner.

1　I'm not a fan of dramas.　　　　Neither am I.　　　　I'm not, either.

2　I love animated movies.　　　　_____　　　　_____

3　I'm not interested in action movies.　_____　　_____

4　I'm interested in old westerns.　　_____　　　_____

5　I don't watch horror movies.　　　_____　　　_____

6　I don't like science fiction movies.　_____　　　_____

B PAIR WORK Make the sentences in Part A true for you. Respond with *so, too, either,* or *neither*.

A: I'm not a fan of dramas.

B: Neither am I.　　　**OR**　　　Really? I am. My favorite drama is . . .

4 Speaking Movie talk

A Complete the sentences with true information.

I like to eat _____candy_____ at the movies.
　　　　　　　　　(snack)

I really like _____ .
　　　　　　　(actor or actress)

I'm not a fan of _____ .
　　　　　　　　　(actor or actress)

I want to see _____ .
　　　　　　　　(name of movie)

I don't really want to see _____ .
　　　　　　　　　　　　(name of movie)

I often see movies at _____ .
　　　　　　　　　　(name of theater)

I usually see movies with _____ .
　　　　　　　　　　　(name of person)

B PAIR WORK Take turns reading your sentences. Respond appropriately.

A: I like to eat candy at the movies.

B: I don't. I like to eat popcorn.

C GROUP WORK What movies are playing right now? Which ones do you want to see?
Can you agree on a movie to see together?

5 Keep talking!

Go to page 149 for more practice.

I can talk about my movie habits and opinions. ✓

B Any suggestions?

1 Interactions Suggestions

A What do you like to do on weekends? Who do you usually spend weekends with? How do you decide what to do?

B 🎧 Listen to the conversation. What do they decide to do on the weekend? Then practice the conversation.

Douglas	What do you want to do this weekend?	Jocelyn	I hate karaoke, and we went to the movies last week.
Jocelyn	I don't really know. Do you have any suggestions?	Douglas	Let's go to the food festival.
Douglas	Well, there's an outdoor movie in the park, a food festival, and a karaoke contest.	Jocelyn	OK. That sounds good. Have you ever been to one?
		Douglas	No, but it sounds like a lot of fun.

C 🎧 Listen to the expressions. Then practice the conversation again with the new expressions.

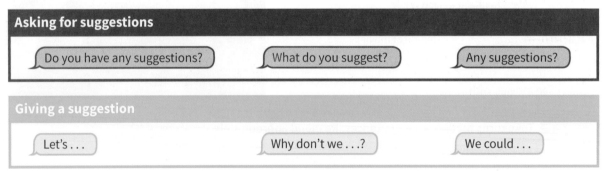

Asking for suggestions

Do you have any suggestions?   What do you suggest?   Any suggestions?

Giving a suggestion

Let's . . .   Why don't we . . .?   We could . . .

D Number the sentences from 1 to 8. Then practice with a partner.

_____	**A** A play? That's not a bad idea.		_____	**B** We always see movies. Why don't we see a play?
_____	**A** I'm not sure. We could see a movie.		_____	**B** OK. And let's have dinner before.
__1__	**A** Let's do something different tonight.		_____	**B** There are two plays. One is a drama, the other a comedy.
_____	**A** Why don't we see the comedy?		__2__	**B** OK. What do you suggest?

2 **Listening** Let's get together!

A 🎧 Listen to three conversations. Check (✓) what the people decide to do.

	What they decide to do		Place	Time
1	☐ go to a movie	☐ watch a movie at home		
2	☐ go out to eat	☐ order take-out food		
3	☐ go to a play	☐ go to a baseball game		

B 🎧 Listen again. Where and when are they going to meet? Write the place and time.

3 **Speaking** This weekend

A **PAIR WORK** Complete the chart with what is happening this weekend where you live.

	Movies	Music	Sports	Festivals
Friday				
Saturday				
Sunday				

B **PAIR WORK** Work with a new partner. Look at your charts. Decide to do three things together.

A: Let's do something fun this weekend.

B: All right. Any suggestions?

A: Well, we could see the new horror movie. Do you like horror movies?

B: No, I don't. Sorry. Why don't we . . . ?

I can ask for and give suggestions. ✓

C All of us love music.

1 Vocabulary Types of music

A 🎧 **Listen to the song clips. Number the types of music you hear from 1 to 10. Then check your answers.**

pop   rock   jazz   country   classical

folk   hip-hop   techno   reggae   blues

B **PAIR WORK** Say the name of a musician for each type of music in Part A. Tell your partner.

"Jennifer Lopez sings pop music."

2 Conversation A music recital

A 🎧 **Listen and practice.**

Ingrid These kids are great musicians. Do all of the students at this school learn a musical instrument?

John No, I don't think so, but most of them do.

Ingrid I see. And do most of the schools in this city have bands?

John I'm not sure. I know a lot of them around here do. Some of the schools even have their own jazz bands.

Ingrid How interesting! Do you know what's next?

John I think there's going to be a violin solo.

B 🎧 **Listen to their conversation after the recital. What type of music do the children prefer to play?**

3 Grammar 🎧 Determiners

100%	All of	
	Most of	
	A lot of	
	Some of	the students learn a **musical instrument**.
	Not many of	
0%	None of	

A Look at the picture of the Branson family. Complete the sentences
with determiners. Then compare with a partner.

1 _____ of them are singing.

2 _____ of them have costumes.

3 _____ of them are sitting.

4 _____ of them are playing an instrument.

5 _____ of them have blond hair.

6 _____ of them are dancing.

B Make true sentences using determiners. Tell your partner.

1 . . . of my favorite songs are pop songs.

2 . . . of my friends play an instrument.

3 . . . of my classmates play in rock bands.

4 . . . of my friends enjoy singing karaoke.

4 Pronunciation Reduction of *of*

A 🎧 Listen and repeat. Notice how *of* is sometimes pronounced /ə/ before consonant sounds.

/ə/	/ə/	/ə/
All of the students	A lot of the schools	None of my friends

B **PAIR WORK** Practice the sentences in Exercise 3A. Reduce *of* to /ə/.

5 Speaking Ask the class.

A **CLASS ACTIVITY** Add a type of music, a song, or a singer to the question.
Then ask your classmates the question.
Write the number of people who answer "yes."

Do you like _____ ? ☐

B Share your information. Use determiners.

"Some of us like hip-hop."

6 Keep talking!

Go to page 150 for more practice. ▶

D Singing shows around the world

1 Reading 🎧

A Read the online article. Which people are most interested in famous singers?

EVERYBODY LOVES A SING-OFF

Every year, thousands of people around the world enter singing competitions on TV, and millions of people watch to see who wins. Why do we love these programs so much?

Kanda, Thailand
Favorite show: The Mask Singer
"I'm a fan because I like seeing regular people become famous. Everybody loves a rags-to-riches story, right? I really enjoy shows where you choose favorites and watch them improve each week. Also, I love when I can vote for a singer – it's fun to help decide who will be the next big star!"

♡ ◯ 34 likes Follow

Andrew, USA
Favorite show: American Idol
"I usually watch singing competitions because I want to see singers before they are stars. Did you know that singers like Justin Timberlake, Beyoncé, and One Direction were all on TV competitions? Not many of the competitors will become famous – but sometimes, I hear a singer and I just know she's going to be great."

♡ ◯ 57 likes Follow

Eduardo, Chile
Favorite show: Festival Internacional de la Canción de Viña del Mar
"Everybody likes to sing – that's why these competitions are so popular. All of my friends sing in the shower, in the car, walking down the street. But I wish it wasn't all pop music. How about a hip-hop competition? Or a techno contest with DJs? That would be really cool."

♡ ◯ 48 likes Follow

Wiktoria, Poland
Favorite show: Eurovision
"I like to watch people sing badly. Seriously, I can hear good singing any time on the radio — it's more fun to hear people who aren't so good. I like to see what happens when people get on stage with a big audience. Will they perform well? Or will they miss a beat? That's really why most of us watch – we like to be the judge."

♡ ◯ 45 likes Follow

B Read the article again. Answer the questions.

1 Why does Kanda watch singing shows? _____

2 What does Andrew want to see? _____

3 What does Yandri not like about competitions? _____

4 Why does Wiktoria like to see people sing badly? _____

C GROUP WORK Do you like to watch singing competitions? Why or why not? Would you enter a competition? What kind of music would you sing? Discuss your ideas.

2 **Listening** Classical music hour

A 🎧 Listen to a radio host talk about the musician Lang Lang. Where is Lang Lang from?

B 🎧 Listen again. Check (✓) the correct answers.

1. 1. Lang Lang had his first music lessons at age:
   ☐ three   ☐ five

2. He received his first award at age:
   ☐ five   ☐ fifteen

3. He likes to share music with:
   ☐ young people   ☐ older people

4. He also works with:
   ☐ UNICEF   ☐ United Nations University

5. Besides classical music he loves:
   ☐ jazz and rock ☐ jazz, hip-hop, and pop

3 **Writing** A popular musician

A Think of your favorite musician or a popular musician. Answer the questions.

- Where is this person from?
- What is this person's best song?
- What type of music is this person famous for?
- What is interesting about this person?

B Write a short description about the musician. Use the model and your answers from Part A to help you.

> *My Favorite Singer*
> *My favorite singer is Thalia. She's from Mexico. She sings different types*
> *of music, but mostly she sings pop and dance music. My favorite song is*
> *"No, No, No." She records songs in many languages. She sings in English,*
> *Spanish, French, and Tagalog.*

C GROUP WORK Share your writing. Did any of you write about the same musician?

4 **Speaking** Make a playlist

A PAIR WORK Make a list of the most important singers, bands, or musicians from your country. What are their most popular songs?

B PAIR WORK Create a five-track playlist. Use your notes.

A: *I think . . . is very important.*

B: *So do I. A lot of young people like his music.*

C GROUP WORK Present your playlist and explain your choices. Ask and answer questions to get more information.

I can describe important singers and musicians.

Wrap-up

1 Quick pair review

Lesson A **Find out!**

What are two types of movies that both you and your partner like? You have two minutes.

A: I like action movies. Do you?

B: No, but I like animated movies. Do you?

Lesson B **Do you remember?**

Match the questions with the suggestions. You have one minute.

1 We should see a movie. Do you have any suggestions? _____

2 I'm hungry. Any suggestions? _____

3 Let's get some exercise. What do you suggest? _____

4 Where should we go shopping? Any suggestions? _____

5 We need to take a vacation? What do you suggest? _____

a We could take a walk.

b Why don't we go to the market?

c We could see a comedy.

d Why don't we go to Mexico?

e Let's make pizza!

Lesson C **Brainstorm!**

Make a list of types of music. How many do you know? Take turns. You and your partner
have two minutes.

Lesson D **Guess!**

Describe a popular band or singer, but don't say the name. Can your partner guess
the name? Take turns. You and your partner have two minutes.

A: She sings pop music. She sings in Korean and Japanese. She's also an actress.

B: BoA?

A: Yes. Her real name is Kwon Bo-ah.

2 In the real world

What were some of the top movies this year? Go online and find information about one
of them in English. Then write about it.

● What's the name of the movie?

● What actors are in it?

● What type of movie is it?

● What songs are in the movie?

A Top Movie

. . . . was one of the top movies this year.
It's an animated movie . . .

12 Time for a change

LESSON A
- Personal goals
- Infinitives of purpose

LESSON B
- Reacting to bad news
- Reacting to good news

LESSON C
- Milestones
- *Will* for predictions; *may*, *might* for possibility

LESSON D
- Reading: "An Olympic Dream Flies High"
- Writing: A dream come true

Warm-up

A The people in the pictures have made changes in their lives. What change do you think each person made?

B Would you like to make any of these changes? Which ones?

A Personal change

1 Vocabulary Personal goals

A 🎧 Match the words and the pictures. Then listen and check your answers.

a	get a credit card	**d**	lose weight	**g**	save money
b	join a gym	**e**	make more friends	**h**	start a new hobby
c	learn an instrument	**f**	pass a test	**i**	work / study harder

1

2

3

4

5

6

7

8

9

B **PAIR WORK** Which things in Part A are easy to do? Which are more difficult? Why? Tell your partner.

"It's difficult to learn an instrument. It takes a long time!"

2 Language in context I'm making it happen!

A 🎧 Listen to three people talk about changes. Who's learning something new?

My friends and I are starting our own band next year. I can sing, but I can't play an instrument, so I'm taking a class to learn the guitar.

–Leonardo

I joined a gym last month to lose weight. I only want to lose a couple of kilos, but I'm finding it difficult. But I'm making some new friends, so that's good.

–Mark

I hated taking the bus to work, so I saved money to buy a bike. Now I ride it to work every day, and I feel a lot healthier and happier.

–Tina

B Talk about a change you made.

3 **Grammar** 🎧 Infinitives of purpose

I'm taking a class **to learn** the guitar.	(= because I want to learn the guitar)
I joined a gym last month **to lose** weight.	(= because I want to lose weight)
She'd like to save money **to buy** a bike.	(= because she wants to buy a bike)
We're starting a book club in July **to make** more friends.	(= because we want to make more friends)

A Match the sentence parts. Then compare with a partner.

1 I joined a gym last week   to buy a car.

2 I'm saving my money   to get better grades.

3 I'd like to go to the U.S.   to relax.

4 I studied harder   to improve my English.

5 I listen to music   to lose weight.

B Rewrite these sentences. Use an infinitive of purpose. Then compare with a partner.

1 I'd like to go to a hair salon because I want to get a new hairstyle.

   I'd like to go to a hair salon to get a new hairstyle.

2 I listen to songs in English because I want to improve my listening.

   _____

3 I saved my money because I wanted to buy a new computer.

   _____

4 I'm studying on weekends because I want to get a better job.

   _____

C **PAIR WORK** Which sentences from Part B are true for you?
Tell your partner.

4 **Speaking** Three changes

A Complete the chart with three changes you would like to make. Then think about the reasons why you would like to make each change.

	Changes	Reasons
1		
2		
3		

B **GROUP WORK** Discuss your changes. Are any of your changes or reasons the same?

"I'd like to go to Canada to study English. I hope to be an English teacher someday."

5 **Keep talking!**

Go to page 151 for more practice. ▶

I **can** give reasons for personal changes. ✓   117

B I'm happy to hear that!

1 Interactions Good and bad news

A Do you ever see old classmates or friends around town? What kinds of things do you talk about?

B 🎧 Listen to the conversation. What's changed for Emily? Then practice the conversation.

Joe Hey, Emily. Long time no see.

Emily Oh, hi, Joe. How are you doing?

Joe Fine. Well, actually, I didn't pass my driving test – again. That's three times now.

Emily **That's too bad.**

Joe Yeah, I wanted to drive to the beach this weekend. So, what's new with you?

Emily Well, I'm playing guitar in a band. I'm really enjoying it.

Joe **That's wonderful!** What kind of music?

Emily Rock. We have a show next week. Do you want to come? I'll email you the information.

Joe Thanks. I'll be there!

C 🎧 Listen to the expressions. Then practice the conversation again with the new expressions.

Reacting to bad news

| That's too bad. | That's a shame. | I'm sorry to hear that. |

Reacting to good news

| That's wonderful! | That's great to hear! | I'm happy to hear that! |

D **PAIR WORK** Share the news below and react appropriately.

I'm learning German.

I bought a car.

I failed my math exam.

I have a part-time job.

I broke my foot.

I lost my wallet.

I won two concert tickets.

I'm going to travel to London.

I'm not sleeping well.

I'm planning to get a pet.

2 Listening Sharing news

A Look at the pictures in Part B. Where are the people?

B 🎧 Listen to four people share news with friends. What news are they talking about? Number the pictures from 1 to 4.

C 🎧 Listen again. Correct the false sentences. Then compare with a partner.

1 Mark has some free time in the afternoons and evenings.
2 Lucia is saving her money to buy a restaurant.
3 Jeff is taking the train because his new car isn't running very well.
4 Wendy and her cousin had a terrible time in Rome and Florence.

3 Speaking Good news, bad news

A Complete the chart with some good news and bad news. (Don't use true news!)

	Good news		Bad news
1		1	
2		2	

B Class activity Share your news. React appropriately.

A: Hi, Mariko. What's new with you?

B: Well, I'm going to Paris next week to study French.

A: That's wonderful!

B: What's new with you?

C GROUP WORK Share the most interesting news you heard.

I can react to good and bad news. ✓ 119

C I think I'll get a job.

1 Vocabulary Milestones

A 🎧 Complete the chart with the correct milestones. Then listen and check your answers.

☐ buy a house

☐ get promoted

☐ go to college

☐ graduate from high school

☐ rent an apartment

☐ retire

☐ start a career

☐ get married

☐ start school

Personal milestones	Educational milestones	Work-related milestones

B Number the milestones from 1 to 9 in the order that they usually happen. Then compare with a partner.

2 Conversation I'll go traveling.

A 🎧 Listen and practice.

Tim Hey, Craig. How are you doing?

Craig Oh, hi, Tim. I'm fine. What's new with you?

Tim Well, I'm graduating from college this summer.

Craig That's wonderful! What do you think you'll do in September?

Tim I think I'll go traveling with some friends.

Craig That sounds fun, but it won't be cheap.

Tim Yeah, so I may get a job this summer to pay for the trip.

B 🎧 Listen to the rest of the conversation. What's new with Craig?

3 Grammar 🎧 *Will* for predictions; *may, might* for possibility

What do you think you'll do?	
Predictions I think **I'll go** traveling with some friends. I **won't get** a roommate. Do you think you**'ll get** a roommate? Yes, I**'ll get** one soon. No. I **won't get** a roommate this year.	*Possibility* I don't really know. I **may get** a job. I'm not really sure. I **might buy** a pet.

A Circle the correct words. Then practice with a partner.

1 A Do you think you'll buy a house next year?

   B No. I don't have enough money. But **I'll / I may** rent an apartment. I don't know.

2 A What do you think you'll do on your next birthday?

   B **I'll / I might** have a big party, but I'm not sure.

3 A When do you think you'll retire?

   B **I'll / I may** retire at 65. Most other people do.

4 A Do you think you'll buy a car this year?

   B No, **I won't / I might**. I don't have enough money for one.

5 A Do you think you'll get married after college?

   B I'm not sure. **I'll / I may** get married someday.

B PAIR WORK Ask and answer the questions in Part A. Answer with your own information.

4 Pronunciation Contraction of *will*

🎧 **Listen and repeat. Notice how these pronouns +** *will* **are contracted into one syllable.**

I'll   you'll   he'll   she'll   we'll   they'll

5 Speaking My future

A Write an idea for each of the things below.

1 an important thing to do: _____

2 an exciting thing to do: _____

3 an expensive thing to buy: _____

4 an interesting person to meet: _____

B PAIR WORK Ask and answer questions about the things in Part A. Use *will*, *may*, or *might* and these time expressions.

A: *Do you think you'll start your career this year?*

B: *Yes, I think I will. I have an interview this week.*

Time expressions	
this week	this month
this weekend	next month
next week	this year

6 Keep talking!

Go to page 152 for more practice.

I can make predictions about the future. ✓

D Dreams and aspirations

1 Reading 🎧

A Look at this quote. What do you think it means?

"The important thing in life is not to win but to try."

–Pierre de Coubertin, founder of the modern Olympic games

B Read the article. Check (✓) the best title.

☐ Skater Loses Olympics but Wins Fans ☐ The Worst Olympian Ever

☐ An Olympic Dream Flies High ☐ Ski Jumper – or Ski Dropper?

At the 1988 Winter Olympics, the most famous competitor wasn't the fastest skier or the strongest ice skater. He didn't win a gold medal – or any medals at all. In fact, Eddie Edwards finished last in the ski jumping competition. But his courage made him a favorite of fans around the world, who nicknamed him "Eddie the Eagle."

Eddie was a construction worker from a small town in England. He had a dream to make the Olympic team.

He was a good skier and almost made the British team in 1984. For the 1988 games, he became England's #1 ski jumper for a simple reason – nobody else wanted to try.

Eddie had no money and no coach. He saved money to buy used equipment – his ski boots were too big, so he wore six pairs of socks. He didn't see very well and wore thick glasses. "Sometimes I take off, and I can't see where I'm going," he said. Before each jump, he was afraid that he might fall. But he worked hard to learn and to improve.

At the Olympic Games in Calgary, Eddie competed in the 70m and 90m jumps. He landed without falling, but came in last in both events.

Many people loved Eddie for his dream and his courage. But others thought he wasn't good enough to compete. To these people, Eddie said, "Where is it written that the Olympics are only for winners?"

Eddie's performance made him famous in England. When he returned home, 10,000 people met him at the airport. Today, Eddie is a construction worker again, but he is also famous thanks to the 2016 film, "Eddie the Eagle."

C Read the article again. Answer the questions.

1 What was Eddie's dream? _____

2 What was Eddie afraid of? _____

3 Why did the crowd like Eddie? _____

4 Why did many people like Eddie? _____

D **GROUP WORK** Do you think it's more important to win or to try? Should the Olympic Games be open to athletes like Eddie, or only the best athletes?

2 Listening An interview with an athlete

A 🎧 Listen to an interview with Suzanne, a marathon runner. Check (✓) the two dreams she's achieved.

- ☐ to run marathons
- ☐ to go back to school
- ☐ to win the Chicago Marathon
- ☐ to run all the big marathons

B 🎧 Listen again. Circle the correct answers.

1 This is Suzanne's **fifth** / **seventh** marathon.
2 She **won** / **didn't win** the Boston Marathon.
3 She finished **first** / **last** in her first race in high school.
4 At age **39** / **43**, she decided to make some changes in her life.
5 The most difficult thing for her was the **training** / **stress**.

3 Writing A dream come true

A Think of a dream that came true for you. Answer the questions.

- What was your dream?
- Why was it a dream for you?
- How did your dream come true?

B Write about your dream. Use the model and your answers in Part A to help you.

> **My Dream**
> My dream was to study Mexican cooking in Oaxaca. I loved to cook, but I wasn't a very good cook. So I went to Oaxaca to study Mexican cooking. I took a two-week class. It was a dream come true. Now I can make great meals. Who knows? I might become a chef someday.

C GROUP WORK Share your writing. Ask and answer questions for more information.

4 Speaking Dream planner

A Complete the chart with a dream for the future. Then add three things you'll need to do to achieve it.

My Dream	How I'll make it happen
	1
	2
	3

B GROUP WORK Tell your group about your dream and how you'll achieve it.

A: My dream is to start my own business someday.

B: That's a great dream. How will you make it happen?

A: Well, first I'll go back to school. Then I'll get a job to get some experience.

I can discuss my dreams for the future. ✓

Wrap-up

1 Quick pair review

Lesson A `Brainstorm!`

Make a list of personal goals that people can have. How many do you know? You have two minutes.

Lesson B `Do you remember?`

Write B for ways to react to bad news. Write G for ways to react to good news. You have one minute.

1 _____ That's too bad.

2 _____ I'm sorry to hear that.

3 _____ That's wonderful!

4 _____ I'm happy to hear that!

5 _____ That's a shame.

6 _____ That's great to hear!

Lesson C `Find out!`

What are two things both you and your partner think you will do in the future? Take turns. You and your partner have two minutes.

A: I think I'll go to college in two years.

B: I don't think I will. I may travel first.

Lesson D `Guess!`

Describe a dream you had when you were a child. Can your partner guess what it was? Take turns. You and your partner have two minutes.

A: I loved swimming. I wanted to win a gold medal.

B: Did you want to swim in the Olympics?

A: Yes, I did.

2 In the real world

What future goals do famous people have? Do you think they will achieve them? Go online and find information in English about a famous person in one of these categories. Then write about him or her.

| an actor | an athlete | a businessperson | a politician | a scientist | a singer |

Bill Gates
Bill Gates wants to improve people's health.
I think he'll achieve this goal . . .

Favorites

GROUP WORK Play the game. Put a small object on *Start*. Toss a coin.

 Move 1 space.   Move 2 spaces.

Heads   Tails

Use the correct form of *be* to ask and answer questions. Can you answer the questions? Take turns.

Yes →   Move ahead.   No ←   Move back.

A: Are you interested in travel?

B: Yes, I am. I'm interested in new places.

An active class?

A Add two things to the chart.

Find someone who . . .	Name	Extra information
goes to the gym		
plays table tennis		
does gymnastics		
plays soccer on the weekends		
plays a sport with a family member		
exercises in the morning		
watches baseball on TV		
listens to sports on the radio		
dislikes sports		

B CLASS ACTIVITY Find classmates who do each thing. Ask more questions. Write their name and extra information you hear.

A: Do you go to the gym, Anna?

B: Yes, I do. I go three times a week.

A: Really? What do you do there?

B: I do yoga, and I swim.

Help box

How often do you . . . ?
Where do you . . . ?
Who do you . . . , with?
What's your favorite . . . ?

C PAIR WORK Share your information.

A: Anna goes to the gym three times a week.

B: Really? What does she do there?

Keep talking!

Are you confident?

A PAIR WORK Take the quiz. Take turns asking and answering the questions.

1   What colors do you often wear?
    a   I wear red, pink, and orange.
    b   I wear yellow and green.
    c   I wear blue and purple.
    d   I wear black, white, and gray.

2   What are you like around your friends?
    a   I'm always very talkative.
    b   I'm talkative, but sometimes I'm quiet.
    c   I'm usually the quiet one.
    d   I don't know.

3   How do you enter a party?
    a   I walk in and say hello to everyone.
    b   I walk in and say hello to one person.
    c   I walk in and look for a friend.
    d   I walk in and stand in a corner.

4   You meet someone new. What do you do?
    a   I say hello and ask questions.
    b   I say "hi" and wait for questions.
    c   I just smile.
    d   I look away.

5   You see someone you like. What do you do?
    a   I walk up and say hello.
    b   I ask a friend to introduce us.
    c   I smile at the person.
    d   I do nothing.

6   The teacher asks a question. What do you do?
    a   I shout out the answer.
    b   I raise my hand.
    c   I check my answer with a friend.
    d   I look down at my desk.

B PAIR WORK Add up and score your quizzes. Are the results true for you?

A: I got 17 points.
B: You're very confident.
A: Really? I'm not sure about that.

a answers = 3 points	c answers = 1 point
b answers = 2 points	d answers = 0 points

12–18	You are very confident. Aren't you ever shy?
6–11	You are confident, but not about everything.
0–5	You're not very confident. Believe in yourself!

Find the differences

Student A

PAIR WORK You and your partner have pictures of the same people, but six things are different. Describe the pictures and ask questions to find the differences. Circle them.

A: In my picture, Brian is young. Is he young in your picture?

B: Yeah, so that's the same. In my picture, he has short straight hair.

A: Mine, too. What color is . . .?

Keep talking!

What's the weather like?

Student A

A PAIR WORK You and your partner have information about the weather in four cities, but some information is missing. Ask questions to get the information.

A: When is spring in Lisbon?

B: It's from March to June. What's the weather like in the spring?

A: It's warm and sunny.

Lisbon, Portugal	Season	Months	Weather
	Spring	March–June	warm and sunny
	Summer	June–September	
	Fall	September–December	
	Winter	December–March	cool and rainy

Seoul, South Korea	Season	Months	Weather
	Spring	March–June	
	Summer	June–September	hot and rainy
	Fall	September–December	
	Winter	December–March	very cold, snowy

Sydney, Australia	Season	Months	Weather
	Spring	September–December	warm and sunny
	Summer	December–March	
	Fall	March–June	
	Winter	June–September	cool and windy

Buenos Aires, Argentina	Season	Months	Weather
	Spring	September–December	
	Summer	December–March	sometimes hot, not rainy
	Fall	March–June	
	Winter	June–September	cold, not rainy

B PAIR WORK Which city's seasons are similar to yours?

Keep talking!

Find the differences

Student B

PAIR WORK You and your partner have pictures of the same people, but six things are different.
Describe the pictures and ask questions to find the differences. Circle them.

A: In my picture, Brian is young. Is he young in your picture?

B: Yeah, so that's the same. In my picture, he has short straight hair.

A: Mine, too. What color is . . .?

Keep talking!

What's the weather like?

Student B

A PAIR WORK You and your partner have information about the weather in four cities, but some information is missing. Ask questions to get the information.

A: When is spring in Lisbon?

B: It's from March to June. What's the weather like in the spring?

A: It's warm and sunny.

Lisbon, Portugal	Season	Months	Weather
	Spring	March-June	
	Summer	June-September	hot, not rainy
	Fall	September-December	warm and windy
	Winter	December-March	

Seoul, South Korea	Season	Months	Weather
	Spring	March-June	warm, not rainy
	Summer	June-September	
	Fall	September-December	sunny and cool
	Winter	December-March	

Sydney, Australia	Season	Months	Weather
	Spring	September-December	
	Summer	December-March	hot and dry
	Fall	March-June	cool and rainy
	Winter	June-September	

Buenos Aires, Argentina	Season	Months	Weather
	Spring	September-December	warm and rainy
	Summer	December-March	
	Fall	March-June	rainy, not cool
	Winter	June-September	

B PAIR WORK Which city's seasons are similar to yours?

Someday . . .

A Write information about things you'd like to do someday.

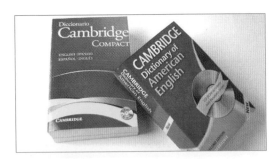

a language I'd like to learn: _____

a person I'd like to meet: _____

a country I'd like to visit: _____

a job I'd like to have: _____

something I'd like to buy: _____

a sport I'd like to try: _____

a place I'd like to live: _____

a game I'd like to play: _____

B GROUP WORK **Share your ideas. Ask and answer questions for more information.**

A: I think I'd like to learn Spanish someday.

B: Really? Why?

A: Because I'd like to visit Costa Rica.

Keep talking!

Home sweet home

A **PAIR WORK** Look at the picture for two minutes. Try to remember the rooms, furniture, and other details.

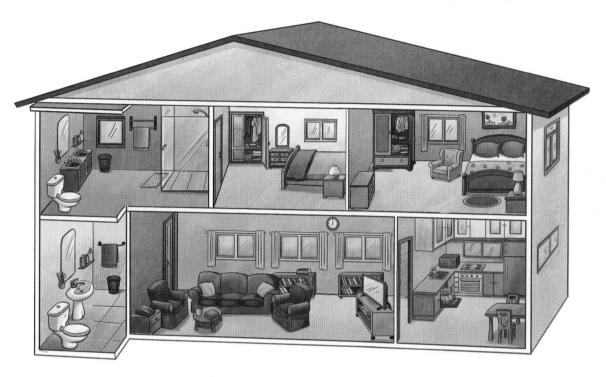

B **PAIR WORK** Cover the picture. Ask and answer these questions. What do you remember?

- How many rooms are there in the house?
- Which rooms are on the first floor? the second floor?
- How much light is there in the living room? How many windows are there?
- Is there much furniture in the living room? What's there?
- What's on the coffee table? What's on the kitchen table?
- Are there many pictures in the house? Where are they?
- How are the two bedrooms different?
- How are the two bathrooms different?
- Is there much space in this house? Do you think there is much noise?

A: How many rooms are there in the house?

B: I think there are . . . rooms.

A: I think so, too. Which rooms are on the first floor?

C Look at the picture again and check your answers.

Cleanup time

PAIR WORK You need to do some chores around the apartment. Decide who does each chore. Be fair!

A: Could you take out the garbage?

B: Sure. I can take it out. Would you clean out the closet?

Keep talking!

Don't get up!

Student A

A `PAIR WORK` Tell your partner to cover the pictures. Describe the exercises. Your partner does the actions. Take turns.

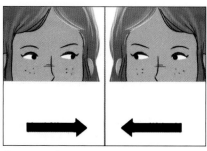

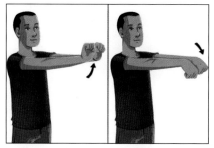

Eye exercises
Move your eyes quickly to the right. Then move them quickly to the left. Repeat five times.

Wrist exercises
Stretch your arms in front of you. Move your hands up and down quickly. Repeat five times.

Shoulder exercises
Lift your shoulders slowly to your ears. Don't move, and hold for three seconds. Then lower your shoulders. Repeat three times.

> **A:** Move your eyes to the right.
>
> **B:** Like this?
>
> **A:** Yes. Now move them to the left.

B `PAIR WORK` How did your partner do? How does your partner feel?

Student B

A `PAIR WORK` Tell your partner to cover the pictures. Describe the exercises. Your partner does the actions. Take turns.

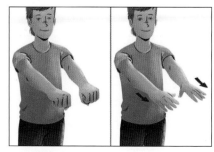

Hand exercises
Stretch your arms in front of you. Close your hands. Then open your hands quickly. Repeat five times.

Neck exercises
Touch your right ear to your right shoulder. Then touch your left ear to your left shoulder. Repeat five times.

Arm exercises
Lift your right arm up and down. Then lift your left arm up and down. Repeat three times.

> **B:** Stretch your arms in front of you.
>
> **A:** Like this?
>
> **B:** Yes. Now close your hands.

B How did your partner do? How does your partner feel?

Keep talking!

How healthy are you?

A PAIR WORK Take the quiz. Take turns asking and answering the questions.

1 How many servings of fruit and vegetables do you eat a day?
- [ ] **a** Five or more
- [ ] **b** Three to four
- [ ] **c** One to two

2 How often do you eat breakfast?
- [ ] **a** Every day
- [ ] **b** Two to six times a week
- [ ] **c** Rarely

3 How many meals do you eat a day?
- [ ] **a** Four or five small meals
- [ ] **b** Three meals
- [ ] **c** One or two big meals

4 How much junk food do you eat?
- [ ] **a** Very little
- [ ] **b** About average
- [ ] **c** A lot

5 How often do you exercise?
- [ ] **a** Every day
- [ ] **b** Two or three times a week
- [ ] **c** Never

6 How long do you spend watching TV or playing video games each week?
- [ ] **a** One to two hours
- [ ] **b** Three to six hours
- [ ] **c** Seven or more hours

7 How well do you sleep at night?
- [ ] **a** Very well
- [ ] **b** Pretty well
- [ ] **c** Not very well

8 How often do you get a checkup?
- [ ] **a** Once a year
- [ ] **b** Every two or three years
- [ ] **c** Hardly ever

9 How happy are you with your health?
- [ ] **a** Very happy
- [ ] **b** Pretty happy
- [ ] **c** Not very happy

a answers = 3 points
b answers = 2 points
c answers = 1 point
21–27 You're very healthy. Congratulations!
15–20 You're pretty healthy. Keep it up!
9–14 You can improve your health. Start now!

B PAIR WORK Add up and score your quizzes. Are the results true for you? Why or why not?

A: My score is 16. It says I'm pretty healthy. I think that's true.

B: My score is 20, but I think I'm very healthy.

Keep talking!

TV listings

A PAIR WORK Look at the TV listings. What types of shows are they?

	Channel 4	Channel 11	Channel 13
7:00–7:30	**Win or Lose** Everyone's favorite game show! Play at home!	**Soap Stars on Ice** See your favorite soap stars ice skate for charity!	**Man's Best Friend** The new sitcom about a talking horse named Fred
7:30–8:00	**Under Arrest** Police drama starring Damien Porter		**Travels with Ryan** This week, Ryan learns how to samba in Brazil.
8:00–8:30	**Mr. and Mrs. Right** The best reality show on TV! Vote for your favorite couple!	**The Year in Sports** The best baseball moments of the year	**The Ina Lopez Show** Tough questions, honest answers. Tonight talk-show queen Ina takes your calls!
8:30–9:00		**Meet My Family** A funny family sitcom	
9:00–9:30	**Lions of Kenya** "An amazing documentary"	**Take It or Leave It** Part game show, part reality show. New!	**My Roommate Ralph** A new sitcom from the creators of *Alien Mom*
9:30–10:00	**The News** Local news with Dinah and Jim	**Family Life** The funny new cartoon for adults	**Kiss and Tell** See the soap everyone is talking about!

B PAIR WORK Look at the information about the Green family. They have only one TV. What shows can they watch together from 7:00 to 10:00?

Dan Green
- enjoys watching sports and news
- hates to watch reality shows

Sarah Green
- hopes to visit Rio de Janeiro
- prefers to watch funny shows

Rick Green
- loves to watch game shows hates soap operas

Rose Green
- enjoys watching soap operas
- doesn't like watching sitcoms

A: They can watch *Win or Lose* at 7:00. Rick loves to watch game shows.

B: And they can watch *Travels with Ryan* at 7:30. Sarah hopes to visit Brazil.

C GROUP WORK What shows do you want to watch?

Keep talking!

My daily planner

A Make a schedule for tomorrow afternoon and evening. Use the ideas below and your own ideas. Write four activities in the daily planner. Think about how long each activity will take.

go grocery shopping	meet friends for coffee	watch a movie on TV
watch sports with friends	chat online with friends	clean my room
exercise at the gym	watch the news	study at the library
_____	_____	_____

Date: / / Sun Mon Tues Wed Thurs Fri Sat	Notes	Date: / / Sun Mon Tues Wed Thurs Fri Sat	Notes
2:00		6:00	
2:30		6:30	
3:00		7:00	
3:30		7:30	
4:00		8:00	
4:30		8:30	
5:00		9:00	
5:30		9:30	

B `CLASS ACTIVITY` Think of three fun activities. Find classmates who want to do the activities with you. Add the information to your planners.

A: What are you doing tomorrow evening at 7:00?

B: I'm meeting some friends for coffee.

A: Oh, OK. Do you want to see a movie at 8:00?

B: I'd love to, but I can't. I'm . . .

Keep talking!

Which product is . . .?

A PAIR WORK Add two more products to the chart. Then think of two examples you know for each product and write their names in the chart.

	Example 1	Example 2	
Video game			Which is newer? Which is more fun? Which is . . .?
Computer			Which is easier to use? Which is faster? Which is . . .?
Cell phone			Which is thinner? Which is less expensive? Which is . . .?
Car			Which is smaller? Which is faster? Which is . . .?

B Compare each pair of products. Use the questions in Part A and your own ideas.

A: I think . . . is newer than . . .

B: That's right. It's more fun, too.

A: I don't really agree. I think . . . is more fun. My friends and I can play it all day!

C Share your comparisons with the class. Which product is better? Why?

They aren't big enough!

Student A

PAIR WORK You and your partner have pictures of the same people, but there are eight differences. Describe the pictures and ask questions about the differences. Circle them.

A: In my picture, Nancy's pants are too baggy. They look very uncomfortable.

B: In my picture, Nancy's pants are too tight. So, that's different.

A: What about Maria's pants? I think they're too short.

B: They're too short in my picture, too. So, that's the same.

Keep talking!

From the past

Student A

A **PAIR WORK** You and your partner have information on six famous people from the past, but some information is missing. Ask these questions and complete the information.

- Where was . . . born?
- When was . . . born?
- What did . . . do?
- Why was . . . famous?

Name	George Washington	Frida Kahlo	Charlie Chaplin
Place of birth	the U.S.	Mexico	England
Date of birth	February 22, 1732	July 6, 1907	_____
What did	_____	painter	actor and director
Why famous	He was the first president of the U.S.	She was very _____, and her art was _____.	He was in a lot of funny black-and-white movies.

Name	Jesse Owens	Marie Curie	Yuri Gagarin
Place of birth	the U.S.	_____	Russia
Date of birth	September 12, 1913	November 7, 1867	March 9, 1934
What did	athlete	scientist	astronaut
Why famous	He was the first American to win _____ gold _____ in track and field in one Olympics.	She was the first person to win two Nobel prizes.	He was the first person in _____.

B **PAIR WORK** Look at the information. What similarities can you find between these famous people and other famous people you know?

8 Lesson A

What can you do here?

A PAIR WORK Think about where you live. Where can you do each of these things? Take notes.

hear live music

see interesting dance

buy fun souvenirs

eat good, cheap food

see statues and art

enjoy beautiful views

go for a walk

visit historical sites

enjoy nature

A: You can often hear live music at the city square.

B: Right. And there's also the university coffee shop.

A: That's true. They have live music on Fridays and Saturdays.

B GROUP WORK Share your information. How similar are your ideas?

Keep talking!

City quiz

A **PAIR WORK** Take the quiz. Ask the questions and guess the answers. Take turns.

1 What is the biggest city in North America?
  a Mexico City **b** Los Angeles **c** Washington, D.C.

2 Where is the biggest soccer stadium in South America?
  a Buenos Aires, Argentina **b** Rio de Janeiro, Brazil **c** Lima, Peru

3 "The Big Apple" is the nickname for what U.S. city?
  a Boston **b** Washington, D.C. **c** New York City

4 Which city is on the Han River?
  a New Orleans, U.S. **b** Venice, Italy **c** Seoul, South Korea

5 What is the most expensive city?
  a Tokyo, Japan **b** London, England **c** Rome, Italy

6 What is the safest big city in the U.S.?
  a New York City **b** Las Vegas **c** Boston

7 The oldest subway system in the world is in what European city?
  a Paris, France **b** Madrid, Spain **c** London, England

8 Which city has the worst traffic in the U.S.?
  a Chicago **b** Los Angeles **c** San Francisco

9 What city is in both Europe and Asia?
  a Berlin, Germany **b** Stockholm, Sweden **c** Istanbul, Turkey

10 The biggest public square in the world is in what city?
  a Beijing, China **b** Moscow, Russia **c** London, England

B Check your answers on the bottom of this page. How many did you get correct?

C **PAIR WORK** Think of another question and three possible answer choices. Ask another pair. Do they know the answer?

"What's the largest city in . . .?"

1.a 2.b 3.c 4.c 5.a 6.a 7.c 8.b 9.c 10.a

Keep talking!

They aren't big enough!

Student B

PAIR WORK You and your partner have pictures of the same people, but there are eight differences. Describe the pictures and ask questions about the differences. Circle them.

A: In my picture, Nancy's pants are too baggy. They look very uncomfortable.

B: In my picture, Nancy's pants are too tight. So, that's different.

A: What about Maria's pants? I think they're too short.

B: They're too short in my picture, too. So, that's the same.

Keep talking!

From the Past

Student B

A **PAIR WORK** You and your partner have information about six famous people from the past, but some information is missing. Ask these questions and complete the information.

- Where was . . . born?
- When was . . . born?
- What did . . . do?
- Why was . . . famous?

Name	George Washington	Frida Kahlo	Charlie Chaplin
Place of birth	the U.S.	_____	England
Date of birth	February 22, 1732	July 6, 1907	April 16, 1889
What did	politician	painter	actor and director
Why famous	He was the first _____ of the _____.	She was very creative, and her art was very interesting.	He was in a lot of _____ black-and-white _____.

Name	Jesse Owens	Marie Curie	Yuri Gagarin
Place of birth	the U.S.	Poland	Russia
Date of birth	_____	November 7, 1867	March 9, 1934
What did	athlete	scientist	_____
Why famous	He was the first American to win four gold medals in track and field in one Olympics.	She was the first person to win _____ Nobel _____.	He was the first person in space.

B **PAIR WORK** Look at the information. What similarities can you find between these famous people and other famous people you know?

What an inspiring person!

A Think of three people you admire. Use the categories below or think of your own. Then complete the chart.

| an athlete | a musician | a writer | an artist | a scientist |
| a politician | an actor/actress | a business leader | a family member | a teacher |

	Name	Why	Notes
1			
2			
3			

B **GROUP WORK** Share your ideas. Ask and answer questions for more information.

A: I really admire Sergey Brin and Larry Page. They started Google.

B: Why do you admire them?

A: Well, I think they're both talented and intelligent.

C: Do you think they're also . . . ?

C Is there a famous person who you *don't* admire? Why not?

Keep talking!

A one-of-a-kind menu

A **GROUP WORK** Imagine you're going to open a restaurant together. Answer the questions and create a menu.

- What's the name of your restaurant?
- What do you want to serve?
- Is it a cheap or an expensive restaurant? Write the prices.

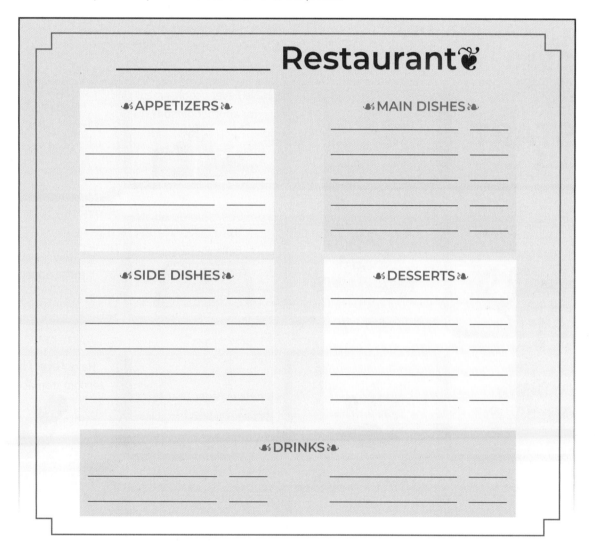

_____ Restaurant

APPETIZERS

MAIN DISHES

SIDE DISHES

DESSERTS

DRINKS

A: Let's have three or four appetizers.

B: OK. How about some garlic bread and onion soup?

C: That sounds good. Let's have a salad, too. How about . . .?

B **GROUP WORK** Exchange your menus. Ask and answer questions about the items. Which dishes would you order?

A: The Mexican salad sounds interesting. What's in it?

B: It has lettuce, tomatoes, onions, peppers, beans, and corn.

Keep talking!

Yes, I have.

GROUP WORK **Play the game. Put a small object on** *Start*. **Toss a coin.**

 Move 1 space.

 Move 2 spaces.

Heads   Tails

Use the words to ask and answer questions. Ask your own *Have you ever . . .?* questions on the **Free question** spaces. Take turns.

A: Have you ever made French fries?

B: Yes, I have.

START

Have / ever / make French fries?

Have / ever / cook a meal for another person?

Have / ever / try Thai food?

Have / ever / eat Indian food?

Free question

Have / ever / bake cookies?

Have / ever / make popcorn?

Free question

Have / ever / have breakfast in bed?

Have / ever / eat at the beach?

Have / ever / have a terrible stomachache?

Have / ever / have a really expensive meal?

Free question

Have / ever / be to a Korean restaurant?

Have / ever / drink coffee late at night?

Have / ever / watch a cooking show on TV?

Have / ever / have a picnic?

Free question

FINISH

Keep talking!

Movie favorites

A Complete the chart with six types of movies that you like. Add a title for each type.

	Type of movie	Title of movie
1		
2		
3		
4		
5		
6		

B **CLASS ACTIVITY** Find classmates who like the same types of movies you like. Then ask questions with *Have you ever . . . ?*

A: I really like animated movies.

B: So do I.

A: Really? Have you ever seen *Despicable Me*?

B: Yes, I have. I love that movie!

Class Survey

A Complete the questions with your own ideas.

1 Do you like the band _____?
(a band) ☐

2 Do you like the song _____?
(a song title) ☐

3 Do you have the album _____?
(name of an album) ☐

4 Do you ever listen to _____?
(a type of music) ☐

5 Do you know the words to the song _____?
(name of a song) ☐

6 Did you listen to _____ as a child?
(a type of music) ☐

7 Would you like to see _____ in concert?
(a singer or band) ☐

B `CLASS ACTIVITY` Ask your classmates the questions in Part A. How many people said "yes" to each question? Write the total number in the boxes.

C `PAIR WORK` Share your information.

A: *A lot of our classmates like the band . . .*

B: *That's interesting. Not many of us like the band . . .*

D Share the most interesting information with the class.

"All of us would like to see . . . in concert."

Keep talking!

Why did I do that?

A Think about things that you did in the past. Check (✓) the things in the first column that are true for you. Then add three more things.

☐ I took a long trip	to _____.
☐ I sent a text to someone	to _____.
☐ I took a test	to _____.
☐ I joined a gym	to _____.
☐ I got a cell phone	to _____.
☐ I uploaded some photos	to _____.
☐ I worked hard	to _____.
☐ I got a part time job	to _____.
☐ _____	to _____.
☐ _____	to _____.
☐ _____	to _____.

B Why did you do each thing? Complete the sentences in Part A with an infinitive of purpose. Use the ideas below or think of your own.

talk with my friends	learn an instrument	show my friends
get my driver's license	get some experience	get a job
share good news	buy a gift	make more friends
save money	lose weight	see my relatives

C **GROUP WORK** Share your sentences. Ask and answer questions for more information.

A: I took a long trip to see my relatives.

B: When was that?

A: Last year.

C: Where did you go?

A: I went . . .

Next year . . .

A Add two future activities to the chart.

Do you think you'll . . . next year?	Name	Other details
take a trip with your family		
start a new hobby		
join a gym		
get married		
buy something expensive		
move to a different home		
start a career		
learn a musical instrument		

B CLASS ACTIVITY Find classmates who will do each thing. Write their names. Ask and answer questions for more information. Take notes.

A: Jun, do you think you'll take a trip with your family next year?

B: Yes, I do.

A: Really? Where will you go?

B: We're planning to go to Australia to visit some friends. I hope to . . .

C GROUP WORK Share the most interesting information.

Keep talking!

Irregular verbs

Base form	Simple past	Past Participle
be	was, were	been
become	became	become
build	built	built
buy	bought	bought
choose	chose	chosen
come	came	come
do	did	done
draw	drew	drawn
drink	drank	drunk
drive	drove	driven
eat	ate	eaten
feel	felt	felt
get	got	gotten
give	gave	given
go	went	gone
hang	hung	hung
have	had	had
hear	heard	heard
hold	held	held
know	knew	known
leave	left	left
lose	lost	lost
make	made	made

Base form	Simple past	Past Participle
meet	met	met
pay	paid	paid
put	put	put
read	read	read
ride	rode	ridden
run	ran	run
say	said	said
see	saw	seen
sell	sold	sold
send	sent	sent
sing	sang	sung
sit	sat	sat
sleep	slept	slept
speak	spoke	spoken
spend	spent	spent
stand	stood	stood
swim	swam	swum
take	took	taken
teach	taught	taught
think	thought	thought
wear	wore	worn
win	won	won
write	wrote	written

Credits

The authors and publishers acknowledge the following sources of copyright material and are grateful for the permissions granted. While every effort has been made, it has not always been possible to identify the sources of all the material used, or to trace all copyright holders. If any omissions are brought to our notice, we will be happy to include the appropriate acknowledgements on reprinting and in the next update to the digital edition, as applicable.

Photography
All below images are sourced from Getty Images.
Front Matter: Hero Images; **U1:** Rob Ball/WireImage; Chris J Ratcliffe/Stringer/Getty Images News; Bulat Silvia/iStock/Getty Images Plus; Rick Doyle/The Image Bank; Maxiphoto/iStock/Getty Images Plus; pashapixel/iStock/Getty Images Plus; empire331/iStock/Getty Images Plus; Shuji Kobayashi/The Image Bank; tioloco/iStock/Getty Images Plus; artisteer/iStock/Getty Images Plus; onurdongel/E+; Digital Vision; KidStock/Blend Images; 4x6/iStock/Getty Images Plus; Kris Timken/Blend Images; Patrik Giardino/Corbis; BakiBG/E+; Donald Miralle/DigitalVision; Robert Daly/OJO Images; Gary Burchell/DigitalVision; Westend61/Brand X Pictures; EXTREME-PHOTOGRAPHER/E+; Thinkstock/Stockbyte; digitalfarmer/iStock/Getty Images Plus; Westend61; JGI/Jamie Grill/Blend Images; Hannah Foslien/Getty Images Sport; **U2:** Alexander Spatari/Moment; Mark Edward Atkinson/Tracey Lee/Blend Images; milehightraveler/E+; damircudic/E+; JGI/Jamie Grill/Blend Images; Blue Images/Corbis; Wavebreakmedia/iStock/Getty Images Plus; Asia Images Group; KaVaStudio2015/iStock/Getty Images Plus; PeopleImages/E+; Purestock; Tanya Constantine/Blend Images; alvarez/E+; Firda Beka; Ronnie Kaufman/Larry Hirshowitz/Blend Images; Image Source; Dominique Charriau/WireImage; **U3:** Andersen Ross/DigitalVision; Matthew Lloyd/Stringer/Getty Images News; SeanPavonePhoto/iStock Editorial/Getty Images Plus; SteffenWalter/iStock Editorial/Getty Images Plus; gpointstudio/iStock/Getty Images Plus; Mats Silvan/Moment; technotr/Vetta; VV-pics/iStock/Getty Images Plus; icholakov/iStock/Getty Images Plus; JodiJacobson/E+; Glowimages; Georgia Immins/EyeEm; Getty Images; Alex Robinson/robertharding; Robert Francis/robertharding; Fouque/iStock/Getty Images Plus; Andrew Lichtenstein/Corbis News; sebastianosecondi/iStock/Getty Images Plus; Shannon Fagan; pavlen/iStock/Getty Images Plus; RichLegg/iStock/Getty Images Plus; Peter Dennen; Chris Speedie; Raimund Linke; hudiemm/iStock/Getty Images Plus; Denyshutter/iStock/Getty Images Plus; PhotoObjects.net/Getty Images Plus; Comstock/Stockbyte; TopPhotoImages/iStock/Getty Images Plus; Chen Liu/EyeEm; **U4:** Jumping Rocks; arnitorfason/iStock/Getty Images Plus; dabldy/iStock Editorial/Getty Images Plus; Aleksandr_Kendenkov/iStock/Getty Images Plus; JazzIRT/E+; Chefmd/iStock/Getty Images Plus; ennesseePhotographer/iStock Editorial/Getty Images Plus; Gunter Marx Photography/Corbis Documentary; Tatjana Kaufmann; Laurie Noble/Stone; Bettmann; Jon Hicks/The Image Bank; NurPhoto; WolfeLarry/iStock/Getty Images Plus; John Rensten/The Image Bank; Siri Stafford/DigitalVision; hulya-erkisi/iStock/Getty Images Plus; Eerik/iStock/Getty Images Plus; fStop Images - Patrick Strattner/Brand X Pictures; TommL/iStock/Getty Images Plus; Eco Images/Universal Images Group; shironosov/iStock/Getty Images Plus; **U5:** Jupiterimages/Pixland/Getty Images Plus; Matthieu Spohn/PhotoAlto Agency RF Collections; Niedring/Drentwett/MITO images; RichVintage/E+; Purestock; Westend61; Peathegee Inc/Blend Images; Hola Images; YKD/iStock/Getty Images Plus; kellll/iStock/Getty Images Plus; energyy/iStock/Getty Images Plus; drbimages/E+; zegers06/iStock/Getty Images Plus; Peter Dazeley/Photographer's Choice; dima_sidelnikov/iStock/Getty Images Plus; laindiapiaroa/Blend Images/Getty Images Plus; Highwaystarz-Photography/iStock/Getty Images Plus; Eva-Katalin/E+; bagotaj/iStock/Getty Images Plus; Clerkenwell/Vetta; Tom Merton/OJO Images; South_agency/iStock/Getty Images Plus; B. Boissonnet; paylessimages/iStock/Getty Images Plus; hxdbzxy/iStock/Getty Images Plus; Image Source/Photodisc; Jose Luis Pelaez Inc/Blend Images; Dougal Waters/DigitalVision; Brand X; Alen-D/iStock/Getty Images Plus; Hero Images; shironosov/iStock/Getty Images Plus; Robert van 't Hoenderdaal/iStock Editorial/Getty Images Plus; Simon McGill/Moment; nensuria/iStock/Getty Images Plus; Peter Dazeley/Photographer's Choice; Velvetfish/iStock/Getty Images Plus; undefined/iStock/Getty Images Plus; onepony/iStock/Getty Images Plus; Olga_k_/iStock/Getty Images Plus; studiocasper/iStock/Getty Images Plus; Pascal Broze/ONOKY; **U6:** Fernando Trabanco Fotografía/Moment; Tara Moore/Corbis; Jacob Wackerhausen/iStock/Getty Images Plus; Chris Ryan/Caiaimage; BJI/Blue Jean Images; Alija/Vetta; Lorado/E+; DreamPictures/Stone; Chud/Moment; Andy Rouse/The Image Bank; Erik Dreyer/Stone; powerofforever/E+; simonkr/E+; Vicki Jauron, Babylon and Beyond/Moment; Klaus Vedfelt/DigitalVision; Charley Gallay/Getty Images Entertainment; hikesterson/iStock/Getty Images Plus; RUNSTUDIO/DigitalVision; Matt Jelonek/WireImage; **U7:** Kathrin Ziegler/Taxi; Mike Watson Images/moodboard/Getty Images Plus; gradyreese/E+; Thomas Barwick/Photodisc; John S Lander/LightRocket; gracethang/iStock Editorial/Getty Images Plus; Jeff Greenberg/Universal Images Group; anyaberkut/iStock/Getty Images Plus; Nerthuz/iStock/Getty Images Plus; Dieter Spears/EyeEm; 3dgoksu/iStock/Getty Images Plus; 3drenderings/iStock/Getty Images Plus; Marco Rosario Venturini Autieri/iStock/Getty Images Plus; luismmolina/iStock/Getty Images Plus; ZargonDesign/E+; Chris Collins/Corbis; mladn61/iStock/Getty Images Plus; PC Plus Magazine/Future; cleotis/iStock/Getty Images Plus; pongky.n/iStock/Getty Images Plus; nevodka/iStock/Getty Images Plus; ItsraSanprasert/iStock/Getty Images Plus; MarkELaw/iStock/Getty Images Plus; Paolo_Toffanin/iStock/Getty Images Plus; digitalskillet/iStock/Getty Images Plus; naumoid/iStock/Getty Images Plus; richjem/iStock/Getty Images Plus; rasslava/iStock/Getty Images Plus; arogant/iStock/Getty Images Plus; momcilog/iStock/Getty Images Plus; emreogan/iStock/Getty Images Plus; lypnyk2/iStock/Getty Images Plus; Wulf Voss/EyeEm; Tarzhanova/iStock/Getty Images Plus; panic_attack/iStock/Getty Images Plus; Feng Li/Staff/Getty Images Entertainment; Chen Chao; Maremagnum/Photolibrary; Martin_Szczepaniak/iStock Editorial/Getty Images Plus; DC_Colombia/iStock Editorial/Getty Images Plus; **U8:** guruXOOX/iStock/Getty Images Plus; Pawel.gaul/E+; Kevin Forest/Photodisc; studyoritim/iStock/Getty Images Plus; Grant Faint/The Image Bank; Richard Baker/In Pictures; TOLGA AKMEN/AFP; Westend61; FotoDuets/iStock Editorial/Getty Images Plus; csfotoimages/iStock Editorial/Getty Images Plus; Luis Dafos/Moment; imantsu/iStock/Getty Images Plus; rache1/iStock/Getty Images Plus; Martin Wahlborg/iStock/Getty Images Plus; Ed-Ni-Photo/iStock Editorial/Getty Images Plus; Richard T. Nowitz/Corbis Documentary; bluejayphoto/iStock Editorial/Getty Images Plus; VitalyEdush/iStock/Getty Images Plus; baona/iStock/Getty Images Plus; MAURO PIMENTEL/AFP; holgs/iStock/Getty Images Plus; shomos uddin/Moment; Dmitry Ageev/Blend Images; Cavan Images/Cavan; BRANDONJ74/E+; Carlos Ciudad Photos/Moment; Maskot; Wei Fang/Moment; **U9:** Michael Gottschalk/Photothek; Pablo Cuadra/Getty Images Entertainment; Stock Montage/Archive Photos; Mehdi Taamallah/NurPhoto; Kelvin Ma/Bloomberg; Jason LaVeris/FilmMagic; RG-vc/iStock/Getty Images Plus; kickers/iStock/Getty Images Plus; bjones27/E+; Reuben Krabbe/Ascent Xmedia/Photodisc; Jupiterimages/Goodshoot/Getty Images Plus; STR/AFP; DreamPictures/Blend Images; skynesher/E+; Comstock Images/Stockbyte; VANDERLEI ALMEIDA/AFP; ben radford/Corbis Sport; Apic/Hulton Archive; Library of Congress/Corbis Historical/VCG; David Levenson/Getty Images Entertainment; JOSE CENDON/AFP; Bettmann; Mahmoud Khaled/Anadolu Agency; THOMAS COEX/AFP; Chris Ratcliffe/Bloomberg; Wavebreakmedia; **U10:** Blulz60/iStock Editorial/Getty Images Plus; john shepherd/iStock/Getty Images Plus; Anastassios Mentis/Stockbyte; kajakiki/E+; Inna Zakharchenko/iStock/Getty Images Plus; WolfeLarry/iStock/Getty Images Plus; Sunwoo Jung/DigitalVision; Vostok/Moment; Jon Hicks/Corbis Documentary; effrey Greenberg/Universal Images Group; Photodisc; bhofack2/iStock/Getty Images Plus; rebeccafondren/iStock/Getty Images Plus; Asia Images Group; HariKarki2003/iStock/Getty Images Plus; naruedom/iStock/Getty Images Plus; mikdam/iStock/Getty Images Plus; NightAndDayImages/E+; margouillatphotos/iStock/Getty Images Plus; Amarita/iStock/Getty Images Plus; 3dsguru/iStock/Getty Images Plus; Boogich/iStock/Getty Images Plus; EmirMemedovski/E+; whitewish/iStock/Getty Images Plus; India Today Group; PeopleImages/E+; Eurngkwan/iStock/Getty Images Plus; **U11:** Hero Images; Emmanuel Faure/The Image Bank; Joe McBride/The Image Bank; izusek/iStock/Getty Images Plus; Hugh Sitton/Stone; John Lamb/The Image Bank; Denkou Images/Cultura; Chud/Moment; Westend61; Hill Street Studios/Blend Images; Michael Klippfeld/Moment; mmac72/E+; Stephanie Rausser/DigitalVision; andresr/E+; Crazytang/E+; Anadolu Agency/Anadolu Agency; Ryan Smith/Corbis; olmozott98/iStock Editorial/Getty Images Plus; Rubberball/Mike Kemp; Onradio/iStock/Getty Images Plus; JGI/Tom Grill/Blend Images; Mlenny/iStock/Getty Images Plus; Inti St. Clair/DigitalVision; Bokeshi/iStock/Getty Images Plus; DreamPictures/Blend Images; Alexei Cruglicov/iStock/Getty Images Plus; piovesempre/iStock/Getty Images Plus; Michael Luhrenberg/iStock/Getty Images Plus; JGI/Tom Grill/Blend Images; Jose Luis Pelaez Inc/Blend Images; moodboard/Cultura; Gabriel Rossi/LatinContent WO; Nilanka Sampath/iStock/Getty Images Plus; Vera_Petrunina/iStock/Getty Images Plus; John Parra; BaloOm Studios/Moment; **U12:** Kemter/iStock/Getty Images Plus; Jetta Productions Inc/DigitalVision; PJPhoto69/iStock/Getty Images Plus; Westend61; Caia Image/Mix: Subjects; Studio CJ/E+; shank_ali/E+; Dougal Waters/DigitalVision; john shepherd/iStock/Getty Images Plus; Neustockimages/E+; laughingmango/iStock/Getty Images Plus; Eakachai Leesin/EyeEm; Jose Luis Pelaez Inc/Blend Images; JGI/Tom Grill/Blend Images; Tomas Rodriguez/Corbis stockyimages/iStock/Getty Images Plus; Michael H/DigitalVision; Thinkstock Images/Stockbyte; Blend Images; Design Pics; Paul Bradbury/OJO Images; Predrag Vuckovic/E+; Moma7/iStock/Getty Images Plus; aldomurillo/E+; fstop123/iStock/Getty Images Plus; Blend Images - JGI/Jamie Grill/Brand X Pictures; Erstudiostok/iStock/Getty Images Plus; tommaso79/ iStock/Getty Images Plus; David Cannon/Allsport; John Lamparski/Getty Images Entertainment; **End Matter:** golovorez/iStock/Getty Images Plus; afe207/iStock/Getty Images Plus; ugurv/iStock/Getty Images Plus; Doug Byrnes/Corbis; GoodLifeStudio/iStock/Getty Images Plus; Mongkhon bualaphum/iStock/Getty Images Plus; C Squared Studios/Photodisc; Raquel Pedrosa/Moment Open; Fandrade/Moment Open; PeopleImages/iStock/Getty Images Plus; John Greim/LightRocket; Alex Robinson Photography/Moment; Wavebreak/iStock/Getty Images Plus; Westend61; SolStock/E+; Icon Sportswire; Kenny McCartney/Moment; JGI/Jamie Grill/Blend Images; Geber86/E+; Purestock; YinYang/E+; skynesher/E+; Maskot; Squaredpixels/E+; Caiaimage/Paul Bradbury; Image Source/DigitalVision; PhonlamaiPhoto/iStock/Getty Images Plus; fazon1/iStock/Getty Images Plus; zhudifeng/iStock/Getty Images Plus; mifilippo/iStock/Getty Images Plus; Dougal Waters/Photographer's Choice; Juanmonino/iStock/Getty Images Plus; Ron Levine/Stockbyte; Fuse/Corbis; Jon Feingersh/Blend Images; Igor Emmerich/Corbis/VCG/Corbis; Saro17/E+; Brand X Pictures/Stokebyte; Sergey Nazarov/iStock/Getty Images Plus; Gwengoat/iStock/Getty Images Plus; Hulton Archive; Popperfoto; Barna Tanko/iStock Editorial/Getty Images Plus; John W Banagan/Photographer's Choice; Pattilabelle/iStock/Getty Images Plus; SAM YEH/AFP; Jeffrey Greenberg/Universal Images Group; QQ7/iStock/Getty Images Plus; yogysic/DigitalVision Vectors; elenaleonova/E+; DonNichols/E+; mukesh-kumar/iStock/Getty Images Plus; Jupiterimages/Photolibrary; KatarzynaBialasiewicz/iStock/Getty Images Plus; Studio_Dagdagaz/iStock/Getty Images Plus; bonchan/iStock/Getty Images Plus; ChesiireCat/iStock/Getty Images Plus; Roberto Ricciuti/WireImage; rusm/E+; chameleonseye/iStock Editorial/Getty Images Plus; chameleonseye/iStock/Getty Images Plus; QQ7/iStock/Getty Images Plus; Hulton Archive; Popperfoto; Bloomberg; Bruno Vincent/Staff/Getty Images News.

Front cover by Hero Images; Eva-Katalin/E+. Back cover by Monty Rakusen/Cultura.
The following images are sourced from other libraries:
U1: Frank Veronsky; Media Bakery; MBI/Alamy; **U2:** FogStock/Alamy; Frank Veronsky; Kathy deWitt/Alamy; **U3:** Shutterstock; Photo Library; **U4:** AP/Wide World Photos; Frank Veronsky; George Kerrigan; Douglas Keister; Shutterstock; Reuters; Alamy; Scott Jenkins; **U5:** Frank Veronsky; **U6:** Frank Veronsky; CBS/Everett Collection; **U7:** Shutterstock; Frank Veronsky; Photo Edit; **U8:** Shutterstock; Media Bakery; Scott Olson; **U9:** NASA; AP/Wide World Photos; Frank Veronsky; AP/Wide World Photos; Newscom; Media Bakery; AP/Wide World Photos; **U10:** Shutterstock; Martin Lee/Alamy; Media Bakery; Carlos Davila/Alamy; Frank Veronsky; Ninja Akasaka; Jack Carey/Alamy; **U11:** Media Bakery; Inmagine; **U12:** Media Bakery; Shutterstock; Frank Veronsky; Courtesy of Suzanne Lefebre; **End Matter:** Shannon99/Alamy; US mint; Media Bakery; Adventure House; Shutterstock; Everett Collection; Mary Evans Picture Library/Everett Collection; Newscom.

Illustration
Front Matter: John Goodwin; Kim Johnson; **U1:** QBS Learning; John Goodwin; **U2:** QBS Learning; Kim Johnson; **U3–7:** QBS Learning; **U9:** Rob Schuster; **U11–12, End Matter:** QBS Learning.

QBS Learning pp5, 16, 19, 20, 21, 23, 30, 31, 32, 36, 40, 46, 49, 50, 59, 60, 66, 69, 70, 71, 106, 110, 111, 119, 128, 130, 133, 134, 135, 140, 144

Art direction, book design, and layout services: QBS Learning
Audio production: CityVox, NYC and John Marshall Media
Video production: Steadman Productions

FOUR CORNERS

Second Edition Video Activity Sheets

2

JACK C. RICHARDS & DAVID BOHLKE

CAMBRIDGE
UNIVERSITY PRESS

Credits

The authors and publishers acknowledge the following sources of copyright material and are grateful for the permissions granted. While every effort has been made, it has not always been possible to identify the sources of all the material used, or to trace all copyright holders. If any omissions are brought to our notice, we will be happy to include the appropriate acknowledgements on reprinting and in the next update to the digital edition, as applicable.

Photography
The following images are sourced from Getty Images.

Teacher's Edition
U1: JessAerons/iStock/Getty Images Plus; miljko/E+; akiyoko/iStock/Getty Images Plus; alla_snesar/iStock/Getty Images Plus; U4: hedgehog94/iStock/Getty Images Plus; Tom Merton/OJO Images; beyond foto; Shen Lung/EyeEm; AndreyPopov/iStock/Getty Images Plus; Albasir Canizares/EyeEm; U6: moodboard/Cultura; U7: Hero Images; U8: flavijus/iStock Editorial/Getty Images Plus; U10: rez-art/iStock/Getty Images Plus; Massimo Rubino/EyeEm; Almaje/iStock/Getty Images Plus; rez-art/iStock/Getty Images Plus; Andrew Bret Wallis/Photodisc; Aik Meng Seow/EyeEm; simona flamigni/iStock/Getty Images Plus; szefei/iStock/Getty Images Plus; U11: Niedring/Drentwett/MITO images; eli_asenova/E+; AIMSTOCK/E+; Paul Natkin/WireImage; U12: trinamaree/iStock/Getty Images Plus; yvonnestewarthenderson/iStock/Getty Images Plus; GMVozd/E+; Tetra Images; MDoubrava/iStock/Getty Images Plus.

Front cover by Hero Images; Eva-Katalin/E+.
Back cover by Monty Rakusen/Cultura.

Illustration
Teacher's Edition
Illustrations by QBS Learning.

Art direction, book design, and layout services: QBS Learning
Audio production: CityVox, NYC and John Marshall Media
Video production: Steadman Productions

This page left intentionally blank

Before you watch

A Look at the picture. Answer the questions. Then compare with a partner.

1 Where is Emi?

She is

2 What is Emi's job?

_____

3 What is Emi doing?

She is interviing

Emi

B Match the words and the pictures. Then compare with a partner.

| a collect buttons ✓ b make a sweater c make jewelry d play chess |

1 ☑ d

2 ☑ c

3 ☑ a

4 ☑ b

While you watch

Jurry.

A Who does each thing? Check (✓) the correct answers. (More than one answer is possible.)

	Emi	Tim	Alicia	The man in the park
1 Who collects buttons?	☐	☑	☐	☐
2 Who plays chess?	☐	☐	☐	☑
3 Who makes jewelry?	☐	☐	☑	☐
4 Who makes sweaters?	☑	☐	☐	☐

B Read the sentences about Tim's collection. Write T (true) or F (false).

1 Tim has about a thousand buttons. _False_

2 He buys them on vacation. _True_

3 Friends and family members also give the buttons to him. _true_

4 Emi doesn't like the button from Tim's sister. _False_

5 His sister lives in Brazil now. _False_

6 Tim gives Emi a button. _False._

C Read the sentences about Alicia's interest. Circle the correct answers.

1 Alicia makes jewelry because it's _Fun_ .

   a hard   b fun   c boring

2 The necklace takes a few _minutes_ to make.

   a minutes   b hours   c days

3 _earrings_ are a little difficult to make.

   a Necklaces   b Earrings   c Necklaces and earrings

4 Alicia doesn't _Sell_ her jewelry.

   a buy   b make   c sell

5 Alicia makes jewelry as a _hobby_ .

   a job   b hobby   c homework assignment

After you watch

A PAIR WORK What do you think about Emi, Tim, and Alicia's interests? Do you know anyone with the same interests as them? Tell your partner.

A: I think Tim's hobby is interesting.

B: Me, too. Do you collect buttons from different places?

A: No, I don't. But I collect postcards.

B GROUP WORK Interview four classmates about their interests. Complete the chart with their information.

Name	Interest or hobby	Why he or she likes it
Roberto	does karate	It's good exercise.

C GROUP WORK Tell another group about your classmates' interests and hobbies.

"Roberto does karate. He likes karate because it's good exercise."

Happy birthday, Eric!

Before you watch

A Complete the sentences with the correct names. Then compare with a partner.

1 _____Dad_____ has short curly brown hair.

2 _____Lizzy_____ has long straight blond hair.

3 _____Mom_____ has short straight brown hair.

4 ___Grandpa Joe___ has short gray hair.

5 _____Dad_____ and _____Mom_____ are middle-aged.

6 ___Grandpa Joe___ is elderly.

7 _____Lizzy_____ is young.

B What do your family and friends usually do on your birthday? Check (✓) the items.

- [✓] eat out with me
- [ ] give me a gift
- [ ] go dancing with me
- [✓] have a party for me
- [ ] make a video for me
- [ ] make special food for me
- [✓] sing "Happy Birthday!" to me
- [ ] other:

C **GROUP WORK** Share your information from Part B. Ask and answer questions for more information.

A: My mother usually makes me a special meal on my birthday.

B: That's nice! What does she make?

While you watch

A Circle the correct answers.

1 Right now, Eric is _in Italy_

  a at home   b in California   c in Italy

2 He is __a__ there.

  a at school   b on vacation   c working

3 Today is Eric's _20th_ birthday.

  a 18th   b 20th   c 22nd

4 Eric's Aunt Lily has the _video camera_

  a birthday cake   b gift   c video camera

5 Eric's family __b__ .

  a eats the cake   b shows Eric pictures   c sings "Happy Birthday"

B Write T (true) or F (false).

1 Now Eric has blond hair. F

2 Eric plays the guitar. F

3 Eric draws pictures. T

4 His sister Lizzy plays the piano. T

5 Eric's family took a trip to Florida. F

C Who describes Eric with the words below? Check (✓) the correct answers.
(More than one answer is possible.)

		Mom	Dad	Lizzy	Grandpa Joe
1	creative	✓	☐	☐	☐
2	funny	☐	☐	✓	☐
3	handsome	✓	☐	☐	☐
4	hardworking	☐	☐	☐	✓
5	serious	☐	☐	✓	☐
6	short	✓	☐	☐	☐
7	tall	✓	☐	☐	☐

After you watch

A PAIR WORK Do you like Eric's birthday video? Do you want a birthday video from your family? Why or why not? Tell your partner.

B PAIR WORK Interview your partner about a friend or family member. Complete the chart with his or her answers.

Questions	Name: _____
1 Is this person a friend or family member?	
2 What is his or her name?	
3 What is he or she like?	
4 What does he or she look like?	

C GROUP WORK Tell another pair about your partner's friend or family member.

"Sandra's sister is friendly and talkative. She's tall and thin, and has long, wavy hair."

Before you watch

A Look at the pictures of Vancouver, Canada. Number the pictures from 1 to 3. Then compare with your partner.

1 Vancouver is a great place to ski in the winter.

2 You can ride your bike in Vancouver in the spring or summer when it's warm.

3 You can see many colorful leaves in the park in the fall.

☐   ☐   ☐

B **PAIR WORK** Would you like to go on vacation in Vancouver? What would you like to do there? Tell your partner.

While you watch

A Circle the correct answers.

1 Ben has a _____ .

   a website   b live travel blog   c TV show

2 Ben and Nick want to get _____ .

   a emails and letters   b phone calls and texts   c emails and texts

3 The date is Thursday, _____ 14.

   a January   b May   c July

4 Ben and Nick would like to talk about _____ Vancouver.

   a the people in   b the food in   c a good time to visit

5 Ben and Nick have a problem because they want to _____ in Vancouver.

   a do different things   b eat different food   c visit different friends

B Check (✓) the correct answers. (More than one answer is possible.)

	Ben	Ben's mom	Nick	Nick's mom
1 Who likes to ski?	☐	☐	☐	☐
2 Who wants to ride a bicycle?	☐	☐	☐	☐
3 Who doesn't like the snow?	☐	☐	☐	☐
4 Who thinks they should go in the spring?	☐	☐	☐	☐
5 Who thinks Ben and Nick's apartment isn't clean?	☐	☐	☐	☐

C Write T (true) or F (false).

1 Ben and Nick both want to go to Vancouver. _____

2 Ben wants to go in January. _____

3 Nick likes hot weather. _____

4 Nick and Ben's mothers are watching Ben's blog. _____

5 Ben and Nick agree on when to go to Vancouver. _____

After you watch

A Complete the summary with the correct words and expressions. Then compare with a partner. (There are two extra words.)

fall	park	problem	snows quite a bit	summer
opinion	pretty warm	ski	spring	winter

Ben and Nick have a _____. Ben wants to go to Vancouver in

the _____. He'd like to go to the _____.

But Nick wants to go in the _____ because he'd

like to _____. Nick's mom has a different

_____. She thinks spring is a good time because

it's _____ in the city, but it

_____ in the mountains.

C PAIR WORK What's your opinion? When is a good time to visit Vancouver? Why?

"I'd say summer is a good time. I'd like to swim and walk in the park."

Before you watch

A Match the pictures and the descriptions. Then compare with a partner.

1 ☐

2 ☐

3 ☐

4 ☐

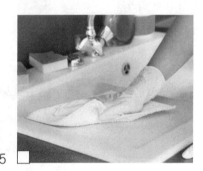

5 ☐

6 ☐

a There are a lot of dishes in the sink.

b He is wiping off the counter.

c There are a few magazines on the coffee table.

d He is putting away his clothes.

e There is a lot of light.

f The room is a mess.

B Label the pictures in Part A with the correct names of the rooms. Then compare with a partner.

| bathroom   bedroom   kitchen   living room |

While you watch

A Write T (true) or F (false).

1 Tim and Bo's kitchen is a mess. _____

2 Bo usually puts the dishes away. _____

3 Tim watches TV and studies in the living room. _____

4 Tim and Bo's living room is clean. _____

5 Tim has a big bedroom, but there is a small closet. _____

B What's in Tim's apartment? Check (✓) the correct answers.

☐ a big closet   ☐ a few boxes   ☐ a lot of clothes   ☐ a sofa

☐ books   ☐ a few magazines   ☐ a lot of garbage   ☐ some noise

☐ a cat   ☐ a guitar   ☐ a lot of light   ☐ a TV

☐ a dishwasher   ☐ a lot of CDs   ☐ a roommate   ☐ two bedrooms

C Circle the correct answers.

1 Tim lives _____ his parents.

   a near   b far away from   c next door to

2 Tim washes the dishes _____ .

   a every day   b once a week   c once a month

3 Bo is Tim's _____ .

   a student   b classmate   c roommate

4 Bo plays _____ .

   a the guitar   b the piano   c the drums

5 Tim says that Bo is a _____ guy.

   a fun   b creative   c boring

6 Bo is a _____ person.

   a clean   b noisy   c hardworking

After you watch

A What do you like about Tim's apartment? What don't you like? Make a list.

Things I like	Things I don't like
There is a big kitchen.	The kitchen is a mess.

B PAIR WORK Make a request for each of the things you don't like in Part B. Your partner agrees to the requests. Take turns.

A: The kitchen is a mess. Could you clean it up, please?

B: No problem.

Before you watch

A Match the stressful situations and the ways to manage them. Then compare with a partner.

1 Your computer broke, but you don't have enough money to buy a new one. _____

2 You have a big test tomorrow, but you don't know the information well. _____

3 You have a lot of work to do, but you don't have enough time to do it. _____

4 You want to exercise, but you don't have enough time. _____

a Get help from other students in the class. Study with them.

b Go to an Internet café or use a computer in a public library.

c Walk to class more often and do quick exercises in the morning at home.

d Ask someone to help you or decide which things you can do later.

B PAIR WORK What do you do in each of the stressful situations in Part A? Tell your partner.

While you watch

A How does Marco manage his stress? Check (✓) the correct answers.

☐ He cleans up his apartment.

☐ He does aerobics.

☐ He does nothing.

☐ He does yoga.

☐ He listens to relaxing music.

☐ He meditates.

☐ He plays soccer.

☐ He plays video games.

☐ He reads a book.

☐ He talks to someone.

☐ He uses a stress ball.

☐ He watches a funny video.

B Marco explains how to meditate. Number the steps from 1 to 9.

_____ Close your eyes.

_____ Relax and watch your breath.

___1___ Sit comfortably.

_____ Breathe slowly and deeply.

_____ Cross your legs.

_____ Count the breaths silently.

_____ Put your hands on your knees.

_____ Keep your neck and back straight.

_____ Continue to breathe slowly and deeply.

C Write T (true) or F (false).

1 Marco is a student. _____

2 He has one part-time job. _____

3 He has a really hard class. _____

4 He has a big French test tomorrow. _____

5 Marco's number one tip is: Talk to somebody. _____

After you watch

A **PAIR WORK** Which of Marco's tips for managing stress is your favorite? Why?

"My favorite tip is the stress ball. I use one of those, too."

B **GROUP WORK** Interview four classmates about their stress. Complete the chart with their answers.

Name	What makes you stressed?	How do you manage your stress?
Li-ming	biology class; boss at work	swimming; TV; talk to friends

C **CLASS ACTIVITY** What is your number one tip for managing stress? Tell the class.

Before you watch

Emi   Alicia   Ian

A Look at the pictures. Complete the sentences with the correct words.
Then compare with a partner.

competition	contestants	judges	reality	star	win

This is a _____ show. There are three _____.

They sing and dance on the show. Each one wants to be a _____.

Emi, Alicia, and Ian are the _____. They make comments

about the singers and the dancers. They help decide which one is going to

_____. Let the _____ begin!

B PAIR WORK Can you make a new sentence with each of the words in Part A?
Tell your partner.

While you watch

A Write T (true) or F (false).

1 The contestants are shy and hardworking. _____

2 Some judges are friendly. _____

3 All of the contestants sing about TV shows. _____

4 Contestant 2 doesn't think Ian is nice. _____

5 Ian thinks Contestant 3 raps well. _____

B Who does each thing? Check (✓) the correct answers.

	Contestant 1	Contestant 2	Contestant 3
1 Who dances?	☐	☐	☐
2 Who writes songs?	☐	☐	☐
3 Who sings a song about love?	☐	☐	☐
4 Who sings a song about rainy day activities?	☐	☐	☐
5 Who sings a song about TV?	☐	☐	☐
6 Who does Ian tell to learn a new activity?	☐	☐	☐

C Which contestants are the judges talking about? Number the judges' comments 1, 2, or 3.

Judge	Comment	Contestant
Emi	I think you're really good!	
	You're hardworking and very noisy.	
	You're a really creative performer.	
Alicia	He's pretty cool!	
	You're funny and very exciting to watch!	
	That's a very interesting song.	
Ian	Do not sing again. Ever!	
	You dance like a refrigerator.	
	He's boring.	

After you watch

A PAIR WORK Judge each contestant. Explain your opinions.

"Contestant number 3 is my favorite. He's a funny dancer. I didn't like . . ."

B GROUP WORK Discuss the questions.

- Do you enjoy watching TV talent shows? What is your opinion of them?
- Do you usually agree or disagree with the judges?
- Which singers are now famous for being on a TV talent show?

Before you watch

A Look at the picture. Circle the correct answers. Then compare with a partner.

1 What is this a picture of?

   a a supermarket   b a farmers' market   c a bake sale

2 What kind of food is *not* in the picture?

   a fast food   b fresh food   c fruits and vegetables

3 Who usually sells the food there?

   a waiters   b cooks   c vendors

B **PAIR WORK** How many food items can you identify in the picture?

While you watch

A What does Ben buy at the farmers' market? Check (✓) the correct answers.

☐ apple cider	☐ bread	☐ eggs	☐ pasta
☐ apple juice	☐ carrots	☐ flowers	☐ a plant
☐ apples	☐ cheese	☐ jam	☐ potatoes
☐ bananas	☐ donuts	☐ milk	☐ tomatoes

B Write T (true) or F (false).

1 The carrots at the supermarket are usually three dollars. _____

2 Ben sometimes bargains for a lower price at the farmers' market. _____

3 Apple cider is like apple jam. _____

4 The bread at the farmers' market is very fresh. _____

5 Nick usually goes grocery shopping at the supermarket. _____

C Circle the correct answers.

1 The food at the farmers' market is _____ than the food at the supermarket.

    a too fresh   b not fresh enough   c fresher

2 The food in the supermarket is _____ than the food at the farmers' market.

    a more expensive   b less expensive   c too expensive

3 The farmers' market has great apples in the _____.

    a summer   b fall   c spring

4 Ben's favorite jam is _____.

    a blueberry   b strawberry   c apple

5 Ben says jam and bread are great for _____.

    a breakfast   b lunch   c a snack

6 Ben bought a plant for his _____.

    a kitchen   b bedroom   c living room

After you watch

GROUP WORK Discuss the questions.

- What things would you buy at Ben's farmers' market? Why?
- Is there a farmers' market where you live? Do you ever go there?
- Where do you usually buy your food? Why?
- What's better to buy at a farmers' market than at a supermarket? Why?
- What's better to buy at a supermarket than at a farmers' market? Why?
- Do you bargain for a lower price when you shop for food? Why?

Things to do in New York City for less than $5.00

Before you watch

A Match the words and the places. Then compare with a partner.

a bridge	b ferry	c library	d museum	d statue

1 ☐

2 ☐

3 ☐

4 ☐

5 ☐

B Circle the correct answers. Then compare with a partner.

1 A ferry is a kind of _____.

   a train   b bus   c boat

2 A food cart is a small shop _____ where you can buy food.

   a on the street   b in a restaurant   c at home

3 If something is free, it costs _____.

   a five dollars   b less than five dollars   c nothing

While you watch

A What cheap activities in New York City does Soon-mi recommend? Check (✓) the correct answers.

☐ eat from a food cart ☐ go to a mall ☐ go to a zoo ☐ see a famous statue

☐ go to a dance club ☐ go to a museum ☐ ride a ferry boat ☐ take a train

☐ go to a library ☐ go to a park ☐ see a Broadway play ☐ walk across a bridge

B Match Soon-mi's comments and the places they describe.

1 You can see it for free on the ferry. _____   a New York Public Library

2 I really love the lion statues. _____   b Metropolitan Museum of Art

3 I think it's about 150 years old. _____   c Staten Island Ferry

4 Here's one thing you shouldn't miss. _____   d Brooklyn Bridge

5 Everyone thinks it costs twenty dollars. _____   e Statue of Liberty

C Write T (true) or F (false).

1 Soon-mi lives in New York City. _____

2 The Staten Island Ferry goes between Staten Island and Manhattan. _____

3 The Brooklyn Bridge connects Brooklyn and Staten Island. _____

4 Food carts have a lot of expensive food. _____

5 Canal Street is the busiest street in Chinatown. _____

6 You can use the Internet for free in the Metropolitan Museum. _____

7 The recommended cost to enter the museum is one dollar. _____

After you watch

A PAIR WORK Would you like to do any of the activities Soon-mi describes in New York City? What other things would you like to do there? Tell your partner.

"I'd like to ride the Staten Island Ferry and walk across the Brooklyn Bridge. I'd like to see a Broadway play, too."

B GROUP WORK What fun activities are free or cheap to do in your town or city? Tell your group.

Before you watch

A Match the verbs and the definitions. Then compare with a partner.

1 admire _____
2 inspire _____
3 study _____
4 teach _____

a to learn about something
b to give someone knowledge or information
c to like someone for what he or she does
d to make someone want to do something

B Complete the sentences with the correct words. Then compare with a partner.

beautiful	exciting	modern	passionate

1 I am _____ about music. I listen to it every day.
2 Soccer is my favorite sport. I think it's so _____ to watch!
3 This computer uses new technology. It is very _____.
4 I went to Grenada two years ago. The weather was _____ there!

While you watch

Aunt Gloria

Alicia

A In what ways did Aunt Gloria inspire Alicia? Check (✔) the correct answers.
(More than one answer is possible.)

☐ Gloria gave Alicia drawing lessons.
☐ She taught Alicia how to paint.
☐ She took Alicia to art museums.

☐ She taught Alicia about art.
☐ She is a famous artist.
☐ She is passionate about art.

B Circle the correct answers.

1 In the video, Alicia _____.

   a calls her aunt   b goes to a museum with her aunt   c visits her aunt

2 Alicia wants to _____.

   a thank her aunt   b give her aunt a gift   c both a and b

3 Alicia's family is from _____.

   a a very small town   b a big city   c a small city

4 The museums in the city had many _____ paintings.

   a simple and boring   b old and modern   c big and small

5 Alicia gives Aunt Gloria _____.

   a some jewelry   b a painting   c an art book

C Write T (true) or F (false).

1 Alicia is a high school student. _____

2 She can make her own jewelry. _____

3 She wants to be an actress. _____

4 Aunt Gloria and Alicia went to museums about once a year. _____

5 They want to go to a museum again soon. _____

After you watch

A PAIR WORK Interview your partner. Take notes.

Questions	Name:
1 Do you know anyone like Aunt Gloria? Who? How are they similar?	
2 Like Alicia, do you have any of the same talents or interests as a family member? Who?	
3 Who inspires you?	
4 How does he or she inspire you?	
5 What personality adjectives describe him or her?	
6 What is he or she passionate about?	

B PAIR WORK Tell another classmate about your partner's answers. Do your partners have similar stories about the people who inspired them?

Before you watch

A Label the pictures with the correct words. Then compare with a partner.

> blueberries   a hamburger   soda   strawberries

1 _____ 2 _____ 3 _____ 4 _____

B Circle the correct answers. Then compare with a partner.

1 What is a diner?

   a a type of restaurant   b a meal   c a waiter

2 What is a fresh fruit plate?

   a a plate with fruit painted on it   b a fruit salad   c a bag of apples

3 What is dessert?

   a breakfast   b sweet food you eat after a meal   c a side dish

While you watch

A Which food items do Ben and Marco say are on the menu? Check (✓) the correct answers.

☐ carrot juice	☐ hamburgers	☐ oysters	☐ spring rolls
☐ cheesecake	☐ lamb chops	☐ rice	☐ squid
☐ crab cakes	☐ mixed vegetables	☐ seaweed salad	☐ steak
☐ fruit salad	☐ onion rings	☐ soy milk	☐ tomato soup

A Who orders what? Draw a line from each food item to Marco or Ben.

fresh fruit plate

a hamburger

onion rings

mixed vegetables

carrot juice

a large soda

frozen yogurt

apple pie with vanilla ice cream

Marco   Ben

B Write T (true) or F (false).

1 The menu at Olga's Diner is really big. _____

2 The service is very fast. _____

3 Olga's Diner is very expensive. _____

4 After dinner, Ben has a stomachache. _____

5 Marco and Ben take a taxi home. _____

Olga's Diner

After you watch

A PAIR WORK Ask and answer the questions.

1 What would you order at Olga's Diner?

2 What wouldn't you try at Olga's Diner?

3 What's the name of a restaurant you haven't been to but want to try? Why?

4 Have you ever had a stomachache after eating in a restaurant? What happened?

5 What restaurant would you recommend in your city or town? Why?

B Imagine you have a restaurant. Make a menu of the foods you would serve.

C GROUP WORK Tell your classmates about the foods on your menu.

"My restaurant's name is Sofia's Diner. I'd serve . . ."

Before you watch

A Look at the pictures. Number the pictures from 1 to 3. Then compare with a partner.

1 Someone is interviewing someone else.

2 Someone is telling a story to someone else.

3 Someone is translating a word for someone else.

B **PAIR WORK** When is the last time you did each thing in Part A? Who were you with? Tell your partner.

While you watch

A What types of music do they say they listen to? Check (✓) the correct answers.
(More than one answer is possible.)

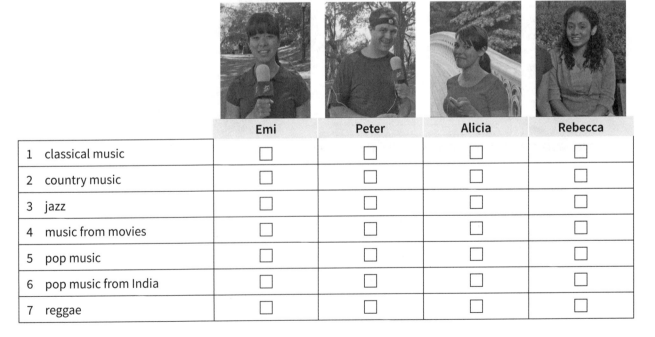

	Emi	Peter	Alicia	Rebecca
1 classical music	☐	☐	☐	☐
2 country music	☐	☐	☐	☐
3 jazz	☐	☐	☐	☐
4 music from movies	☐	☐	☐	☐
5 pop music	☐	☐	☐	☐
6 pop music from India	☐	☐	☐	☐
7 reggae	☐	☐	☐	☐

B Write T (true) or F (false).

1 Emi thinks reggae music is relaxing. _____

2 Bob Marley is a famous singer from Nigeria. _____

3 Peter says most of the people in Texas listen to reggae. _____

4 Alicia thinks most Indian pop songs are about pop culture. _____

5 Emi and Rebecca are friends. _____

C Circle the correct answers.

1 Peter loves country music because the words are really _____.

   a inspiring   b intelligent   c interesting

2 Peter says a lot of country music songs _____.

   a are serious   b tell a story   c are on the radio

3 Alicia thinks that Indian musical movies are _____.

   a fun   b boring   c interesting

4 Some of Alicia's friends can _____ the words.

   a sing   b spell   c translate

5 Emi and Rebecca plan to go to a _____ concert together.

   a jazz   b reggae   c rock

After you watch

A PAIR WORK Do you listen to any of the same music as Emi, Peter, Alicia, or Rebecca? Why or why not? Tell your partner.

"I listen to reggae like Emi and Rebecca, because it's relaxing. But I don't listen to classical music like Emi. It's too relaxing. It makes me fall asleep!"

B Make a playlist of songs. Choose songs from all of the types of music that you like.

Name of song	Singer, musician, group	Type of music
"One Love"	Bob Marley	Reggae

C PAIR WORK Tell your partner about your playlist. Ask and answer questions for more information.

A: I love the song "One Love" by Bob Marley.

B: Why do you love it?

A: It's a really cool, relaxing reggae song.

Before you watch

A Label the pictures with the correct words. Then compare with a partner.

| coffee | cookies | a cupcake | a muffin | a recipe |

1 _____ 2 _____ 3 _____ 4 _____ 5 _____

B Check (✓) the correct answers. Then compare with a partner.

1 What is a business?

☐ It's a job you get after you graduate.

☐ It's a company or organization that sells something to make money.

2 Who are customers?

☐ They're people who buy things.

☐ They're people who sell things.

3 What does it mean to do research?

☐ It means you look for information about something and study it.

☐ It means you prepare for an exam.

While you watch

A Write T (true) or F (false).

1 Tim's dream is to have a cookie store. _____

2 Tim's friends don't think he should open a cookie store. _____

3 Tim talks to Amelia because she has her own shop. _____

4 Amelia says it's really important to know your cupcakes. _____

5 Amelia didn't have any problems making her dream come true. _____

Tim and Amelia

B Circle the correct answers.

1 Tim's video is for his business _____.

    a class   b bank   c plan

2 Tim asks Amelia for _____.

    a her cupcake recipe   b business advice   c a job

3 At first, Amelia sold only _____.

    a coffee and muffins   b coffee and donuts   c coffee and cupcakes

4 Amelia thinks Tim might have a problem selling only _____.

    a coffee   b cookies   c cupcakes

5 A business plan shows that a new business will _____.

    a sell cookies   b buy new products   c make money

6 Amelia offers Tim _____.

    a a business plan   b a job   c a cup of coffee

C How did Amelia's dream come true? Number the steps from 1 to 7.

_____ She went to the bank for a loan, but the bank said "no."

_____ She used her research to write a business plan.

___1___ She worked part-time at a coffee shop to learn about the business.

_____ The bank liked Amelia's business plan, and it gave her the money.

_____ She went to a second bank, and that bank said "no," too.

_____ She did a lot of research.

_____ She took a class to learn about business.

After you watch

A PAIR WORK How will Tim make his dream happen? Make predictions. Use the expressions below and your own ideas.

do research	get a job	learn about his customers	take another class
finish his video report	get a loan	save money	write a business plan

    A: I think Tim will write a business plan.

    B: I think he might get a loan.

B GROUP WORK Share your predictions with another pair. How many different predictions did you make?

This page left intentionally blank

FOUR CORNERS

Second Edition   Workbook

2

JACK C. RICHARDS & DAVID BOHLKE

CAMBRIDGE
UNIVERSITY PRESS

This page left intentionally blank

Contents

Credits

The authors and publishers acknowledge the following sources of copyright material and are grateful for the permissions granted. While every effort has been made, it has not always been possible to identify the sources of all the material used, or to trace all copyright holders. If any omissions are brought to our notice, we will be happy to include the appropriate acknowledgements on reprinting and in the next update to the digital edition, as applicable.

My interests

A I'm interested in fashion.

1 Complete the puzzle and the sentences with words for people's interests.

Crossword grid answers:
- 1 Down: SPORT
- 2 Down: POLITICS
- 3 Across: FASHION
- 4 Across: ART
- 5 Down: TECHNOLOGY
- 6 Down: CULTURE
- 7 Down: TRAVEL
- 8 Across: LANGUAGES

Across

3 I'm interested in ___fashion___.
   I like new and different clothes.

4 Tonya is interested in ___art___.
   She loves the old paintings at the museum.

8 Dennis is interested in ___languages___ (lenguilles).
   His favorites are Spanish, Portuguese, and Chinese.

Down

1 Mario is interested in ___Sports___.
   He likes basketball and soccer.

2 Jonathan is interested in ___Politics___ (polilles).
   He works with the mayor.

5 Mrs. Wilson doesn't like ___Technology___ (teqnololli).
   She hates computers!

6 Penny is interested in pop ___culture___ (pop coucher).
   She loves popular music and art.

7 Are you interested in ___Trave___ (treit)?
   Let's go to China for a month!

2 **Match the questions and the answers.**

1 Where is Daniel from? ___e___   a Yes, she is.
2 How old is Ricardo? ___c___   b My name's Sophia.
3 Is he married? ___g___   c He's 24 years old.
4 Is she interested in literature? ___g___   d They're from Colombia.
5 Are you interested in travel? ___h___   e He's from Australia.
6 What's your name? ___b___   f I'm interested in pop culture.
7 Where are they from? ___d___   g No, he isn't.
8 What are you interested in? ___f___   h No, I'm not.

3 **Look at Yolanda's information. Then answer the questions.**

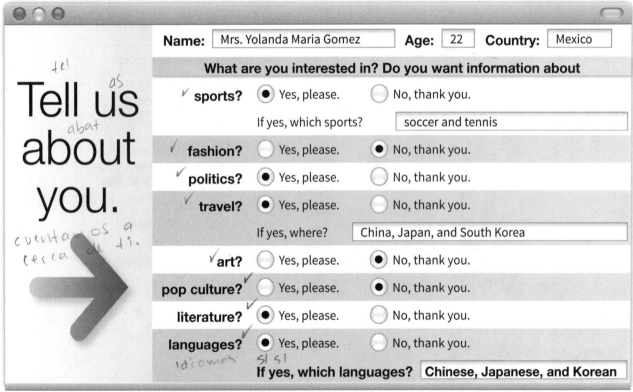

1 What's Yolanda's last name?   It's Gomez.
2 Is she married?   No, she isn't
3 Is Maria her full name?   No, it isn't
4 How old is she?   she is 22 years old
5 Where is she from?   she is from Mexico
6 What sports is she interested in?   she is interested in Soccer and tennis
7 Is she interested in Japanese?   yes, she is interested in Japanese.
8 What countries is she interested in? she is interested in china, Japan, and South Korea

2

4 Write about Yolanda's interests with the information from Exercise 3 on page 2.
Use the simple present of *be*.

1   Yolanda is interested in sports.
2   She's not interested in fashion.
3   Yolanda is interested in politics
4   Yolanda is interested in travel
5   She's not interested in art
6   She's not interested in pop culture
7   Yolanda is interested in literature
8   Yolanda is interested in languages

5 Complete the conversation with questions.

Lynne   Hello?

Judy   Hello. This is Judy from *Speak Magazine*.
Can I ask you some questions?
puedo hacerle algunas preguntas

Lynne   Sure.

Judy   Thank you. _____What's your name_____ ?
                                1

Lynne   I'm Lynne Roberts.

Judy   Hello, Ms. Roberts. __where are you From__ ?
                                        2

Lynne   I'm from Chicago.

Judy   How old are you ?
                        3

Lynne   I'm 31.

Judy   Are you married or single?
                    4

Lynne   I'm married.

Judy   How old is your husband ?
                        5

Lynne   My husband is 30 years old.

Judy   how many languages do you speak ?
                        6

Lynne   Yes, we are. I'm interested in Spanish, and my husband speaks French.

Judy   *grit*
Great. do you travel ? *genial viajas*
genial   7

Lynne   Yes, we're interested in travel.

Judy   OK. Are you and your husband interested in *Speak Magazine*?

Lynne   Hmm . . .

3

B Can you repeat that, please?

1 Write the lines of the conversation in the correct order.

R-O-D-R-I-G-U-E-Z.

Hello, Gina. What's your last name?

Could you say that again, please?

Sure. Rodriguez.

✓ Hi. This is Gina.

My last name is Rodriguez.

Oh, OK, Ms. Rodriguez. How do you spell that?

Cómo se deletrea eso

Gina	Hi. This is Gina.
Clerk	Hello, Gina. what's your last name?
Gina	My last name is Rodriguez
Clerk	Could you say that again, please?
Gina	Sure. Rodriguez
Clerk	Oh, ok, Ms Rodriguez. How do you spell that?
Gina	R - O - D - R - I - G - U - E - Z

2 Complete the conversations with *repeat* or *more slowly*.

1 **A** It's on page 122.

   B Can you say that ___more slowly___, please?

2 **A** What's your phone number?

   B It's 324-555-1908.

   A Could you speak _____, please?

3 **A** Her name is Na Young Park.

   B Could you _____ that, please?

4 **A** What's your last name?

   B Lowery.

   A Could you say that _____, please?

5 **A** The train is at 10:40 a.m.

   B Can you _____ that, please?

4

Do you play sports?

1 Label each picture with the correct word from the box.

baseball	golf	karate	swim	yoga
bowl	✓gymnastics	ski	table tennis	

UPTOWN SPORTS CENTER

1 _____gymnastics_____
Monday and Wednesday
2:00 p.m.

2 _____
Monday and Friday
5:00 p.m.

3 _____
Tuesday
7:00 a.m. and 4:00 p.m.

4 _____
Tuesday and Thursday
6:00 p.m.

5 _____
Wednesday
1:00 p.m. and 4:30 p.m.

6 _____
Thursday
6:30 p.m.

7 _____
Friday
3:30 p.m.

8 _____
Saturday
9:00 a.m.

9 _____
Saturday
2:30 p.m.

2 Complete the sentences with the words from Exercise 1. Use *play* or *do* when necessary.

1 You can _____*do gymnastics*_____ on Monday and Wednesday at 2:00 p.m.

2 You can _____ on Wednesday at 1:00 p.m. and 4:30 p.m.

3 You can _____ on Saturday at 9:00 a.m.

4 You can _____ on Tuesday at 7:00 a.m. and 4:00 p.m.

5 You can _____ on Friday at 3:30 p.m.

3 Put the words in the correct order to make questions and answers.

1 play / does / she / What / sports / ?   A   *What sports does she play?*
  table / plays / tennis / She / .   B   *She plays table tennis.*

2 gymnastics / they / do / Where / do / ? A _____
  school / do / at / They / gymnastics / . B _____

3 like / Does / he / karate / ?   A _____
  he / Yes / , / does / .   B _____

4 play / golf / When / do / you / ?   A _____
  the / golf / I / play / in / morning / . B _____

5 you / Do / sell / skis / ?   A _____
  don't / No / , / we / .   B _____

6 they / afternoon / the / Do / swim / in / ? A _____
  don't / No / , / they / .   B _____

4 Circle the correct words to complete the conversation.

Joe   Hey, Mari. Do you (like) / likes karate?

Mari No, I **doesn't** / **don't**. I **like** / **likes** yoga.
                    2   3

Joe   **Do** / **When do** you do yoga?
          4

Mari I usually **do** / **does** yoga after work.
                     5

      Do / **What do** you like yoga?
         6

Joe   No, I **do** / **don't**. But my brother **like** / **likes** it.
              7   8

Mari **Do** / **Where do** you like golf?
         9

Joe   Yes! I **play** / **plays** golf a lot. Do you
                 10

      do like / **like** golf?
              11

Mari Yes, I **do** / **does**.
                 12

Joe   Great! Let's play golf on Saturday.

Mari OK.

6

5 Complete the text with the simple present forms of the verbs in parentheses.

HOLE	Linda	Debbie
1	3	4
2	5	5
3	2	3
4	7	4
5	4	6
6	4	2
7	5	4
8	3	3
9	6	6

HOLE	Linda	Debbie
10	3	4
11	1	3
12	2	3
13	3	4
14	5	4
15	3	2
16	4	5
17	1	4
18	4	3
Total	65*	69

Linda _____ likes _____ (like) the game miniature golf. A miniature golf course
1
_____ (have) 18 holes, but the course is very small. At the end of
2
the game, the person with the lowest score _____ (win).
3
Linda _____ (play) miniature golf with her friend Debbie. They
4
_____ (play) in the park on Saturdays, and Linda usually
5
_____ (win) the game. But that's OK with Debbie.
6
She _____ (like) the game, too, and they always
7
_____ (have) a lot of fun.
8

6 Read the text in Exercise 5. Use the answers below to complete the questions.

1	_What game does_	Linda like?	miniature golf
2	_Does a miniature golf course have_	18 holes?	Yes, it does.
3	_____	with?	with her friend Debbie
4	_____	miniature golf?	in the park
5	_____	miniature golf?	on Saturdays
6	_____	the game, too?	Yes, she does.

7 Answer the questions about a sport you like.

1 What is the sport? _____

2 When do you play it? _____

3 Where do you play it? _____

D Free time

1 **Read the text. Check (✓) the events that are in a decathlon.**

1 ✓ the 100-meter run   4 ☐ the 500-meter run

2 ☐ the high jump   5 ☐ the low jump

3 ☐ the 1500-meter hurdles 6 ☐ the long jump

The decathlon is a sports competition with ten different events. Athletes compete in all ten events for two days. After the ten events, the person with the best score wins.

There are four races, or track events, in the decathlon: the 100-meter run, the 400-meter run, the 1500-meter run, and the 110-meter hurdles. In the 110-meter hurdles, athletes run and jump. Athletes also compete in six field events. In the long jump, people run and jump. In the high jump, they run and jump over a high bar. In the pole vault, athletes run and jump over a high bar with a long

pole. In the shot put, the javelin throw, and the discus throw, athletes throw different things. The shot is a large heavy ball. The javelin is a long thin pole. The discus is like a large round disk or plate.

The women's decathlon started in 2001. Before 2001, only men competed in the decathlon. Women now compete in the same ten events, but there are some differences. For example, the hurdles are lower and women jump over hurdles on a 100-meter course, not on a 110-meter course, like the men's decathlon. The shot, the javelin, and the discus in the women's decathlon are not as heavy as in the men's events.

2 **Read the text again. Rewrite the sentences. Correct the underlined words.**

1 The decathlon has <u>twelve</u> events.   _The decathlon has ten events._

2 Athletes throw things in <u>five</u> events.   _____

3 The shot is a large heavy <u>disk</u>.   _____

4 <u>Women</u> jump over hurdles on a 110-meter course. _____

5 The <u>men's</u> decathlon started in 2001.   _____

Descriptions

A He's talkative and friendly.

1 Put the letters in the correct order to make personality adjectives.

1 iyfldrne _____ friendly _____
2 vittkaael _____
3 nidfnecto _____
4 nsueogre _____
5 ysh _____

6 vceirtae _____
7 nuyfn _____
8 gdnkwhrraoi _____
9 rssuieo _____

2 Complete the sentences with some of the adjectives from Exercise 1. Use the simple present of *be*.

1 Ethan ___ is shy ___ but ___ confident ___.

2 Rita _____ and _____ .

3 Tom and Ed _____ and _____ .

4 Paul and Yoko _____ _____ .

5 Ms. Perez _____ _____ .

6 Emma _____ _____ .

3 Rewrite the sentences with the words in parentheses.

1 Laura is shy but confident. (person)
   Laura is a shy but confident person.

2 Sue and Kelly are hardworking. (students)
   _____

3 Dana is talkative and funny. (girl)
   _____

4 He's serious but friendly. (guy)
   _____

5 She's generous. (mother)
   _____

6 They're creative and confident. (musicians)
   _____

7 I'm friendly. (person)
   _____

8 Mr. Nelson is talkative but serious. (teacher)
   _____

4 Complete the conversation with *What . . . like*? questions.

Doug   Hi, Isabel. How's your art class?

Isabel I love it! My teacher is Mrs. Linden.

Doug   What's she like _____ ?
                        1

Isabel She's great. She's creative but serious. There are
        12 students in the class.

Doug   _____ ?
                        2

Isabel They're shy, and they're not very friendly. But my
        friend John is in the class.

Doug   _____ ?
                        3

Isabel John is a talkative guy.

Doug   And _____ ?
                        4

Isabel Me? I'm a serious and hardworking student!

5 Read Part 1 of Jenny's job evaluation. Then complete the evaluation in Part 2 with the simple present and the correct adjectives.

ACE ACCOUNTANTS
EMPLOYEE EVALUATION FORM

Employee's Name: Jenny Lewis   Job: Accountant   Date: May 24

Part 1: Which words describe the employee? Check the words.

☑ serious   ☑ confident   ☑ hardworking   ☑ creative

☐ talkative   ☐ funny   ☑ shy   ☑ friendly

Part 2: Write an evaluation of the employee.

Jenny ___is a serious___ accountant and very _____ . She
⠀⠀⠀⠀⠀⠀⠀⠀⠀¹⠀⠀⠀⠀⠀⠀⠀⠀⠀⠀⠀⠀⠀⠀⠀⠀⠀⠀⠀⠀⠀²

_____ . She works late every day. Jenny _____ person
⠀⠀⠀⠀³⠀⠀⠀⠀⠀⠀⠀⠀⠀⠀⠀⠀⠀⠀⠀⠀⠀⠀⠀⠀⠀⠀⠀⠀⠀⠀⠀⠀⠀⠀⠀⠀⠀⁴

and has many good ideas. She is not very talkative or funny. Jenny _____

⠀⠀⠀⠀⠀⠀⠀⠀⠀⠀⠀⠀⠀⠀⠀⠀⠀⠀⠀⠀⠀⠀⠀⠀⠀⠀⠀⠀⠀⠀⠀⠀⠀⠀⠀⠀⠀⠀⠀⁵

but _____ . People like her.
⠀⠀⠀⠀⠀⁶

6 Write conversations for the pictures with your own ideas. Use *What . . . like?* questions and *be* + adjective (+ noun).

Examples: **A** ___What are they like?___   **A** ___What's he like?___

⠀⠀⠀⠀⠀⠀⠀**B** ___They're friendly and funny.___   **B** ___He's a confident and creative actor.___

Tina Fey and Amy Poehler, comedians

Johnny Depp, actor

1 **A** _____ ?   2 **A** _____ ?

⠀⠀**B** _____ .   ⠀⠀**B** _____ .

7 Write conversations for another actor or actress, singer, or musician.

1 Actor or actress: _____   2 Singer or musician: _____

⠀**A** _____ ?   ⠀**A** _____ ?

⠀**B** _____ .   ⠀**B** _____ .

B I don't think so.

1 Circle the correct sentence to complete the conversation.

1 **A** Is Mia hardworking?

    B (I think so.) / I don't think so. She always works late.

2 **A** Does your teacher give a lot of homework?

    B I believe so. / I'm not really sure. It's the first day of class.

3 **A** Is Jay-Jay talkative?

    B I guess so. / I don't believe so. He's shy.

4 **A** Are Mr. and Mrs. Trandall generous?

    B I believe so. / I don't believe so. They sometimes help me.

2 Look at the pictures. Complete the conversations with expressions from Exercise 1.
More than one answer is possible.

1 **A** Is Larry funny?

    B _I don't think so. / I don't believe so._

2 **A** Does Paula take a dance class?

    B _I believe so_

3 **A** Are Tina and Jordan friendly?

    B _I guess so_

4 **A** Does Eric like baseball?

    B _I believe so_

C What do they look like?

1 Match the descriptions with the people in Joe's family. Then write about them.

A ✓	B ✓	C ✓	D	E
young	middle-aged	bald	middle-aged	short and
tall and thin	long blond hair	a gray mustache	curly hair	overweight
wavy shoulder-	little round	elderly and	a short black	young
length hair	glasses	medium height	beard	straight black hair

B   C   Z   A   d

1   This is my mother.
    She's middle-aged.
    She has long blond hair.
    She has little round glasses.

2   This is my grandfather.
    He has bald

3   These are my brothers.
    they has

4   This is my sister.
    she is

5   This is my father.

13

2 Read the clues and label the pictures with the correct names.

- Ken's hair isn't straight, long, or brown.
- Megan doesn't have short or black hair.
- Diane's hair isn't brown.
- Mario's hair isn't long or blond.

  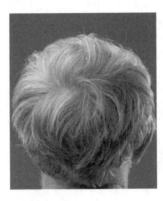 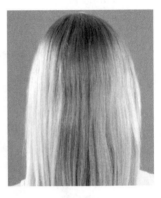

long black hair   short brown hair   wavy blond hair   straight blond hair

1 _Diane_   2 _Mario_   3 _Ken_   4 _Megan_

3 Answer the questions. Use the information from Exercise 2.

1 What does Ken look like?   He has wavy blond hair.

2 What does Mario look like?   He has short brown hair.

3 What does Megan look like?   She has straight blond hair.

4 What does Diane look like?   _____

4 Look at the answers. Write the questions with *What . . . like?* or *What . . . look like?*

1 _What does he look like?_   He has a brown mustache.

2 _What's he like?_   He's confident and serious.

3 _____   She has long straight hair.

4 _____   They're tall and overweight.

5 _____   They're friendly and talkative people.

6 _____   I'm short and thin.

7 _____   He's pretty funny.

8 _____   I'm creative and hardworking.

9 _____   We have curly red hair.

5 Complete the chart with the words from the box.

black	curly	green	long	new	round	straight	wavy
blond	elderly	✓little	middle-aged	red	short	tall	young

Size	Age	Shape	Color
little			

6 Put the words in the correct order to make sentences.

1 hair / straight / John / has / brown / .   John has straight brown hair.

2 short / He's / a / elderly / man / .

3 round / Wendy / glasses / has / little / .

4 have / eyes / green / They / small / .

5 beard / long / He / a / has / gray / .

6 We / hats / blue / new / have / .

7 Look at the pictures. Write sentences. Use some of the words from Exercise 5.
More than one answer is possible.

1   He has short brown
     hair.
     He's young.

2

3

4

D People's profiles

1 Read the text. Write the name of the artist and the cartoon under the correct picture.

1 _____

2 _____

3 _____

Famous Cartoonists

Jim Davis

Jim Davis is famous for his comic strip, *Garfield*. It's about a cat named Garfield. This cat is lazy and eats a lot of lasagna. Garfield also sleeps a lot. Jim's comic is about a cat. Jim played with lots of cats when he was a boy, and he has a pet cat and a dog now. This helps him draw and write about Garfield. Jim lives and works in Albany, Indiana.

Matt Groening

Matt Groening is famous for the cartoon *The Simpsons*. The characters in *The Simpsons* have the same names as the people in Matt's family, but they don't look like his family. The father in the cartoon, Homer, is bald. The mother, Marge, has big blue hair. They have three children. The sister, Lisa, is extremely serious, and Maggie is a baby. Bart is talkative and funny. Matt says Bart is like him. Matt is from Portland, Oregon, but he lives near Los Angeles, California now.

Cathy Guisewite

Cathy Guisewite also lives in California, but she's from Dayton, Ohio. For 34 years she wrote a comic strip called *Cathy*. *Cathy* is about a woman's life. She and her mother do not always see things the same way. In the cartoon, Cathy likes to eat, and her mother thinks she's overweight. Cathy also has problems at work. The real Cathy is retired, and she has one daughter.

2 Read the text again. Then circle the correct answer.

1 Jim's cartoon is **Garfield** / *The Simpsons*.

2 The cartoon of Marge **looks like** / **doesn't look like** Matt's mother.

3 In *The Simpsons*, Lisa is very **serious** / **talkative**.

4 **Jim and Cathy** / **Matt and Cathy** live in California now.

5 The real Cathy has a **daughter** / **son**.

Rain or shine

A It's extremely cold.

1 Label each picture with the correct word from the box.

cloudy
✓cold
cool
hot
rainy
snowy
sunny
warm
windy

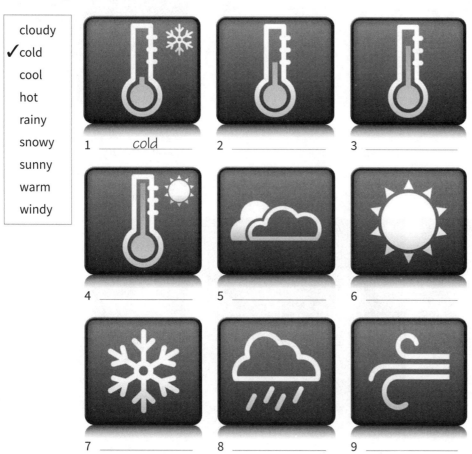

1 _cold_   2 _____   3 _____

4 _____   5 _____   6 _____

7 _____   8 _____   9 _____

2 Look at the map. Write sentences about the weather. Use the simple present of *be* and words from Exercise 1.

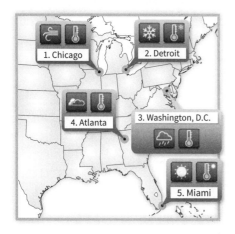

1 _It's windy and cool in Chicago._
2 _____
3 _____
4 _____
5 _____

3 Circle the correct answer for each picture.

1 What season is this?
  a It's warm.
  b It's the rainy season.
  ⓒ It's the dry season.

2 What season do you like?
  a I like summer.
  b I like winter.
  c I like fall.

3 What season is it now?
  a It's the dry season.
  b It's the rainy season.
  c It's snowy.

4 What season is it in Toronto?
  a It's winter.
  b It's spring.
  c It's summer.

5 What's your favorite season?
  a It's fall.
  b It's winter.
  c It's the rainy season.

6 What season does he like?
  a He likes sun.
  b He likes winter.
  c He likes spring.

4 Cross out the word that doesn't belong in each list.

1	extremely	really	~~fairly~~	very
2	somewhat	a lot	pretty	fairly
3	summer	spring	sunny	fall
4	cold	warm	snowy	cool
5	summer	windy	snowy	rainy
6	cloudy	winter	sunny	snowy

5 Put the words in the correct order to make sentences.

1 very / winter / It's / cold / the / in / .

It's very cold in the winter.

2 spring / lot / in / It / rains / a / the / .

3 New York City / windy / It's / pretty / in / .

4 in / cool / It's / fairly / Quito / .

5 season / in / It / dry / much / doesn't / rain / very / the / . .

6 summer / in / at / snow / It / doesn't / all / the / .

7 a / It / Canada / bit / snows / quite / in / .

8 extremely / It's / Bangkok / in / hot / .

6 Circle the correct words to complete the sentences.

1 It's (pretty) / a little sunny today.

2 It rains **pretty** / **a lot** in London.

3 It's **extremely** / **a lot** hot in Istanbul.

4 It's **somewhat** / **very much** cool in March.

5 It doesn't snow **somewhat** / **very much** in Sydney.

6 It's **very** / **a lot** cloudy in Seattle.

7 It doesn't snow **extremely** / **at all** in Lima.

8 It's **at all** / **fairly** windy in Iceland.

9 It rains **a little** / **very** in December.

10 It's **really** / **quite a bit** hot in Mexico City.

7 Write about the weather in your town. Use the words in parentheses.

Example: (snow) _It snows a lot in the winter._ or _It doesn't snow at all._

1 (snow)

2 (rain)

3 (windy)

4 (hot)

5 (sunny)

6 (cloudy)

B In my opinion, . . .

1 Complete the conversations with the words from the box.

| I'd   opinion   think   thoughts   what   what's |

A. **Rosa**   Hey, Marcos. Let's have a party for Mom.

   Marcos   OK. When?

   Rosa   Hmm . . . I don't know. _____ What _____ do you think?
                                    1

   Marcos   I _____ Saturday is a good day.
                        2

   Rosa   OK. That sounds good.

B. **Jake**   Hi, Todd. When are you coming to see me?

   Todd   Well, I'm not sure. What are your _____?
                                                1

   Jake   In my _____ , winter is a good time. It usually
                            2

                snows a lot. We can ski!

   Todd   OK. That would be great.

C. **Hiro**   So, Julie. When is a good time for you to visit?

   Julie   _____ say in the winter. It's cold and snowy here.
                        1

   Hiro   OK. Where should we meet?

   Julie   Hmm . . . _____ your opinion?
                                    2

   Hiro   How about Kyoto? Then you can meet my parents. It's somewhat cool in
                the winter, but it doesn't usually snow.

   Julie   That's a great idea!

2 Match the pictures to the conversations in Exercise 1. Label the pictures with the correct conversation letter.

1 ☐

2 ☐

3 ☐

C I'd like to play chess.

1 Complete the sentences with a word from each box. Use the simple present form of the verbs.

| bake | ✓do | make | play |
| do | make | play | take |

| a board game | ✓a jigsaw puzzle | a video | cookies |
| a crossword | a nap | chess | popcorn |

I usually _do a jigsaw puzzle_ with
my children.
₁

Sometimes, we _____
with friends.
₂

Sometimes, my wife and I _____
_____ on Friday evenings.
₃

But we always _____
on Sunday mornings.
₄

On Sunday afternoon, the kids _____
_____ .
₅

And my mom _____
for us.
₆

My wife _____ .
₇

And I sometimes _____
like this one.
₈

2 Look at the chart. Then answer the questions.

Healthy Pines Recreation Center

NAME	PLAY CHESS	PLAY A BOARD GAME	DO A JIGSAW PUZZLE	BAKE COOKIES	DO YOGA
Ethan			✓		
Carolyn	✓				
Paul	✓				
Marina				✓	
Emma		✓			
Doug		✓			
Jenny					✓
Mark					✓

Activities for Wednesday Afternoon

1 What would Ethan like to do?   He'd like to do a jigsaw puzzle.
2 Would Carolyn and Paul like to play chess?   Yes, they'd like to play chess.
3 What would Marina like to do?
4 Would Emma like to bake cookies?
5 Would Doug like to play a board game?
6 What would Jenny and Mark like to do?

3 Look at the answers. Write the questions about the underlined parts.

1 _What would she like to play?_   She'd like to play <u>a board game</u>.
2 _____   He'd like <u>to take a nap</u>.
3 _____   I'd like to play <u>baseball</u>.
4 _____   <u>No, they wouldn't</u>. They don't like gymnastics.
5 _____   I'd like to do yoga <u>in the park</u>.
6 _____   <u>Yes, she would</u>. She loves chess.
7 _____   <u>No, I wouldn't</u>. I never take naps.
8 _____   They'd like to make a video <u>at the school</u>.

22

4 Write sentences about what the people would like and wouldn't like to do.

1 Kara _would like to play table tennis._
She wouldn't like to play soccer.

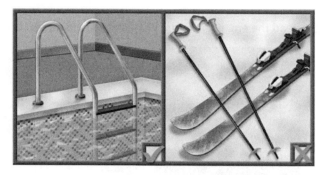

2 Dan _____

_____

3 Sheila and Greg _____

_____

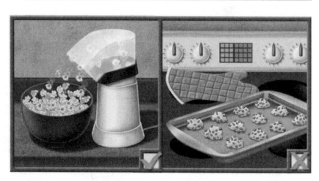

4 Mr. and Mrs. Jones _____

_____

5 Larry _____

_____

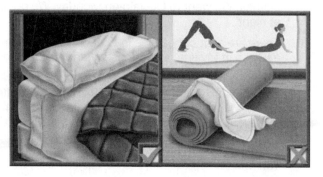

6 Claudia _____

_____

5 Answer the questions with your own information.

1 Would you like to play chess tonight? _____

2 Would you like to take a nap on Saturday? _____

3 Would you like to play soccer tomorrow? _____

4 Would you like to do your homework in a park? _____

5 Where would you like to go for vacation? _____

6 When would you like to go to bed? _____

D Where would you like to go?

1 Read the email. Write the names of the places and the weather under the correct pictures.

1   _Otavalo_
           cool
      pretty cold

2 _____

3 _____

4 _____

Hi, Rachel!

I'm having a great time in Ecuador with my family. We're in Quito right now. It's the capital of Ecuador. The city is big, and there's a lot to do. It's warm in the day and cool at night now. It sometimes rains a lot in Quito, but it's not the rainy season now. We're walking around the city a lot.

The weather is really different in other parts of Ecuador. In the town of Otavalo, the weather is cool all day and pretty cold at night. There's a famous market in Otavalo with many handmade clothes. We went to Otavalo on Monday. We got beautiful sweaters at the market to wear at night!

There are a lot of beaches in Ecuador. The beaches are usually sunny and very hot. We went to a beach in Muisne on Wednesday and had a great time! It was sunny and hot!

Cotopaxi National Park is close to Quito. The park is very big, and it has a large volcano in it. The volcano is also called Cotopaxi. It snows quite a bit on Cotopaxi, and it's extremely cold and snowy at the top. You can walk to the top. The kids can't do it, but Helena and I would like to walk up there this weekend.

How are you? Say hi to Mike and the kids.

Your friend,
Martin

---

2 Read the email again. Then write T (true), F (false), or NI (no information).

1 Quito is the capital of Ecuador. ___T___

2 There isn't a market in Quito. _____

3 Martin and his family liked the beach in Muisne. _____

4 Martin's children are very young. _____

5 Martin and Helena are in Cotopaxi National Park now. _____

6 Rachel would like to go to Ecuador. _____

Life at home

A There's a lot of light.

1 Cross out the word that doesn't usually belong in each list.

1	**bedroom:**	dresser	closet	~~dishwasher~~
2	**bathroom:**	sink	sofa	shower
3	**living room:**	armchair	coffee table	toilet
4	**kitchen:**	bathtub	refrigerator	cupboards
5	**bedroom:**	curtains	stove	bed

2 Complete the sentences with some of the words from Exercise 1.

STUFF FOR SALE

I'm selling my ____*bed*____
____1____
and _____ . They're
____2____
two years old. $150.

For sale: an old

_____ . $50.
____3____
Email r27@cup.org.

We're selling our

_____ and
____4____
_____ . Click
____5____
here to respond.

House for sale. Two bedrooms,
a big _____ with a
____6____
dishwasher.

I can make _____ for
____7____
your bedroom or living room!
Call Susie at 222-5678.

I can fix your _____
____8____
and _____ !
____9____
Email Jason at Jfix@cup.com.

3 What's in your home? Complete the chart with the words from the box.

Example: Kitchen ___*three cupboards, a sink, a refrigerator*___

armchair	closet	curtains	refrigerator	sink
bathtub	coffee table	dishwasher	shelves	sofa
bed	cupboards	dresser	shower	stove

Living Room	Kitchen	Bedroom	Bathroom

4 Write about your home. Use *some*, *a few*, *many*, and *any* and the words in parentheses.

Example: ___There are a few cupboards in my kitchen.___ or
___There aren't many cupboards in my kitchen.___

1 (cupboards / kitchen) _____

2 (shelves / bedroom) _____

3 (armchairs / living room) _____

4 (closets / house) _____

5 (bedrooms / house) _____

5 Circle the correct word or phrase to complete each sentence about Sandra's house.

1 There's **a lot of** / **many** noise on the street.

2 There's **some** / **a few** light in the living room.

3 There isn't **many** / **any** space in the closets.

4 There's **a little** / **a few** light in the bedroom.

5 There aren't **many** / **a little** cupboards in the kitchen.

6 There are **much** / **a few** shelves in the bathroom.

6 Complete the questions with *much* or *many*.

1 How _____*much*_____ light is there in the kitchen?

2 How _____ closets are there in the bedrooms?

3 Are there _____ shelves in the closets?

4 How _____ street noise is there?

5 Is there _____ space in the kitchen?

7 Complete the conversation with the questions from Exercise 6.

Mr. Clark So, this is the house for sale.

Andrew Oh, it's nice. _How much street noise is there?_
                                           1

Mr. Clark Oh, it's fairly quiet.

Lydia Now about the house!

_____
                2

Mr. Clark There's quite a bit of light.

Andrew That's good. We love cooking.

_____
                3

Mr. Clark No, not really. It's pretty small, but there are a lot of cupboards.

Lydia And the bedrooms? _____
                                              4

Mr. Clark There are two closets in the big bedroom, and there's one closet in the small bedroom.

Andrew Oh, that's good. _____
                                            5

Mr. Clark I'm not sure about the shelves. Let's look at the house!

Lydia That's a good idea!

8 Read the answers. Then write the questions.

1 _How much noise is there in the living room?_   There isn't any noise in the living room.

2 _____   There is some light in the bathroom.

3 _____   There are a lot of cupboards in the kitchen.

4 _____   There isn't much space in the dresser.

5 _____   There are a few shelves in the bedroom.

6 _____   Yes, there are four armchairs in the living room.

B Can you turn down the music?

1 Check (✓) all the words that complete the request.

_____ you open this cupboard, please?

☑ Could   ☐ How   ☐ When   ☐ Where

☐ Would   ☐ Do   ☐ Can

2 Check (✓) all the responses to the request in Exercise 1.

☑ No problem.   ☐ Oh, really?   ☐ A little.

☐ In my opinion.   ☐ Sure.   ☐ I'd be happy to.

3 Complete the request and the response in each conversation. Use different words and expressions from Exercises 1 and 2.

A. **Karen** Hey, Jeff. It's Karen from upstairs.
Would you turn down ¹
your TV, please? It's too noisy, and I'm studying.

    Jeff _____ ² .
Sorry about the noise.

    Karen Thanks.

B. **Tessa** It's hot in here.

    Megan I know. _____ ¹
the window, please?

    Tessa _____ ² .

    Megan Thanks. That's better.

C. **Don** Hey, Liv. _____ ¹
the phone?

    Liv _____ ² .

    Don Thanks. I can't talk right now.

C I always hang up my clothes!

1 Complete the household chores with *away*, *off*, *out*, or *up*.

1 wipe _____*off*_____ the counter

2 take _____ the garbage

3 hang _____ the clothes

4 clean _____ the yard

5 drop _____ the dry cleaning

6 pick _____ the magazines

7 put _____ the dishes

8 clean _____ the closets

2 What household chores can you do with these items? Label the pictures with some of the phrases from Exercise 1.

  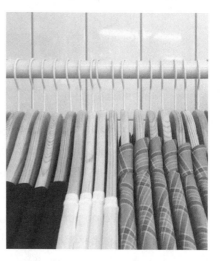

1 _____clean up the yard_____ 2 _____ 3 _____

4 _____ 5 _____ 6 _____

3 Rewrite the sentences.

1 Please pick up those magazines.   *Please pick those magazines up.*

2 Can you take out the garbage?   _____

3 Dennis cleans his yard up every week.   _____

4 I usually put away the dishes at night.   _____

5 Would you drop this letter off at the post office?   _____

6 My son and daughter never hang their clothes up.   _____

4 Complete the answers with the phrasal verb and *it* or *them*.

1 Where do you drop off your dry cleaning?   I ___*drop it off*___ at Super Clean.

2 Where do you hang your coat up?   I _____ in the closet.

3 Who can clean up the living room?   David can _____ .

4 Who can clean out the closets?   Marta and Vern can _____ .

5 Do your children put away their toys?   No, they don't _____ .

6 Does your husband take the garbage out?   No, I _____ .

7 How often do you wipe off the counters?   I _____ three times a day.

8 How often does Miho clean the garage out?   She _____ once a year.

5 Rewrite the questions in Exercise 4 with *it* or *them*.

1 *Where do you drop it off?*

2 _____

3 _____

4 _____

5 _____

6 _____

7 _____

8 _____

6 Look at the chart. Who does each chore? Write two sentences about each chore. Use *it* or *them* in the second sentence.

	Sunday	Monday	Tuesday	Wednesday	Thursday	Friday	Saturday
1. put the dishes away				Kelly and Tim			Dad
2. take out the garbage			Dad			Kelly	
3. drop off the dry cleaning		Mom				Tim	
4. pick up the dry cleaning	Kelly			Dad			
5. hang the clothes up			Kelly		Tim		
6. clean up the yard		Mom and Kelly					Dad and Tim
7. clean up the bathrooms			Mom and Tim			Kelly	
8. clean out the cars	Kelly and Tim			Mom and Dad			

1   Kelly and Tim put the dishes away on Wednesday.   Dad puts them away on Saturday.

2   _____   _____

3   _____   _____

4   _____   _____

5   _____   _____

6   _____   _____

7   _____   _____

8   _____   _____

7 Answer the questions with your own information. Use *it* or *them*.

1   Who takes out the garbage in your home?   _____

2   How often do you wipe off the counters in your kitchen?   _____

3   When do you put away the dishes?   _____

4   How often do you drop off the dry cleaning?   _____

5   Where do you hang up your clothes?   _____

6   How often do you clean up the kitchen?   _____

D What a home!

1 Read the article. Then complete each sentence with one word.

1 Jake: "When I travel, my bed is on a _____."

2 Maria: "When I travel, I sleep in a _____ bed."

3 Tom and Riana: "The virtual _____ is very clean."

Other Homes

Do you have another place you call "home"? Four people describe their "other homes."

JAKE LONDON'S TOUR BUS

I'm a musician. I play the guitar and sing. I travel quite a bit with my band, so my other home is a big bus. There's a kitchen and a bathroom on the bus. There's a small living room with a TV. There are six beds on the bus, one for each person in the band!

MARIA MILLER'S HOTEL ROOM

I'm a flight attendant. Because of my job, I stay in hotels a lot. The hotel rooms usually have a big bed, a small kitchen, and a desk. So, hotel rooms are my "other homes." I always bring a few personal items when I travel for work. I take a nice dress, a few T-shirts, and my favorite jeans. I take a small pillow, and I always take a good book. I'm usually in one place only for a day, so I can put my things away in five minutes!

TOM AND RIANA PETERSON'S VIRTUAL HOUSE

Our "other home" isn't real! We love computer games. We play a game on our computer in a virtual world. We have avatars in this virtual world, and they have a home! Our real home is a small apartment, but the virtual house is big. In the virtual home, our avatars do the household chores. They clean up the rooms, put away the dishes, and take the garbage out. The virtual house is very clean, but our real house is a mess!

2 Read the text again. Answer the questions.

1 What does Jake do? _He's a musician._

2 Is there a TV on Jake's bus? _____

3 What does Maria do? _____

4 How much time is Maria usually in one place? _____

5 Who does the household chores in Tom and Riana's virtual home? _____

Health

A Breathe deeply.

1 Label the parts of the body with the correct words from the box.

ankle	eye	hand	leg	nose	teeth
arm	finger	✓head	mouth	shoulder	toe
ear	foot	knee	neck	stomach	˙wrist

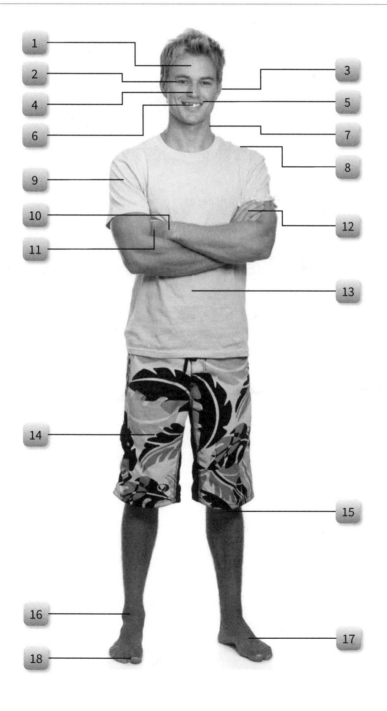

1 _____ head
2 _____
3 _____
4 _____
5 _____
6 _____
7 _____
8 _____
9 _____
10 _____
11 _____
12 _____
13 _____
14 _____
15 _____
16 _____
17 _____
18 _____

2 Match the objects to the corresponding parts of the body. Label each picture with the correct word from the box.

| ✔back | eyes | feet | finger | neck | wrist |

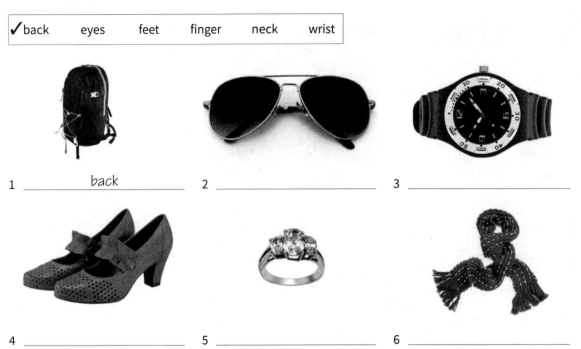

1 _____back_____   2 _____   3 _____

4 _____   5 _____   6 _____

3 Complete the instructions with the correct form of the verb in parentheses.

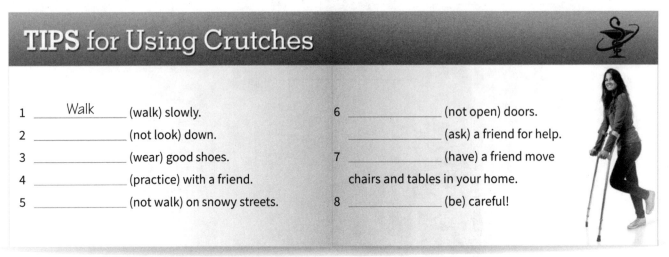

TIPS for Using Crutches

1 _____Walk_____ (walk) slowly.

2 _____ (not look) down.

3 _____ (wear) good shoes.

4 _____ (practice) with a friend.

5 _____ (not walk) on snowy streets.

6 _____ (not open) doors.

_____ (ask) a friend for help.

7 _____ (have) a friend move chairs and tables in your home.

8 _____ (be) careful!

4 Complete the chart with the correct adverbs.

Adjective	Adverb
1 careful	carefully
2 deep	
3 heavy	
4 noisy	
5 quick	
6 quiet	
7 slow	

5 **Circle the correct adverb to complete each sentence.**

1 Raise your arms _____ .
   a noisily   b deeply   (c) quickly

2 Please talk _____ in the library.
   a slowly   b quietly   c noisily

3 Walk _____ , please. I can't walk quickly.
   a heavily   b slowly   c quietly

4 Don't talk _____ . The baby is taking a nap.
   a noisily   b slowly   c heavily

5 Lower your head _____ .
   a heavily   b noisily   c carefully

6 Breathe _____ in yoga. Relax and breathe slowly.
   a deeply   b noisily   c quickly

6 **Write sentences with the words in parentheses. Use the simple present or the imperative form of the verbs and the adverb form of the adjectives.**

1 ___Jim stretches slowly._____ (Jim / stretch / slow)

2 _____ (breathe / deep / for ten minutes)

3 _____ (not breathe / heavy)

4 _____ (Millie / talk / quiet / on the phone)

5 _____ (not walk / quick / after lunch)

6 _____ (we / listen / careful / to our teacher)

7 **Answer the questions with your own information.**

Example: ___I talk quickly.___ or ___I talk slowly.___

1 Do you talk slowly or quickly? _____

2 Do you drive quickly or carefully? _____

3 Do you walk quietly or noisily? _____

B I'm not feeling well.

1 Complete the puzzle with words for health problems. What's the mystery word?

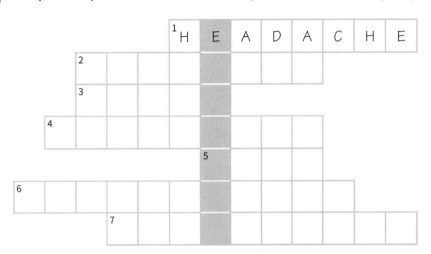

1

2

3

4

5

6

7

2 Complete each conversation with two different expressions from the box.

Get well soon.	I feel awful.	✓ I'm not feeling well.
I don't feel so good.	I hope you feel better.	Take it easy.

A. **Ed** Hi, Pat. How are you?

Pat _I'm not feeling well._
1

Ed What's wrong?

Pat I have a bad cough.

Ed That's too bad. _____
2

B. **Meg** Hey, Tim. How are you?

Tim _____
1

Meg What's wrong?

Tim I have the flu.

Meg Oh, no! _____
2

C How healthy are you?

1 Put the letters in the correct order to make phrases about healthy habits.

1 tae a ablnadec tide
   eat a balanced diet

2 ttpeocr uyor sink

3 tea a ogod fraeskbat

4 tge gnhueo pesel

5 sreeecxi idyla

6 shaw yrou dashn

7 og rfo a klwa

8 flit gwsieth

2 Look at the pictures. How often do you do these things? Write sentences about your habits using some of the phrases from Exercise 1 and *always*, *usually*, *hardly ever*, or *never*.

Example: _I usually eat a balanced diet._

 1 _____

 2 _____

 3 _____

 4 _____

5 _____

6 _____

3 Complete the questions with *How long, How many, How much, How often,* or *How well.*

1 <u>How many</u> vegetables do you eat at dinner?   Hmm . . . Not many.

2 _____ do you walk in the mornings?   For about 30 minutes.

3 _____ do you play soccer?   Pretty well.

4 _____ meals do you cook a week?   Ten meals.

5 _____ coffee do you drink each day?   Two or three cups.

6 _____ do you do karate?   Once a week.

7 _____ do you do yoga?   For about an hour.

8 _____ sleep do you get?   Quite a bit.

4 Look at Greg's answers to an online health quiz. Write the questions.

ARE YOU HEALTHY?
Choose the answers that best describe your habits.

1 **Q:** <u>How often do you eat breakfast?</u>

A: I eat breakfast *every day*.

2 **Q:** _____

A: I follow my diet *pretty well*.

3 **Q:** _____

A: I exercise *daily*.

4 **Q:** _____

A: I drink *a lot* of water.

5 **Q:** _____

A: I *don't get much* sleep.

6 **Q:** _____

A: I wash my hands *three times* a day.

7 **Q:** _____

A: My eating habits are *somewhat healthy*.

8 **Q:** _____

A: I spend *four hours a day* at the gym.

5 Write questions with *How* and the words in parentheses to complete the conversation. Use the answers to help you.

Tae Ho Hi, Fran. How is your mom feeling?

Fran She's not well. She's always tired and doesn't eat well.

Tae Ho <u>How much fruit *does she eat*?</u> (fruit / eat)
　　　　　　　　　　　　1

Fran A lot. She eats apples or bananas every day.

Tae Ho _____ (eat / vegetables)
　　　　　　　　　　　　2

Fran She always eats vegetables at dinner.

Tae Ho _____ (meals / eat / a day)
　　　　　　　　　　　　3

Fran Two. Breakfast and dinner. Is that OK?

Tae Ho Well, three is better. _____
（go to the gym）　　　　　　　　　　　　4

Fran About three times a week.

Tae Ho _____ (spend at the gym)
　　　　　　　　　　　　5

Fran Oh, about an hour. She lifts weights, and she does yoga.

Tae Ho _____ (sleep / get)
　　　　　　　　　　　　6

Fran About four hours a night.

Tae Ho That's not much sleep. In my opinion, that's why she's always tired!

6 Rewrite the questions from Exercise 5 with *you*. Then answer the questions with your own information.

1 <u>How much fruit *do you eat*</u> ?
　　I _____ .

2 _____ ?
　　_____ .

3 _____ ?
　　_____ .

4 _____ ?
　　_____ .

5 _____ ?
　　_____ .

6 _____ ?
　　_____ .

D Don't stress out!

Read the text. Write the instructions from the box in the correct places.

> Move your arms to the right.
> Raise your body.
> Sit carefully on the ball.
> Then lower your head and arms.

The New **HealthyYou** Exercise Ball

Repeat these exercises 20 times for each activity.

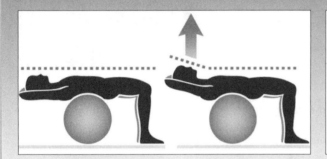

THE SIT UP

1 Put your back carefully on the ball. Place your feet on the floor.
2 Put your hands behind your head.
3 Raise your head and arms slowly. Hold your stomach in.
4 _____

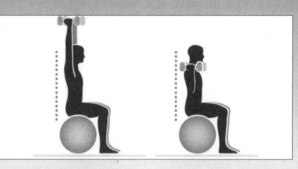

THE WEIGHT LIFT

1 _____
   Place your feet on the floor.
2 Hold a weight in each hand.
3 Lift the weights over your head. Keep your back straight.
4 Lower the weights to your shoulders.

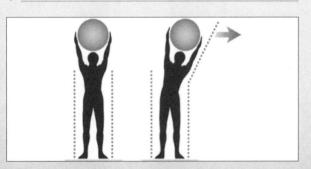

THE REACH

1 Stand up and hold the ball. Stretch your arms and raise the ball over your head.
2 Move your arms to the left. Keep your legs straight. Don't move your feet.
3 _____

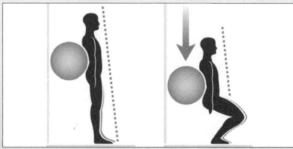

THE SQUAT

1 Place the ball against the wall. Put your back against the ball.
2 Lower your body, bending your knees. Keep your back straight.
3 _____

What's on TV?

A I love watching game shows.

1 Look at the pictures. Circle the correct answer.

1 What type of shows do they like?
- (a) Documentaries
- b Cartoons
- c Talk shows

2 What type of shows does Jim watch?
- a Reality shows
- b Sitcoms
- c Cartoons

3 What's his favorite type of TV show?
- a Game shows
- b The news
- c Soap operas

4 What do they watch at night?
- a The news
- b Talk shows
- c Dramas

5 What type of shows does his family watch?
- a Sitcoms
- b Documentaries
- c Game shows

6 What does Sarah watch after work?
- a Sitcoms
- b Dramas
- c The news

7 What's on TV?
- a A game show
- b A cartoon
- c A talk show

8 What's that?
- a A cartoon
- b A reality show
- c A soap opera

9 What are they watching?
- a The news
- b A drama
- c A talk show

2 Complete the chart. Write the verbs from the box in the correct column.

dislike	✔hate	like	prefer
enjoy	hope	love	want

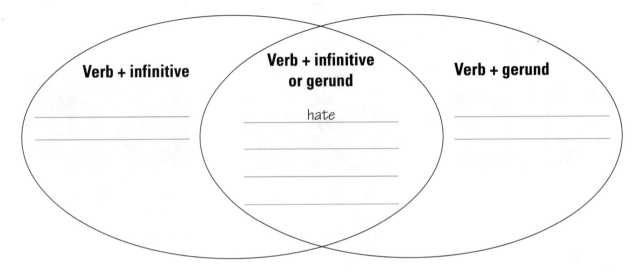

Verb + infinitive

_____

_____

Verb + infinitive or gerund

_____hate_____

_____

_____

_____

Verb + gerund

_____

_____

3 Put the words in the correct order to make sentences.

1 at night / shows / watch / I / like / reality / to / .

    I like to watch reality shows at night.

2 to / new / Melvin / buy / TV / next week / hopes / a / .

    _____

3 on the Internet / TV shows / dislikes / My / mother / watching / .

    _____

4 do / What / love / of TV shows / types / watching / you / ?

    _____

5 favorite / hate / We / our / missing / show / .

    _____

6 on the radio / listen / Sarah and Mike / prefer / to / to the news / .

    _____

4 In four of the sentences from Exercise 3, the verb can be followed by either a gerund or an infinitive. Rewrite those sentences in the other way.

1   I like watching reality shows at night.

2   _____

3   _____

4   _____

42

5 Answer the questions with the words in parentheses. Use the correct form of the verbs. Sometimes two answers are possible.

1 What shows do you watch on TV?
   I love watching sitcoms. / I love to watch sitcoms. .... (love / watch / sitcoms)

2 Does your sister like reality shows?
   Yes. .... (enjoy / watch / them)

3 Do you listen to the radio?
   No, I don't. .... (prefer / listen / to music on my computer)

4 Why is Jack at the store?
   .... (want / buy / a new TV)

5 Why is Laura at the bookstore?
   .... (hope / see / that famous writer)

6 What types of movies does Paul like?
   .... (like / watch / dramas)

7 Why aren't Dan and Susan at the mall?
   .... (hate / shop)

8 Do you and Mary watch a lot of TV?
   No. .... (dislike / watch / TV)

6 Circle the correct words to complete the conversation.

Mara   Hey, Ken. What's wrong?

Ken   Well, I **hate** / **dislike** to watch TV.
          1

Mara   Oh, OK. What do you **enjoy** / **want** to do?
          2

Ken   Hmm . . . Well, I **like** / **want** riding bikes.
          3

Mara   But it's really cold outside!

Ken   You're right. I **hope** / **enjoy** playing board games.
          4

Mara   Well, I **prefer** / **enjoy** to play chess.
          5

Ken   OK. Let's play chess! Could you turn off the TV?

Mara   Well, actually . . . I **want** / **dislike** to watch it
          6
          while we play.

Ken   Oh, no!

B I don't really agree.

1 **Complete the conversation with *agree* or *disagree*.**

Tim	I think cartoons are great!
Aisha	I _____*agree*_____ . They're funny!
	₁
Wendy	I don't really _____ , Aisha.
	₂
	Cartoons aren't funny. They're boring.
Aisha	Wendy, don't you like soap operas?
Wendy	Yes, I do. Why?
Aisha	Well, I think soap operas are boring!
Wendy	I _____ . They're interesting!
	₃
Tim	I'm afraid I _____ , Wendy.
	₄
	They are pretty boring!
Wendy	Well, what do you think of reality shows?
Tim	Oh, they're great . . . interesting and funny!
Aisha	I _____ with you, Tim!
	₅
Wendy	Hey, I think so, too. Let's watch a reality show.

2 **Complete the conversations with your opinion. Use some of the expressions from Exercise 1.**

A. **Tim**   I think cartoons are great.

   Aisha   I think so, too. They're funny.

   You   _____
                            ₁

   Wendy   I think cartoons are boring.

   You   _____
                            ₂

B. **Aisha**   Do you like soap operas?

   Wendy   Yes! I think soap operas are interesting!

   You   _____
                            ₁

   Tim   I think soap operas are boring!

   You   _____
                            ₂

C I'm recording a documentary.

1 Complete the sentences and the puzzle with television words.

Across

2 Jenny likes to watch _____ of old sitcoms on TV. She watches the same shows from the 1990s every night.

5 Do you _____ the sad parts of movies? I never watch them.

6 I'm going to work. Can you _____ my favorite show? Thanks!

7 I like watching TV shows online. I _____ through the boring parts!

Down

1 I don't pay for any TV channels, but there are some good shows on _____ *public* _____ TV.
1

2 Where's the _____ control? I want to turn the TV on.

3 Do you have _____ TV? You have great channels, but I didn't see a dish outside.

4 I hate watching TV. I like the shows, but I don't like the _____ .

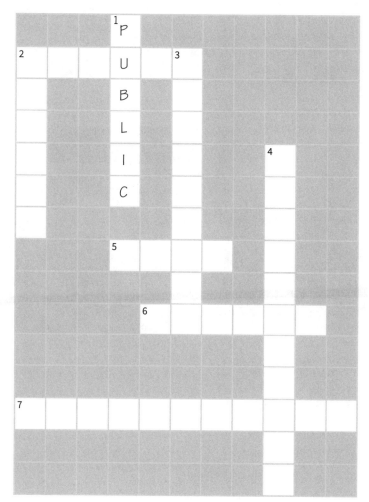

2 **What are they doing on Saturday? Read the sentences. Label the pictures with the correct names.**

- Tom is staying home on Saturday.
- Tonya is taking her school books to the library on Saturday.
- Isabella is going to a club on Saturday.
- Randy is playing a sport on Saturday.
- Emily is driving to her sister's house on Saturday.
- Mateo is meeting a friend at a Japanese restaurant on Saturday.

1 _____Isabella_____   2 _____   3 _____

4 _____   5 _____   6 _____

3 **Match the questions and answers. Use the information in the sentences and the pictures in Exercise 2.**

1 What's Tom doing on Saturday? __*e*__   a He's playing soccer.

2 What's Randy doing on Saturday? _____   b He's eating sushi with Naoki.

3 What's Isabella doing on Saturday? _____   c She's visiting her sister in San Francisco.

4 What's Emily doing on Saturday? _____   d She's doing her homework at the library.

5 What's Mateo doing on Saturday? _____   e He's watching TV.

6 What's Tonya doing on Saturday? _____   f She's going dancing.

4 Rewrite the sentences. Use the present continuous and the words in parentheses.

1 She goes to work.

   _She's going to work on Monday_____ . (on Monday)

2 He watches reruns of his favorite TV show.

   _____ . (tonight)

3 What do you do for fun?

   _____ ? (this weekend)

4 Does he teach English in South Korea?

   _____ ? (next year)

5 We don't record our favorite shows.

   _____ . (on Friday)

6 The Hawks play the Lions.

   _____ . (next week)

7 I don't cook Mexican food.

   _____ . (for the party)

8 Where does she travel for work?

   _____ ? (next month)

5 Look at some of Becky's plans for next week. Then read the answers and complete the questions.

	Thursday	Friday	Saturday	Sunday

	- buy a new TV	- have a party for Mark
		- make and post a
		  video of the party
			- watch the baseball
			  game with Tim
			- record the game for
			  Doug
				- visit my parents
				- go out with Joan

1 _Is Becky buying a new TV_____ on Friday?   No, she isn't. She's buying it on Thursday.

2 _____ on Sunday?   No, they aren't. They're watching it on Saturday.

3 _____ on Saturday?   No, she isn't. She's having it on Friday.

4 _____ of the game?   No, she isn't. She's making a video of the party.

5 _____ for Mark?   No, she isn't. She's recording it for Doug.

6 _____ on Thursday?   No, they aren't. They are going out on Sunday.

7 _____ her grandparents?   No, she isn't. She's visiting her parents.

8 _____ on Saturday?   No, she isn't. She's visiting them on Sunday.

D Popular TV

1 Read the article. Write the headings for each section in the correct place.

Watch on your smartphone   Watch free shows on your computer   Watch on your TV

Great TV through the Internet

Today you can watch great TV through the Internet. You can watch new shows or reruns from around the world.

1 _____

You don't have a smart TV? That's OK. Get a streaming media player. It's a small box, and it's not very expensive. Connect it to your TV, and you can watch shows from the Internet through your TV. You can find good shows through on-demand services. Some services only allow you to watch the most recent episodes. Other services let you watch whole seasons of your favorite shows.

2 _____

Some TV networks allow you to watch their TV shows online for free. Go to the websites of these networks. Look for live streams or past episodes. There are some commercials, but they are usually short.

3 _____

Do you want to take your shows with you everywhere you go? No problem. You can download apps to your smartphone. Search for apps from TV networks or on-demand services. You can watch the shows on a bus, or on a train, or while you are exercising at the gym!

> TV is almost 100 years old! Here are some important dates in the history of television.
> - **1920s** first TV sets
> - **1930s** first TV commercial
> - **1940s** first sitcom, first color TV sets
> - **1950s** first reality show
> - **1960s** first satellite TV

2 Read the article again. Then answer the questions.

1 Are reality shows new? — _No, they aren't._

2 Do free online shows have commercials? — _____

3 Can you watch reruns online? — _____

4 How can you watch TV shows on a bus? — _____

5 What can you connect to your TV to watch shows through the Internet? — _____

Shopping

A It's lighter and thinner.

1 Match the opposites.

1	light _e_	a	loud
2	quiet _____	b	big
3	cheap _____	c	fast
4	small _____	d	thick
5	thin _____	e	heavy
6	slow _____	f	expensive

2 Look at the pictures. Complete the sentences with some of the words from Exercise 1.

1 Joe's car is _____ big _____ and _____ slow _____.

2 Donna's car is _____ and _____.

3 This book is _____ and _____.

4 This book is _____ and _____.

3 Look at the pictures. Then write sentences with the comparative form of the adjectives in parentheses.

tablet, $400   laptop, $1,000

1 The laptop is heavier than the tablet._____ (heavy)
2 _____ (big)
3 _____ (expensive)
4 _____ (light)
5 _____ (cheap)
6 _____ (small)

4 Circle the correct words to complete the email.

To:	MateoG@cup.org
From:	Cassandra92@cup.com
Subject:	My new computer!

Hi, Mateo!

I have a new computer. It's really nice. It's a laptop, so it's **more small / smaller**
1
than my old desktop computer. It's also **faster / less fast**! It was
2
expensiver / more expensive, but that's OK. I love it! The computer store had
3
a **cheaper / less cheap** laptop, but it was very **old / older**. My laptop is
4   5
better / good than that one!
6

Oh, I have a new cell phone, too. It's **nice / nicer** than my old phone. It's pretty
7
small / less small, and it's extremely **lighter / light**!
8   9

How are you? How are your Spanish classes? Are they **more difficult / difficult**
10
than your classes last year? My English class is **bad / worse** than my class last
11
year. The teacher is pretty friendly, but the class is **big / bigger** than the one
12
last year!

Write soon!
Cassandra

5 Complete the conversation with the comparative form of the correct adjective from the box. Use *Which*, *is*, *printer*, and *than* as needed.

cheap	new	quiet	small

Clerk   Hello. Can I help you?

Yoko   Yes, please. I want to buy a new printer.

Clerk   OK. These two printers are great — the Target 1000 and the Excite XL.

Yoko   ___Which printer is smaller___ ?
          1

Clerk   The Target 1000 _____ the
                                    2
          Excite XL. The Excite XL is very big.

Yoko   _____ ?
                        3

Clerk   The Target 1000 _____
                                        4
          the Excite XL. It's only $120.

Yoko   _____ ?
                        5

Clerk   Oh, the Excite XL _____ the Target 1000.
                                        6
          The Target 1000 is pretty loud.

Yoko   Hmm . . . _____ ?
                                    7

Clerk   The Excite XL _____ . The Target 1000 is a year old.
                                    8

Yoko   OK, thanks. I want to buy the Excite XL.

6 Write sentences about the pictures. Use the comparative form of the adjectives.

1   ___The bicycle is smaller than the motorcycle.___   (small)

2   _____   (expensive)

3   _____   (heavy)

4   _____   (quiet)

5   _____   (fast)

bicycle, $1,500

7 What's your opinion? Write sentences about the pictures in Exercise 6. Use the comparative form of the adjectives.

1   _____   (nice)

2   _____   (good)

motorcycle, $4,000

Would you take $10?

1 Write B (bargaining for a lower price) or S (suggesting a different price). Then add the correct punctuation.

1 __B__ Will you take $100 __?__
2 _____ I'll let you have it for $85 _____
3 _____ You can have it for $15 _____
4 _____ How about $35 _____
5 _____ Would you take $12 _____
6 _____ I'll give it to you for $45 _____

2 Complete the conversation with some of the sentences from Exercise 1.

A. **Bin** Excuse me? How much is this plate?

Hai It's only $20.

Bin Oh, that's expensive.
_____Would you take $12_____ ?
                  1
Hai No, I'm sorry. _____ .
                              2
Bin OK, thanks. I'll take it.

B. **Gustavo** Excuse me? How much is this hat?

Ivan It's only $60.

Gustavo Wow, that's expensive.

_____ ?
              1
Ivan No, I'm sorry. $60 is a good price.

Gustavo Well, thanks, anyway.

Ivan Wait! _____ .
                          2
Gustavo Great. I'll take it!

C This hat is too small.

1 Circle the correct word to complete each sentence.

1 These jeans are tight. They're not _____ .
  a bright   b uncomfortable   ⓒ comfortable

2 This gray shirt is very _____ . Can I try on that shirt with flowers on it?
  a plain   b comfortable   c bright

3 I don't like this dress. It's _____ .
  a pretty   b comfortable   c ugly

4 This blouse is too small. It's very _____ .
  a baggy   b tight   c comfortable

5 I really like this tie. It's so _____ .
  a uncomfortable   b nice   c ugly

6 $200! These shoes are _____ .
  a expensive   b baggy   c bright

2 Complete the conversations with the correct adjective from the box.

bright	comfortable	plain	pretty	tight	ugly

A. **Nick** Do you like these pants, Paul?

Paul Well, I like the color. They're _____ bright _____ .
            1
         But . . .

Nick But?

Paul Um, well . . . Do they fit?

Nick Actually, no. They're fairly _____ .
                                        2

Paul Why don't you try on a bigger size?

Nick That's a good idea.

(Later)

Nick OK. What do you think?

Paul Those pants look good on you. And they look more
         _____ .
            3

B. **Mary** Look at this dress, Paula. It's really
          _____ . I love it!
              1

Paula Well, I don't. It's just a black dress. It's very
          _____ .
              2

Mary I know, but it's nice.

Paula Well, I don't think it's pretty. I think it's
          _____ .
              3

Mary Really? Now I don't want to buy it.

3 **Put the words in the correct order to make sentences.**

1 isn't / This / enough / shirt / big / .   _This shirt isn't big enough._

2 clothes / have / He / doesn't / enough / .   _____

3 is / My / tight / jacket / too / .   _____

4 don't / enough / have / We / time / .   _____

5 enough / Her / warm / coat / isn't / .   _____

6 glasses / too / these / Are / expensive / ?   _____

7 shoes / Do / enough / you / have / ?   _____

8 this / cheap / Is / belt / enough / ?   _____

4 **Complete the sentences with _too_ or _enough_.**

A

This blouse is _____*too*_____ big, and these pants aren't
        1
long _____ ! The bag is _____ expensive,
        2   3
and the shoes are _____ tight.
                          4

B

This jacket is _____ small, and these pants
                        1
are _____ baggy. The bag is ugly, and the
           2
shoes aren't big _____ !
                          3

C

This blouse isn't nice _____ , but I like the
                              1
pants. The bag isn't big _____ , and the
                                2
shoes are _____ expensive. I don't have
                3
_____ money. I hate shopping!
        4

5 **Match the pictures to the sentences from Exercise 4. Write A, B, or C.**

1 ☐

2 ☐

3 ☐

54

6 Write sentences in the simple present. Use the words in parentheses and *too* or *enough*.

1 *We don't have enough pasta.*

(we / not have / pasta)

2 _____

(this sofa / not be / big)

3 _____

(she / not be / tall)

4 _____

(these pants / be / short)

5 _____

(it / be / cold)

6 _____

(there be / space / in the closet)

7 _____

(he / not get / sleep)

8 _____

(these weights / be / heavy)

D A shopper's paradise

1 Read the article. Then number the pictures.

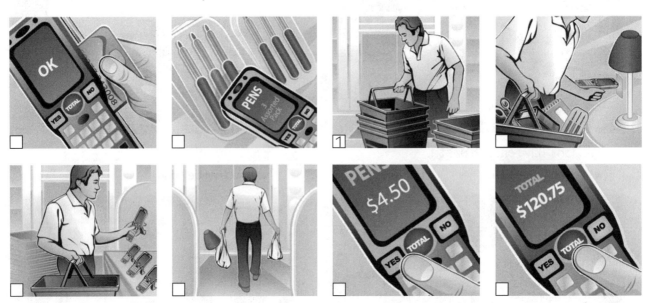

Oh Office has a new way to shop.

Come and try it! It's easier than shopping the old way.

1 Enter our store. Get a shopping basket. Our baskets are bigger than baskets in other stores. You have enough space for pencils, paper, small office lamps, and more!

2 Take a *go-scan* from the shelf next to the baskets. Turn it on.

3 Start shopping! Scan an item you want to buy.

4 Look at the price on the window of the *go-scan*. Do you want the item? Yes! Touch the "yes" button, and scan the item again. Then put it in your basket. You don't want the item? Touch the "no" button, and put the item back on the shelf.

5 Continue shopping and scanning!

6 Are you finished? Touch the "total" button on the *go-scan*. How much is it?

7 Put your credit card in the *go-scan*.

8 Put your things in a bag and go home.

See you soon at Oh Office!

2 Read the article again. Then answer the questions.

1 What kind of store is it?   It's an office store.

2 Where are the *go-scans*?

3 Are Oh Office baskets smaller than baskets in other stores?

4 Which button is for items you want?

5 Which button shows how much everything costs?

Fun in the city

A You shouldn't miss it!

1 Complete the captions under the pictures with the words in the box.

Botanical Garden	Fountain	✓ Palace	Square
Castle	Monument	Pyramid	Statue

1 Grand _Palace_

2 Trim _____

3 _____ of King Leonidas of Sparta

4 Chichen Itza Mayan _____

5 New York _____

6 Arc de Triomphe _____

7 Friendship of the Peoples _____

8 Federation _____

2 Complete the sentences. Write three of the places from Exercise 1.

1 The _____ is in the Park of Soviet Economic Achievement in Moscow.

2 The _____ is in Greece. It's bigger and taller than a real man.

3 The _____ is in Bangkok, Thailand. The queen and king live there sometimes.

3 Complete the conversations with *should* or *shouldn't*.

A. **Eva** I'm going to Peru on vacation. Where _____should_____ I go?

1

   Simone You _____ go to Arequipa. It's beautiful. And

2

   you _____ miss Cuzco. It's amazing!

3

B. **Cory** I want to buy a book. Where _____ I buy it?

1

   Ben You _____ buy it at the mall. It's too expensive.

2

   You _____ buy it online. It's cheaper.

3

C. **Jung Ah** How _____ we get to the restaurant?

1

   Su Ho Well, we _____ take the bus. It's too slow.

2

   Jung Ah _____ we take a taxi?

3

   Su Ho Yes, we _____ .

4

D. **Andres** What time _____ we come to your party?

1

   Santos You _____ come early. You can help me with the food.

2

   Andres _____ I come at 6:00?

3

   Santos No, you _____ . That's too early. How about at 7:00?

4

   Andres OK.

4 Look at the weather information for each city. Then answer the questions.

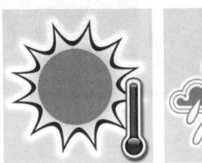   

    Cairo   Seoul   Chicago   Vancouver

1 Mateo hates cold weather. Should he go to Cairo?   _____Yes, he should._____

2 Alison doesn't like rainy weather. Should she go to Seoul? _____

3 Kyle and Casey want to ski. Should they go to Vancouver? _____

4 I don't like hot weather. Should I go to Chicago? _____

5 Paul wants to swim outside. Should he go to Vancouver? _____

6 Mr. and Mrs. Willis like cold weather. Should they go to Cairo? _____

5 Write sentences about Tours 1 and 2. Use *can* or *can't*.

CITY TRAVEL

	go to a museum	see a palace	visit a monument	have lunch at a castle
Tour 1	✗	✓	✗	✓
Tour 2	✓	✗	✓	✗
Tour 3	✗	✓	✓	✗
Tour 4	✗	✓	✗	✓

1 On Tour 1, _you can't go to a museum_ or _____.

   You can see a palace and _____.

2 On Tour 2, _____ or _____.

   _____ and _____.

6 Answer the questions about Tours 3 and 4. Use the information from Exercise 5.

1 Can Susan go to a museum on Tour 3?   _No, she can't._

2 Can we have lunch at a castle on Tour 4?   _____

3 Can you visit a monument on Tour 4?   _____

4 Can Jack see a palace on Tour 3?   _____

5 Can Jean and Paul go to a museum on Tour 4?   _____

7 Circle the correct answer.

1 The main square is great! You _____ go there tomorrow.

   a should   b shouldn't   c can't

2 There are 150 statues in this city. You _____ see them all in one day.

   a should   b can't   c can

3 Julia loves to ski. She _____ go to Canada. There's a lot of snow there in the winter.

   a should   b can't   c shouldn't

4 We _____ eat pasta. There's a good Italian restaurant across the street.

   a. shouldn't   b can't   c can

5 It's extremely hot today. We _____ take our coats on the tour.

   a should   b can   c shouldn't

B I'd recommend going . . .

1 Write the lines of the conversation in the correct order.

> Almost, but I don't know much about Montpellier. What do you think I should do there?
> ✓ Hi, Mari.
> I'd suggest seeing the botanical garden.
> Oh, hi, Ray. Are you ready for your trip to France?
> OK. That sounds good.
> Botanical garden?
> Yes. You can see all of the botanical garden in one day, and it's great.

Ray Hi, Mari. _____

Mari _____

Ray _____

Mari _____

Ray _____

Mari _____

Ray _____

2 Write a conversation with the words and expressions in the box. Use Exercise 1 as a model.

> Italy
> Rome
> the fountains
> I'd recommend . . .
> What would you recommend doing there?

Lina Hi, Sergio. _____

Sergio _____

Lina _____

Sergio _____

Lina _____

Sergio _____

Lina _____

60

C The best and the worst

1 Put the letters in the correct order to make adjectives.

1 edmorn   _modern_
2 ssseutfrl   _____
3 gluy   _____
4 nceal   _____
5 atdaloriitn   _____
6 lbfietauu   _____
7 lxiargen   _____
8 fase   _____
9 aodurnseg   _____
10 iydtr   _____

2 Describe the pictures. Give your opinion. Use some of the words from Exercise 1.

Example: _It's a beautiful and safe city._

1 _____

2 _____

3 _____

4 _____

5 _____

6 _____

3 **Rewrite the sentences with the opposite adjectives.**

1 It's the most modern hotel in the city.

   It's the most traditional hotel in the city.

2 It's the safest city in the world.

   _____

3 It's the most beautiful restaurant in Chicago.

   _____

4 The bookstore is the most expensive store in the mall.

   _____

5 Shannon has the most stressful job in the world!

   _____

6 Market Street is the noisiest street in my town.

   _____

7 It's the cleanest beach in Spain.

   _____

8 It's the smallest café by the park.

   _____

4 **Read the clues. Then answer the questions.**

1 ● Miami is bigger than Naples.
  ● Key Largo is smaller than Naples.
    What's the biggest city in Florida?

    Miami is the biggest city in Florida.

2 ● Oliver is shorter than Ethan.
  ● Matt is taller than Ethan.
    Who's the tallest boy in the class?

    _____

3 ● Main Street is dirtier than Elm Street.
  ● Park Street is cleaner than Elm Street.
    What's the cleanest street in the town?

    _____

4 ● Jane's computer is newer than David's computer.
  ● Wendy's computer is older than Jane's computer.
    Who has the newest computer in the family?

    _____

5 Complete the paragraphs with the superlative form of the adjectives in parentheses.

What's your favorite place?

Posted by: **KateMonk12**

I love going to Thailand. Bangkok is

the biggest (big) city in Thailand. I always stay in
1

_____ (clean) and _____ (safe)
2   3

hotel in the city. It's also close to the markets. I get _____
4

(beautiful) clothes there!

Posted by: **DavidP**

Sometimes I think I have _____ (bad) and
5

_____ (stressful) job in the world! But, not always.
6

I sometimes travel for work, and it's great. My favorite place is a hotel

in San Diego. The pool is _____ (relaxing) place! But it's
7

not my favorite place in the hotel. I love the hotel restaurant. I think it's one of

_____ (good) restaurants in the city.
8

Posted by: **LivLiv**

My favorite city is Tokyo. It's _____ (modern) city
9

in Japan. I think it's _____ (clean) big city in the world. I
10

like visiting the Tokyo National Museum. It's _____ (old)
11

museum in Japan, and it's also one of _____ (traditional).
12

6 Answer the questions with information about your country.

1   What's the oldest city? _____

2   What's the best season to travel? _____

3   What's the coldest city? _____

4   What's the hottest city? _____

5   Where's the biggest park? _____

6   What's the most modern museum? _____

D The best place to go

1 Read the blog. Then circle the correct answer.

1 *Eating a Biscuit Together* is by **Ku BomJu** / **Bukchon**.

2 The statue of the businessman is in **Los Angeles** / **Ernst & Young**.

3 The statue in Australia is a statue of Charles **La Trobe** / **Robb**.

4 The artist of *The Runner* is Costas **Dromeas** / **Varotsos**.

Unusual Statues around the World

I travel a lot for work and for fun. I see a lot of famous landmarks. *The Statue of Liberty* in New York City is my favorite statue, but here are some unusual statues from my travels.

This statue is called *Eating a Biscuit Together*. This statue is actually a bench – you can sit on it! It's by artist Ku BomJu, and it's in front of the Bukchon Art Museum in Seoul, Korea. I think it's very funny!

I don't know the artist or name of this statue, but I really like it! It's a statue of a businessman in Los Angeles, California. It's in front of the Ernst & Young Building. I think he has the most stressful job in Los Angeles. Maybe he is an accountant for a movie star!

You can't miss this statue! It's of Charles La Trobe, a famous politician in Australia in the 1800s. The artist's name is Charles Robb. It's at La Trobe University Bundoora in Melbourne, Australia. Do you think his head hurts?

I love this statue! It's called *Dromeas II*, but people call it *The Runner* in English. It has a lot of glass plates that make the shape of a runner. The artist is Costas Varotsos. It's in front of the Athens Hilton hotel in Athens, Greece. I think it's the fastest statue in the world, but it's not going far!

2 Read the article again. Write T (true), F (false), or NI (no information).

1 The Bukchon Art Museum has traditional Korean art. __NI__

2 The statue of the businessman is in Europe. _____

3 The statue in Australia doesn't have a head. _____

4 The statue *The Runner* is in Greece. _____

5 *The Runner* is the writer's favorite statue. _____

People

A Where was he born?

1 Look at the pictures. Complete the puzzle with career words.

1
2
3
4

5
6
7
8

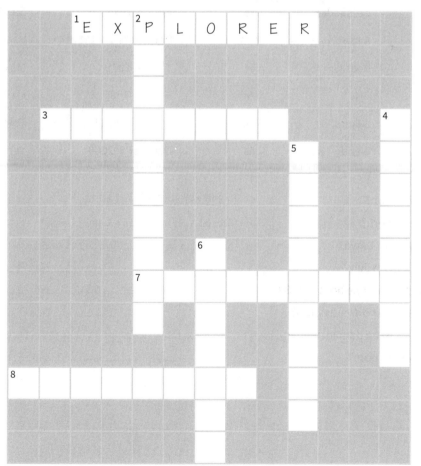

¹E X ²P L O R E R

2 Rewrite the sentences. Use the past of *be* and the words in parentheses.

1 I'm in Chicago right now.

   I was in Chicago last week   . (last week)

2 Tom and Carol are at a basketball game tonight.

   _____ . (last night)

3 Where are you right now?

   _____ ? (yesterday)

4 Stephanie and Kim aren't in class today.

   _____ . (on Tuesday)

5 Is David at the party tonight?

   _____ ? (on Friday night)

6 Tameka isn't tired now.

   _____ . (in the morning)

3 Look at the chart. Then answer the questions.

Family name	First name	Title	Birthday	Place of birth
Balkan	Erol	Mr.	January 17, 1992	Istanbul
Davis	Cassandra	Ms.	April 7, 1986	San Francisco
Ferris	Alicia	Mrs.	December 10, 1950	Vancouver
Gomez	Rodrigo	Mr.	June 4, 1975	Mexico City
Johnson	Kyle	Mr.	May 23, 1986	Melbourne
Kato	Sakura	Mrs.	January 18, 1967	Tokyo
Morgan	Wendy	Ms.	October 8, 2000	Vancouver

1 Where was Erol born?   He was born in Istanbul.

2 When was Alicia born?   _____

3 Was Sakura born in Tokyo?   _____

4 Was Rodrigo born in July?   _____

5 Were Cassandra and Kyle born in 1988?   _____

6 Where were Alicia and Wendy born?   _____

7 Were Erol and Sakura born in January?   _____

8 When was Rodrigo born?   _____

4 Complete the conversation with the correct form of the past of *be*.

Jay   Hey, Shelly. This is really interesting . . .

Shelly What?

Jay   Well, I'm reading about Leonardo da Vinci.

Shelly Oh. _____Was_____ he an explorer?
                    1

Jay   No, he _____ . He _____ a famous artist. Many
                    2   3

        of his paintings _____ famous, such as the *Mona Lisa*.
                              4

Shelly Oh, yeah. That's right.

Jay   But I didn't know this. He _____ also a musician and a writer!
                                          5

Shelly Wow. _____ he born in Italy?
                    6

Jay   Yes, he _____ . He _____ born in Vinci,
                    7   8

        a small town in Italy.

Shelly Vinci, like his last name.

Jay   Yes, "da Vinci" means "from Vinci." Hey, he _____ born on
                                                            9

        April 15, 1452. That's your birthday!

Shelly No, it isn't. I _____ born on April 15. My birthday is April 16.
                              10

Jay   Oh, yeah. Well, listen to this. He _____ also a great scientist with many inventions.
                                                  11

Shelly _____ his inventions popular?
              12

Jay   No, they _____ . And the technology _____
                      13   14

        available then to make his inventions.

5 Answer the questions with your own information.

1   Where were you born?   _____

2   When were you born?   _____

3   When were your parents born?   _____

4   Where were you yesterday afternoon?   _____

5   Were you in your English class yesterday? _____

B I'm not sure, but I think . . .

1 Complete the expressions of certainty and uncertainty in the conversation.

Jerry Hey, Tanya, can you help me with this puzzle?

Tanya Sure.

Jerry Who was Coco Chanel?

Tanya She was a famous designer.

Jerry Are you sure?

Tanya I'm p_____ .
                    1

Jerry OK. D-E-S . . . Yes, that's an eight-letter word.
           It works! And what was the last name of the Mexican
           president in 2002?

Tanya I'm not s_____ , but I think it
                          2

           was Fox.

Jerry Yes, that works. Oh, I know this one. Mozart's first name
           was Wolfgang.

Tanya Are you sure? I think it was Ludwig.

Jerry No, it wasn't Ludwig. I'm c_____
                                          3

           it was Wolfgang. It has eight letters.

2 Complete the conversation with expressions of certainty or uncertainty. More than
one answer is possible.

Jerry OK. Only three more. Who is Elena Ochoa?

Tanya I'm _____ , but I think she was
                              1

           a scientist.

Jerry Hmm . . . That doesn't fit. It starts with an *A* . . . I know, she was an astronaut!

Tanya Are you sure?

Jerry Yes. _____ ! OK. This one's difficult. Who was Eiji Sawamura?
                              2

Tanya _____ , but I think he was a soccer player.
                     3

           No, wait, he was a baseball player! _____ .
                                                              4

Jerry You're right. Thanks!

68

C People I admire

1 Complete the sentences in the evaluations with the words in the box.

brave	caring	determined	honest	inspiring	intelligent	passionate	talented

TOMKINS ACCOUNTING

Name: Orlando Rodriguez   **Position:** Accountant

Overall rating: Very good

Comments:

Orlando is extremely _____ . He learns new things quickly and easily.
₁

He's also very _____ . He tries everything possible to do a good job.
₂

He's always on time, and he's very _____ . He always tells the truth,
₃

even when others don't agree with his opinion.

Perfect Pets Animal Care

Name: Josie Kennedy   **Position:** Assistant

Notes:

I think Josie is good for the job. She is very _____ . She was nice to all
₄

the animals here. She's also very _____ . She wasn't afraid to work
₅

with the bigger dogs. I recommend Josie for this job.

LTC Teamwork Presentation ←→

Overall rating: ☑ Very good   ☐ Good   ☐ Not good

Comments:

The presentation on teamwork was very good. I learned a lot about how to work with

people in groups. Ms. Beck was a great teacher. She was very _____
₆

about teamwork and showed strong feelings about it. She was _____ ,
₇

and now I want to do more teamwork with people at my office! She's also a

_____ writer. She's very good at writing how-to books. I want to buy
₈

her newest book.

2 Complete the email. Use the simple past of the verbs in parentheses.

◀ ▶ ＋ www.email.com/cambridge ⟳

》

TO: Bob@email.com

Hello from San Diego!

I'm having a great vacation! It's very warm here.

Yesterday we _____ went _____ (go) to Balboa Park. It's a really big
                        1

park, so we _____ (decide) to stay all day. In the park,
                        2

we _____ (visit) the San Diego Zoo. It's the biggest zoo
                3

in California! After that, we _____ (walk) around other
                                        4

parts of the park, and we _____ (get) really tired. But we
                                5

_____ (see) some beautiful fountains and statues, and my
                6

brother _____ (meet) a movie star!
                7

We _____ (eat) lunch at a café in the park. We
                8

_____ (have) some good sandwiches, but my parents
                9

_____ (not like) them.
                10

See you soon!

Terri

---

3 Write questions with the words in parentheses and the simple past. Then answer the
questions with the information in Exercise 2.

1 A _Where did Terri go on vacation_____? (Where / Terri / go / on vacation)

  B _She went to San Diego_____.

2 A Did _____? (Terri / go / to the park with her family)

  B _____.

3 A _____? (What / they / visit / in the park)

  B _____.

4 A _____? (they / get / tired)

  B _____.

5 A _____? (Where / they / eat / lunch)

  B _____.

6 A _____? (Terri's parents / like / the food)

  B _____.

4 Look at Miguel's status updates. Then write sentences about his week. Use the simple past and *ago*.

SOCIALSPACE

Miguel Trandall

STATUS UPDATES

I'm eating fish at a Thai restaurant. Yum! ☺
Posted on Monday, 4/12 at 2:40 p.m.

Miranda and I are shopping.
Posted on Tuesday, 4/13 at 7:32 p.m.

I'm watching a boring reality show. ☹
Posted on Wednesday, 4/14 at 9:05 p.m.

I'm not going to the park. It's too cold!
Posted on Thursday, 4/15 at 5:15 p.m.

My mom and I are eating breakfast in a coffee shop.
Posted on Friday, 4/16 at 8:10 a.m.

Martin and I are lifting weights. Ugh!
Posted on Saturday, 4/17 at 11:23 a.m.

My sister and I aren't going out. We're too tired!
Posted on Sunday, 4/18 at 12:00 p.m.

Today is Monday, 4/19.

1   Miguel ate fish at a Thai restaurant seven days ago.

2   _____

3   _____

4   _____

5   _____

6   _____

7   _____

D Making a difference

1 Read the article. Then check (✓) the adjectives that describe each person.

	brave	determined	inspiring	passionate	talented
1 John Muir			✓		
2 Ada Blackjack					
3 Louis Armstrong					

Book Corner
Books in review this week: <u>Biographies</u>

BOOKMAGAZINE

A Passion for Nature: The Life of John Muir by Donald Worster

This biography about John Muir was terrific. John Muir was born in Scotland in 1838, and he moved to the United States in 1849. He was an explorer and a writer, and he was a very inspiring person. He was passionate about nature, and he helped to create many national parks in the United States. In this book, Donald Worster describes Muir's inspiring travel and work. He also writes about Muir's life with his family and friends.

Ada Blackjack: A True Story of Survival in the Arctic by Jennifer Nevin

Ada Blackjack was born in 1898 in Alaska. In 1921, she went with one Canadian and three American explorers to Wrangel Island in the Arctic. The four men wanted to explore the island. Ada was their cook. After two years, they didn't have enough food and had to leave the island. One man was too sick to travel. Three of the men left to find help. Ada stayed with the sick man. After three months, the man died. Then Ada was alone on the island. She was there for five months, but Ada was determined and brave. Finally, a search team found her, and Ada went back to Alaska. It's an exciting book, and Jennifer Nevin tells Ada's story very well.

Pops: A Life of Louis Armstrong by Terry Teachout

Louis Armstrong was born in New Orleans in 1901. He was an extremely talented jazz musician, composer, and singer. He influenced all kinds of musicians and singers, including jazz and pop musicians and singers who are popular today. Louis Armstrong was famous all over the world. In 2001, one hundred years after his birth, the New Orleans airport was renamed Louis Armstrong International Airport in his honor. Terry Teachout writes about Armstrong's music, but he also writes about his life. He shows that Louis Armstrong was an inspiring musician who had an extremely interesting life.

2 Read the article again. Answer the questions.

1 Where was John Muir born?   He was born in Scotland.

2 When did Muir move to the United States?

3 When did Ada Blackjack go to Wrangel Island?

4 How long was Blackjack alone on the island?

5 Where was Louis Armstrong born?

6 What was Armstrong's job?

In a restaurant

A The ice cream is fantastic!

1 Cross out the words that don't belong in each list.

1 **Main dishes:**	chicken stir-fry	~~fruit salad~~	lamb chop	cheese ravioli
2 **Desserts:**	apple pie	ice cream	cheesecake	steak
3 **Side dishes:**	mashed potatoes	French fries	mixed vegetables	tomato soup
4 **Appetizer:**	crab cakes	garlic bread	rice	onion rings

2 Label the food with some of the menu items from Exercise 1.

1 _____

2 _____

3 _____

4 _____

5 _____

6 _____

7 _____

8 _____

9 _____

10 _____

3 Plan a party. Write menu items for each category. Use your own ideas.

PARTY
MENU

Appetizers:

_____
_____

Main dishes:

_____
_____

Side dishes:

_____
_____
_____

Desserts:

_____
_____
_____

4 Circle the correct word in the parentheses at the end of the sentence to complete each conversation.

1 **A** How are the desserts? Any recommendations?

   B I had _____ apple pie. It's great! (an / a / the)

2 **A** Let's order _____ garlic bread. (some / a / an)

   B Not for me, thanks. I don't like garlic.

3 **A** Let's try _____ appetizer! (some / a / an)

   B OK.

4 **A** Do you want coffee?

   B Yes, please. With _____ milk. (some / the / a)

5 **A** What do you want for dinner?

   B I think I'll start with _____ dessert! (an / a / the)

6 **A** Do you want _____ cheese ravioli? (an / a / some)

   B No, thank you.

5 Look at the pictures. Complete the sentences with the names of the people having the food. Then circle the correct words to complete the sentences.

Mi Yon

John

Mateo

Mindy

1 _____ John _____ is having **a** / **some** hamburger, **the** / **some** French fries, and **the** / **some** apple pie.

2 _____ is having **a** / **some** garlic bread, **the** / **some** cheese ravioli, and **a** / **some** cheesecake.

3 _____ is having **a** / **some** steak, **a** / **some** mashed potatoes, and **the** / **some** ice cream.

4 _____ is having **the** / **some** chicken soup, **a** / **the** hot dog, and **a** / **an** fruit salad.

6 Complete the conversations with *a* / *an*, *the*, or *some*.

A. **Randy**   What did you have for lunch today?

    Joe   I had _____*a*_____ hot dog and _____ tomato soup.
                           1   2

    Randy   How were they?

    Joe   _____ hot dog was very good, but _____ soup was cold.
                      3   4

B. **David**   What did you have?

    Marcia   I had _____ garlic bread and _____ cheese ravioli.
                        1   2

    David   How were they?

    Marcia   _____ garlic bread and _____ cheese ravioli were good.
                        3   4

B I'll have the fish, please.

1 Complete the expressions for ordering food and checking information.
Sometimes more than one answer is possible.

Waiter Are you ready to order?

Joshua Yes, I am.

Waiter OK. What would you like?

Joshua I'll _____ *have* _____ the chicken
          ^{1}
          stir-fry and some rice, please.

Waiter Anything else?

Joshua No, thank you.

Waiter OK. Let me _____ that.
          $_2$
          You'd like the chicken stir-fry and

          some rice.

Joshua Yes. Oh, and I'd _____
          some onion soup, too. $_3$

Waiter Is that all?

Joshua Yes, that's all.

Waiter OK. Let me _____ that.
          $_4$
          You'd like the chicken stir-fry, some rice, and
          some onion soup.

Joshua That's right. Oh, wait! Can I

          _____ some water,
          please? $_5$

Waiter Sure. Is that all?

Joshua Yes. Thank you.

Waiter Let me _____ that back.
          $_6$
          The chicken stir-fry, some rice, some onion
          soup, and some water.

Joshua Yes, please. That's all, thank you!

2 Complete the conversation with your own ideas and the expressions in Exercise 1.

Waiter Are you ready to order?
You Yes. _____
Waiter Anything else?
You Um, yes. _____
Waiter OK. Let me _____
You That's right. Thank you.

C Have you ever . . . ?

1 **Put the letters in the correct order to make food words.**

1 aaocsovd ____avocados____
2 ysoetsr ____________
3 asdet ____________
4 idsuq ____________
5 aesdewe ____________
6 naspinlta ____________
7 yso lmik ____________
8 arcort ujeic ____________
9 lbeu ehecse ____________
10 zfeonr goutyr ____________

2 **Complete the order form from an online supermarket. Use some words from Exercise 1.**

FOODMART

	Item	Price
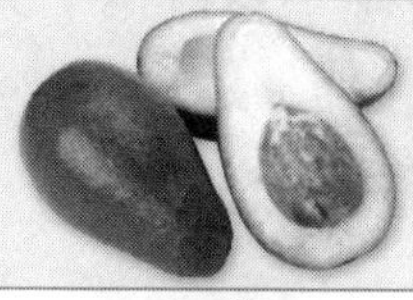	1 ____avocados____	$0.98
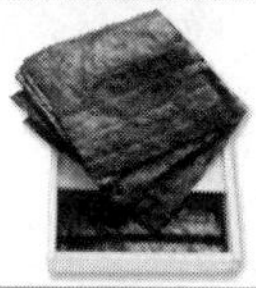	2 ____________	$4.25
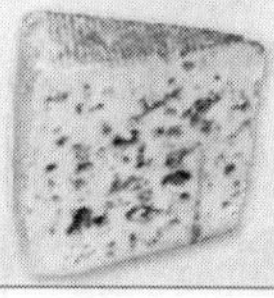	3 ____________	$5.00
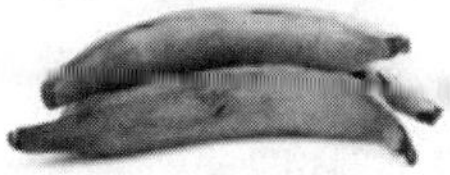	4 ____________	$1.56
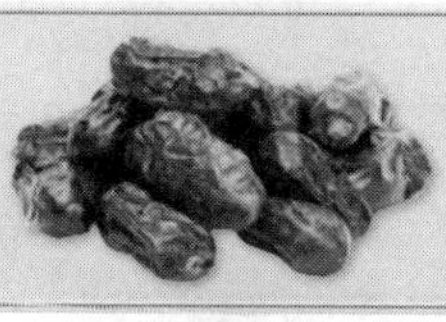	5 ____________	$4.75
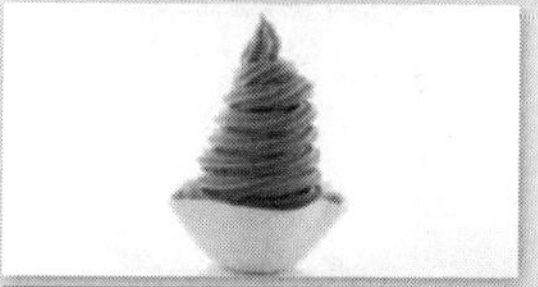	6 ____________	$3.89
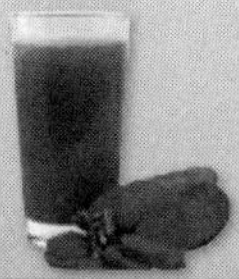	7 ____________	$6.20
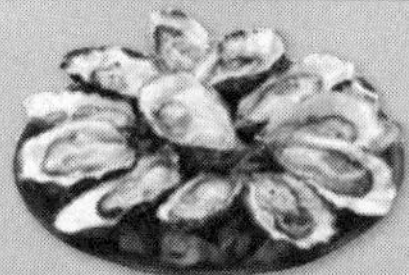	8 ____________	$3.42

3 Complete the chart with the correct past participles.

Verb	Past participle
1 be	been
2 drink	
3 eat	
4 have	
5 try	

4 Look at Ramiro's answers to the quiz. Then write sentences about Ramiro's food experiences. Use the present perfect.

ARE YOU AN ADVENTUROUS EATER?

Answer the questions.

1. How many times have you eaten black spaghetti? — ten times

2. Have you ever drunk seaweed juice? — Yes ● No

3. Have you ever tried squid? — ● Yes No

4. How often have you had unusual food? — many times

5. Have you ever eaten plantains? — ● Yes No

6. Have you ever had fish tacos? — Yes ● No

7. Have you been to restaurants in other countries? — ● Yes No

8. How often have you cooked unusual foods at home? — never

RESULTS: You are a fairly adventurous eater.

1   Ramiro has eaten black spaghetti ten times.
2   He has never drunk seaweed juice.
3   _____
4   _____
5   _____
6   _____
7   _____
8   _____

5 Complete the conversation. Use the present perfect and the words in parentheses.

Mark Hey, Vince. _Have you ever eaten_ (eat) oysters?
　　　　　　　　　　　　　　　 1

Vince No, I _____ . Have you ever
　　　　　　　　　　　2
　　　　 eaten them?

Mark Yes, I _____ . They're delicious!
　　　　　　　　　　　3

Vince _____ (be) to
　　　　　　　　　4
　　　　 the Seascape Restaurant?

Mark No, I _____ . Is it good?
　　　　　　　　　　5

Vince Yeah, it's great! My wife and I _____ (eat)
　　　　　　　　　　　　　　　　　　　6
　　　　 there three times.

Mark _____ (have) the seafood there?
　　　　　　　　7

Vince Um, no, I _____ . I usually have the chicken!
　　　　　　　　　　8

Mark Really?

Vince Yes. But people say the oysters are fantastic.

6 Read the answers. Write the questions.

1　_Have you ever tried squid sushi?_　　No, I haven't. I've never tried squid sushi.
2　_____　　Yes, I have. I've had chicken tacos many times.
3　_____　　Yes, I have. I've drunk carrot juice before.
4　_____　　No, I haven't. I've never been to a Colombian restaurant.
5　_____　　No, I haven't. I've never eaten plantains.
6　_____　　Yes, I have. I've been to Chinese restaurants many times.

7 Answer the questions in Exercise 6 with your own information. Write a short
answer and add a sentence. Use the sentences in Exercise 6 as models.

1　_Yes, I have._　　　　　　　　　_I've eaten squid sushi many times._
2　_____　　　　　_____
3　_____　　　　　_____
4　_____　　　　　_____
5　_____　　　　　_____
6　_____　　　　　_____

D Restaurant experiences

1 Read the webpage. How many seafood items are on the menu?

There are _____ seafood items on the menu.

YOUR MENU Find a restaurant near you!

New Search	Profile and Reviews	Menu

New Search

by rating
★
★★
★★★
★★★★

by price
$
$$
$$$

by type of food

American
Chinese
Colombian
Korean
Mexican
Turkish
Vietnamese

cafés
sandwiches
seafood
traditional
vegetarian

Sun Seafood and Son

Food: ★ ★ ★ ★
Price: $$
Website: www.sss/cup.com
Hours: 12:30 p.m.–10:00 p.m.
Monday–Friday
9:00 a.m.–10:00 p.m.
Saturday–Sunday

Reviews

Posted by RickN on 4/27
The food at this restaurant is delicious! I recommend the crab cakes with blue cheese for an appetizer. I also like the mixed seafood salad. My favorite main dish is the squid stir-fry! All of the seafood is good.

Posted by Carla82 on 5/16
This restaurant is pretty good. I liked the seafood, but I didn't like the juices. I recommend getting water to drink!

Posted by Jake on 6/2
This is the best restaurant in this city. I've had everything on the menu! The side dishes are delicious. Try the mixed vegetables with crab. Oh, and have dessert. The seaweed ice cream is delicious! It really is!

Menu

Appetizers:
crab cakes with blue cheese
onion soup
mixed seafood salad

Main dishes:
squid stir-fry
fish of the day
seafood ravioli

Side dishes:
mixed vegetables with crab
rice
fried mushrooms

Drinks:
carrot juice
seaweed tea
water

Desserts:
cheesecake
seaweed ice cream
fruit salad

2 Read the article again. Check (✓) the items that are definitely true.

☐ RickN liked the crab cakes.

☐ RickN has only tried three items on the menu.

☐ Carla82 tried some juice at the restaurant.

☐ Carla82 does not like seaweed.

☐ Jake has never eaten a main dish at the restaurant.

☐ Jake liked the ice cream.

Entertainment

A I'm not a fan of dramas.

1 Look at the pictures. Circle the correct type of movie to label each picture.

1 a a science-fiction movie
  (b) an action movie

2 a a comedy
  b a horror movie

3 a a horror movie
  b a musical

4 a an animated movie
  b a science-fiction movie

5 a a western
  b a comedy

6 a a drama
  b a comedy

7 a an action movie
  b an animated movie

8 a a western
  b a musical

2 Respond to the statements. Complete the sentences with *so* or *neither* and *am* or *do*.

1 A I love horror movies!

  B _So do_____ I.

2 A I'm not a fan of musicals.

  B _____ I.

3 A I never go to the movies on Sundays.

  B _____ I.

4 A I'm really tired.

  B _____ I.

5 A I have a lot of homework tonight.

  B _____ I.

6 A I don't like seafood.

  B _____ I.

3 Rewrite the responses in Exercise 2 using *too* or *either*.

1 A I love horror movies!

  B _I do, too._____

2 A I'm not a fan of musicals.

  B _____

3 A I never go to the movies on Sundays.

  B _____

4 A I'm really tired.

  B _____

5 A I have a lot of homework tonight.

  B _____

6 A I don't like seafood.

  B _____

4 Circle the correct words to complete the conversations.

1 A (I like) / I don't like tacos.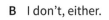

 B So do I.

2 A I like / I don't like westerns.

 B I don't, either.

3 A I'm / I'm not a fan of science fiction movies.

 B Really? I am. I love them!

4 A I'm always / I'm never on time.

 B Neither am I.

5 A I'm / I'm not cold!

 B I am, too.

6 A I eat / I don't eat a lot of pizza.

 B Really? I don't. I hardly ever eat pizza.

5 Complete the conversations with your own responses.

1 A I'm not a fan of horror movies.

 You _Neither am I._ or _Really? I am. I like horror movies._

2 A I love doing laundry.

 You _____

3 A I always get up late on Saturdays.

 You _____

4 A I don't usually eat a big breakfast in the morning.

 You _____

5 A I'm not a fan of action movies.

 You _____

6 A I'm usually late for class.

 You _____

B Any suggestions?

1 Put the words in the correct order to make expressions to ask for and give suggestions.

1 suggestions / Any / ? — _Any suggestions?_

2 any / you / suggestions / Do / have / ? — _____

3 an / see / movie / action / Let's / . — _____

4 a / we / Why / movie / don't / to / go / ? — _____

5 you / suggest / What / do / ? — _____

6 TV / could / We / watch / . — _____

2 Complete the conversation with the sentences from Exercise 1. Use each sentence once.

Ivan   So, what do you want to do today?

Emily I don't know. _Do you have any suggestions_ ?
                                          1

Ivan   _____ .
                          2

Emily Sorry. I don't really want to watch TV.

Ivan   OK. _____ ?
                          3

Emily _____ ?
                          4

Ivan   Good idea. What type of movie do you want to see?

Emily Hmm, I don't know. _____ ?
                                              5

Ivan   Yes. _____ .
                          6

Emily That sounds good. There's a new action movie with Matt Damon.

Ivan   Great!

3 Complete the conversations with your own suggestions.

1 **Friend** I'd like to have something nice for dinner. Any suggestions?

  You _____

2 **Friend** I want to do something different tonight. Do you have any suggestions?

  You _____

3 **Friend** I want to watch a good drama. What do you suggest?

  You _____

C All of us love music.

1 Look at the music calendar. Complete the words for the types of music.

SWEET SOUND
Café and Club

Monday, 8:00 p.m.

Listen to p*op*_____ singer Laura Bee. She's singing, and
1
DJ Strong is playing t_____ music. Don't miss it!
2

Tuesday, 9:30 p.m.

Tuesday is b_____ night. Listen to Elsa Ford sing her
3
sad songs.

Wednesday, 10:00 p.m.

Do you prefer a quiet evening? Then stay home on Wednesday night!
The music is going to be loud. Listen to Heavy Sushi play
r_____ music.
4

Thursday, 7:00 p.m.

Melinda May is a great co_____ singer from Texas.
5
Listen to her new songs Thursday night.

Friday, 7:00 p.m., 9:00 p.m.

Listen to the best j_____ music in town. Monty Miles
6
plays twice!

Saturday, 8:30 p.m.

On Saturday night, r_____ musicians Kipp and Kyle play their cool
7
instruments, and h_____ star Bee Cool sings with them.
8

Sunday, 2:00 p.m., 7:00 p.m.

Do you like slow, quiet music? Lydia Saad sings f_____ songs
9
at lunch. At night, Daniel Avilez plays beautiful cl_____ music
10
on his guitar.

2 Put the words in the correct place in the chart.

✓all of   a lot of   most of   none of   not many of   some of

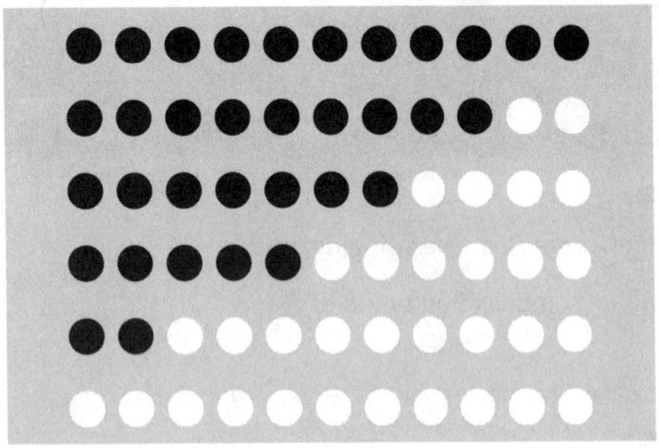

all of _____

_____

_____

_____

_____

3 Look at the survey. Then circle the correct answers to complete the sentences.

What kind of music do you like?
We asked 100 students, and here are their answers.

Type of music	Yes	No	Type of music	Yes	No
classical	14	86	jazz	23	77
rock	82	18	blues	38	62
pop	100	0	country	8	92
reggae	35	65	hip-hop	95	5
folk	0	100	techno	86	14

1 (**Not many of**) / **Most of** the students like classical music.
2 **All of** / **A lot of** them like rock music.
3 **All of** / **None of** them like pop music.
4 **Not many of** / **Some of** them like reggae.
5 **All of** / **None of** them like folk.
6 **A lot of** / **Not many of** them like jazz.
7 **All of** / **Some of** them like blues music.
8 **Not many of** / **None of** them like country.
9 **Some of** / **Most of** them like hip-hop.
10 **All of** / **A lot of** them like techno music.

4 Look at the picture. Then rewrite the sentences to correct the underlined mistakes.

1 <u>Some of</u> the runners are tired.   *Many of the runners are tired.*

2 <u>None of</u> them are running. _____

3 <u>Many of</u> them are sitting. _____

4 <u>Most of</u> them are running fast. _____

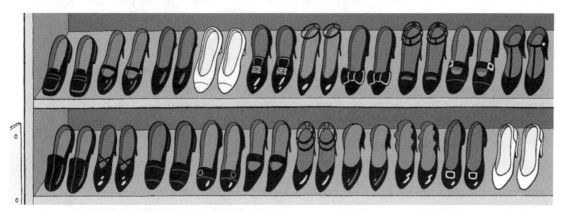

5 <u>All of</u> the shoes are black. _____

6 <u>Many of</u> them are white. _____

7 <u>A lot of</u> them are gray. _____

8 <u>None of</u> the people are listening to music. _____

9 <u>Not many of</u> them are reading. _____

10 <u>Most of</u> them are sitting. _____

D Singing shows around the world

1 Read the webpage. What four things does Mark like? Which one doesn't anyone write about?

Mark likes _____ .

None of them write about _____ .

Posted by Mark at 6:15

Hi! I'm new to this town. What can I do for fun this weekend? I like listening to music, eating at restaurants, and going to museums. I also love going to the movies! Any suggestions? Thanks for your help.

Posted by Dennis102 at 6:18

Hey, Mark. Welcome to our town. It's small, but it's great. There's a movie theater downtown on Maple Street. Do you like scary movies? There's a great horror movie playing this weekend — *Terror in Texas*. There's a terrific jazz club next to the movie theater. They have different musicians every weekend. A lot of them are from New Orleans.

Posted by SandraMN at 6:32

Hi, Mark. Do you have children? *Trudy Goes to Paris* is also playing. It's a terrific animated movie. There are a lot of good restaurants here. All of them are downtown. You can eat food from around the world. There's a Chinese restaurant, a Mexican restaurant, a Turkish restaurant, and a Vietnamese restaurant. Have you ever tried Vietnamese food? They play great folk music at this restaurant, too.

Posted by LeroyLee at 6:45

Welcome to our town, Mark! Sandra's recommendation is good. The food at the Vietnamese restaurant is delicious! My favorite place to hear music is Club 64. They usually have musicians from all over the world. This weekend Farah Fields is singing. She's a great blues singer. And next week, a rock band from England is playing.

Posted by Mark at 6:59

Thanks, everyone! I want to try the Vietnamese restaurant, and my wife and I will go to Club 64 next week. We love rock music! OK, I'm in a hurry . . . We're going to see *Terror in Texas* at 7:30! Thanks!

---

2 Read the article again. Answer the questions.

1 Where is the jazz club? _next to the movie theater_

2 Where are a lot of the jazz musicians from? _____

3 Who recommends an animated movie? _____

4 What kinds of music are recommended? _____

Time for a change

A Personal change

1 Complete the conversations with the phrases from the box.

get a credit card	lose weight	save money
join a gym	make more friends	start a new hobby
learn an instrument	✓pass a test	study harder

A. **Jake**   So, Wendy. What are you doing these days?

Wendy   Oh, I'm studying a lot to <u>_pass a test_</u>.
                                                    1

Jake   That's great! But why are you shopping right now?

Wendy   I don't know. I think I should go home
             and _____ !
                              2

B. **Doug**   Hey, Akio. Do you want to go to the movies?

Akio   No. It's too expensive. I'm trying to _____ .
                                                                        1
             I want to _____ .
                                    2

Doug   Really? Why? Do you want to _____ ?
                                                        3

Akio   Not really. I just want to exercise more.

C. **Mick**   Hey, Brenda. How can I _____ ?
                                                    1

Brenda   Oh, it's easy. You can go online. But why do you want a credit card?

Mick   I want to _____ , so I'm going to take guitar lessons!
                                    2

Brenda   That's cool!

Mick   Yeah. But now I need to buy a guitar!

D. **Jen**   I'd like to do something different. Any suggestions?

Ted   Why don't you _____ , like taking pictures?
                                        1

Jen   Well, I have a camera, but I'm not very good at using it.

Ted   You could take a class. That's also a good way
           to _____ .
                        2

Jen   Yeah, thanks. That's a good idea.

2 Put the words in the correct order to make sentences.

1 house / a / saving / buy / We're / money / to / new / .
We're saving money to buy a new house.

2 get / English / better job / Are / a / learning / you / to / ?
_____

3 new friends / to / Lisa / gym / joined / a / make / .
_____

4 movies / see / went / to / comedy / Ethan and Ruben / to / the / a / .
_____

5 take / to / yoga / relax / I / classes / .
_____

6 a / buy / more clothes / credit / Rita / Is / getting / card / to / ?
_____

3 Look at the chart. Why are the people taking the classes? Write sentences with the present continuous and infinitives of purpose.

Team Time Sports Center

Name	Exercise / Class	Purpose / Goal
Kim Rawlings	take soccer lessons	play better
Ed Hendricks	lift weights	get stronger
Jim Franklin	take a salsa class	dance better
Hannah Park	take yoga	relax
Tina Madding	do gymnastics	have fun
Josh Sparks	learn karate	lose weight

1 *Kim is taking soccer lessons to play better.*

2 _____

3 _____

4 _____

5 _____

6 _____

4 Complete the flyer. Write sentences with the words in parentheses. Use the imperative and infinitives of purpose.

One-on-One ENGLISH

Do you want to improve your English? Here are six easy ways.

1 _Study harder to get better grades._ (study harder / get better grades)

2 _____ (take a writing class / improve your writing)

3 _____ (talk to English speakers / improve your pronunciation)

4 _____ (listen to music in English / improve your listening)

5 _____ (read websites in English / learn new words)

6 _____ (email Kate / take an English class)

Kate Harrison: kateH@cup.org   *Classes start every Monday.*

5 Read the conversations. Complete the sentence about each person. Use infinitives of purpose.

1 **Julia** Why are you going to Peru?

Lynn Because I want to see Machu Picchu.

Lynn _is going to Peru to see Machu Picchu._

2 **Paul** Why did you join a gym?

Doug Because I want to lose weight.

Doug _____

3 **Wesley** Why are you saving money?

Sandra Because I want to buy a car.

Sandra _____

4 **Jill** Why did you start an English club?

Tom Because I want to make more friends.

Tom _____

6 Answer the questions with your own information. Use infinitives of purpose.

Example: _I'd like to visit Japan to see the botanical gardens._

1 What country would you like to visit? Why? _____

2 What famous person would you like to meet? Why? _____

3 Why are you taking English classes? _____

4 What other language would you like to learn? Why? _____

B I'm happy to hear that!

1 Write the lines of the conversation in the correct order.

> I'm good, thanks. But I had the flu last month.
> I'm sorry to hear that!
> Oh, hi, Ken. How are you doing?
> ✓ Hey, Sam. Long time no see.
> That's great to hear!
> That's wonderful! Have a great time!
> Yeah. And guess what? I'm going to Paris on Saturday.
> Yeah. I was sick for two weeks, but I feel better now.

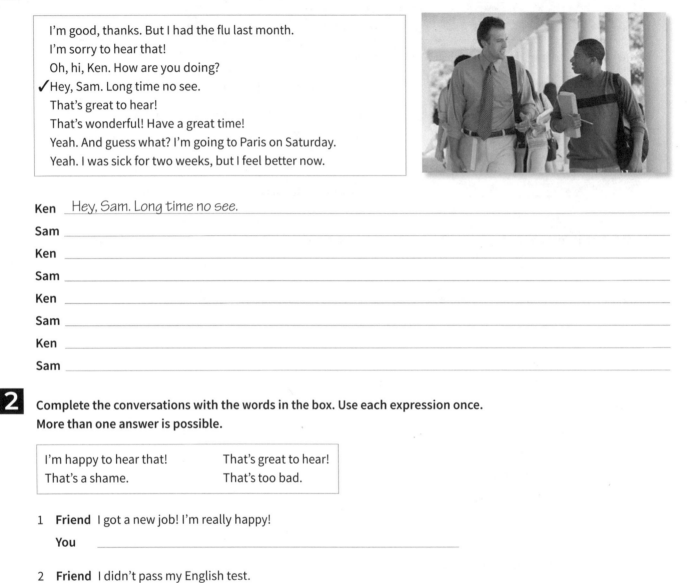

Ken _Hey, Sam. Long time no see._

Sam _____

Ken _____

Sam _____

Ken _____

Sam _____

Ken _____

Sam _____

2 Complete the conversations with the words in the box. Use each expression once.
More than one answer is possible.

I'm happy to hear that!	That's great to hear!
That's a shame.	That's too bad.

1 **Friend** I got a new job! I'm really happy!

   You _____

2 **Friend** I didn't pass my English test.

   You _____

3 **Friend** My mother is not feeling very well.

   You _____

4 **Friend** I learned to play the guitar, and I have a concert next week!

   You _____

C I think I'll get a job.

1 Complete the sentences with the words in the box and the simple past. Then number the pictures in the correct order.

buy a house	go to college	retire
✓get married	graduate from high school	start a career
get promoted	rent an apartment	start school

Dorothy was born in 1945. This is the story of her life . . .

☐ She _got married_ to Leonard in 1970.

☐ In 1967, she _____ _____ .

☐ Dorothy _____ in 1950.

☐ They _____ for five years.

☐ She _____ 13 years later.

☐ Dorothy _____ in 1980, and again in 1994.

☐ She _____ in 2010.

☐ Then, in 1975, they _____ _____ .

☐ She _____ in 1963.

Now, she wants to travel around the world with her husband . . .

2 Match the sentences.

1 I'll never retire. ___e___

2 I may retire when I'm 65. _____

3 I might save enough money for a new car. _____

4 I'll save enough money for college by July. _____

5 I won't go to Mexico in the summer. _____

6 I might go to Spain next year. _____

a That's the age my parents retired.

b I start classes in September.

c But I have to finish school first.

d I need one to drive to work.

e I love working!

f It's too hot!

3 Complete the email. Use *will*, *won't*, or *might* and the words in parentheses.
(++ = very certain, + = less certain)

Hello, Aunt Sarah!

How are you? I'm great. I have big plans for the future. I _'ll graduate_____
                                                                    1
(++ graduate) from high school next month. My brother _____ (+ come)
                                                                    2
for my graduation. In June, my friend Christopher and I _____ (++ go)
                                                                    3
to Mexico. We _____ (++ stay) at our friend Mateo's house. Christopher
                    4
_____ (+ leave) in July, but I _____ (++ stay) until August. In
        5   6
September, I _____ (+ go) to college, or I _____ (+ work) for
                    7   8
a year first. I _____ (++ not decide) until August.
                    9

Take care,
Ryan

4 Complete the email with the correct form of the words in parentheses. Use *will*, *won't*, or *may*.

Dear Ryan,

It was great to hear from you! You're graduating! Congratulations! I _may come_____
                                                                          1
(come) to your party. I'm not sure. Paul _____ (have) a soccer game that weekend.
                                                2
We'll know for sure next week. But Uncle Dan and I want to take you to a new Korean restaurant.

We _____ (go) in May to celebrate! We don't have many plans in May, so we
        3
have time. I know you _____ (love) Mexico!
                                4
Uncle Dan and I _____ (not go) there this year because we need to save money.
                        5
We don't know yet, but we _____ (go) to Canada. It will be cheaper because we
                                    6
can stay with friends in Canada.

See you soon!
Love,
Aunt Sarah

94

5 Look at Hiro's notes. Then answer the questions about his plans.
Use *will* or *won't*.

SUMMER PLANS

go to Vancouver to see friends, June	✓ buy ticket next week
visit Uncle Kazu in Vancouver	✗ no time
run a marathon, July	✓ running every day
get a job	✓ look for a job, July
take guitar lessons, August	✗ too expensive

Aya So, Hiro . . . Do you think you'll go to Vancouver this summer?

Hiro ___Yes, I will.___ I'll buy my ticket next week.
　　　　　　1

Aya Great. And do you think you'll visit Uncle Kazu?

Hiro _____ I'm not going to have time.
　　　　　　2

Aya Oh, do you think you'll run the marathon in July? I'll be in it!

Hiro _____ I'm running every day now.
　　　　　　3

Aya We should practice together.

Hiro That'd be great. We can run together in the morning or afternoon.
I'm not working right now.

Aya Really? Do you think you'll get a new job soon?

Hiro _____ I'll look for a job in July when I get back
　　　　　　4
from Vancouver.

Aya Hey, how about the guitar . . . Do you think you'll take those lessons?

Hiro _____ They're too expensive. I need a job first!
　　　　　　5

6 Complete the sentences so they are true for you. Use *will, won't, may,* or *might*.

1 I _____ buy a new car next year.

2 I _____ get a new computer this year.

3 It _____ snow this week.

4 I _____ visit relatives next month.

5 My teacher _____ give us homework next week.

6 **A** Do you think you'll run a marathon next year?

　 You _____ .

7 **A** Do you think you'll ever be on a reality show?

　 You _____ .

D Dreams and aspirations

1 Read the webpage and article. Write the quotes in the correct place in the article.

Search by authors: A B C D E F G H I J K L M N O P Q R S T U V W X Y Z

Search by subject:
art
life
love
marriage
movies
politics
sports
work

QUOTES OF THE DAY:
"Life isn't a matter of milestones, but of moments."
– Rose Kennedy

"All life is an experiment. The more experiments you make the better."
– Ralph Waldo Emerson

"There are people who have money and people who are rich."
– Coco Chanel

This week with Joan!

Hello, readers! This week I'm writing about life. I found three interesting quotes about life. One quote is " _____ ." I agree!
   1
I think it means you should experiment — change your habits and try new things — to make life interesting. So last week, I tried these experiments: I ate seaweed tacos, I ran a marathon, and I went salsa dancing! Next week, I might go skiing or buy a new computer.

Another person said, " _____ ." I really like this one.
   2
I don't have a million dollars, but I still feel rich. I have a great family and good friends. I enjoy a rich, happy life with them.

My favorite quote is " _____ ." This means the small
   3
things in life are important. Sure, milestones are important, like graduating from college, starting a career, or getting married. But little things, moments, make life great. For example, I went shopping with my daughter. It wasn't a milestone, but we had fun, and I'll remember this day forever.

So, my advice? Work on your dreams and aspirations, but have fun, too. Life is short.

2 Read the article again. Write P (past) or F (future) for Joan's experiences and plans.

1 eat seaweed tacos ___P___

2 run a marathon _____

3 go skiing _____

4 buy a new computer _____